Donald E. Westlake was the author of ove[r] non-fiction books, including *Under an Engl[ish]* crime fiction, and is perhaps best-known for criminal characters who featured in long-ru... ...g ...d mighly successful series: Parker (which Westlake wrote under the pseudonym Richard Stark), and John Dortmunder. Westlake won three Edgar Awards, and in 1993 the Mystery Writers of America named him a Grand Master, the greatest honour given by the organisation. He passed away in 2008.

UNDER AN ENGLISH HEAVEN

Donald E. Westlake

SILVERTAIL BOOKS • *London*

First published in Great Britain in 1972 by Simon & Schuster

This edition published by Silvertail Books in 2018
www.silvertailbooks.com

978-1-909269-81-1

If I were to write something here thanking everyone who helped me in any way while I assembled this book, the result would be a second volume as long as the first. I can't do that, not and remain on good terms with my publisher, but I did thank them all privately, and I have tried in the book itself to offer them something even better than gratitude: accuracy. If I have failed even in that—and I surely have, at least a few times, despite my best efforts—I offer my apologies.

Having said that, there is one individual I must single out for thanks. His name is Colin Rickards, he is a British journalist and author, and he has been an incredibly kind and well-informed Vergil in guiding me, a confirmed fiction writer, through the descending circles of Fact. He has spent more than fifteen years as a reporter of West Indian affairs, and he knows more about Anguilla and St. Kitts than either of us would dare to print. He has, in fact, written a book on the Anguillan secession himself, which would have been published long before mine but that it ran into mysterious problems. The book was already in page proofs when the British publisher—part of a conglomerate, other parts of which have business dealings with the British Government—decided for some strange reason not to bring it out after all. At this moment, the book's future is still clouded, but I wish it well; never have I so heartily welcomed competition.

I once read that the Navajo Indians in making their intricately designed blankets always insert one purposeful flaw in the pattern, the idea being that perfection is the exclusive right of the gods, who would be angry at a mortal who did something without defect. I have no deliberate flaws in this book, yet somehow I doubt the gods will be annoyed with me.

—DONALD E. WESTLAKE

To anybody anywhere
who has ever believed anything
that any Government ever said
about anything …

If I should die, think only this of me:
That there's some corner of a foreign field
That is for ever England. There shall be
In that rich earth a richer dust concealed;
A dust whom England bore, shaped, made aware,
Gave, once, her flowers to love, her ways to roam,
A body of England's, breathing English air,
Washed by the rivers, blest by suns of home.
And think, this heart, all evil shed away,
A pulse in the eternal mind, no less
Gives somewhere back the thoughts by England given;
Her sights and sounds; dreams happy as her day;
And laughter, learnt of friends; and gentleness,
In hearts at peace, under an English heaven.

RUPERT BROOKE, "The Soldier"

Contents

"Now tell us all about the war,
And what they fought each other for."
—Robert Southey, "The Battle of Blenheim"

When in the spring of 1967 the tiny Caribbean island of Anguilla rebelled against independence and in favor of colonialism, the action was so misunderstood by the islanders' ex-mother country, Great Britain, that two years later the English invaded the place with 315 paratroopers in a witless attempt to put the rebellion down. Since British rule was exactly what the Anguillans had been asking for, this was a military expedition doomed by its presumptions to plunge into defeat, humiliated rather than slaughtered, but resoundingly trounced for all that.

This triumph was the third in Anguilla's unbroken string of victories over foreign assailants. The first military invasion of the island took place in 1745, when a force of six or seven hundred French soldiers landed at Crocus Bay, determined to wrest the place from the fifteen hundred mostly-English settlers. The settlers, already thinking of themselves as Anguillans, had no army as such, then or now; but some of them did have guns and none of them particularly liked being invaded.

The invaders had been spotted before they reached shore. A small posse of Anguillans dug itself in at strategic spots on the ridge overlooking the beach and in fifteen minutes of sharpshooting killed thirty-two Frenchmen and wounded twenty-five more, including the French commander, named De la Touche. There were no casualties among the defenders. The French decided that 7-to-1 odds were insufficient and tried to leave, but in the confusion of departure the Anguillans came down onto the beach and captured fifty invaders. Thus ended the first invasion.

The second military invasion of Anguilla took place in 1796, when two French warships landed three hundred troops at Rendezvous Bay, on the western end of the island, with orders to kill every man and woman and child on the island and destroy all buildings and crops. There ensued one of the oddest one-day battles of military history.

Once again the Anguillans had seen the enemy coming ashore. This time they'd sent a fast cutter off to the nearest English settlement at St. Kitts, seventy miles to the south, to ask for help, while in the meantime they made some effort to organize their defenses. They were given ample opportunity to do so since the French, in landing, had failed to keep their powder dry. Everybody on both sides waited while the French spread out their powder on sheets in the sun.

Some Anguillans wanted to toss burning sticks onto the sheets, but their leader, Deputy Governor Benjamin Gumbs, said No; that would be "ungentlemanly." (There are still today some Anguillans who want to shoot flaming arrows onto sheets of gunpowder, and there are still the others who reject it as ungentlemanly.)

Eventually the French powder dried and the French troops attacked. They were professionals against amateurs, the islanders didn't have the same handy heights at Rendezvous Bay as they'd had at Crocus Bay fifty-one years earlier, and the Anguillans were driven gradually backward across the island. The invaders killed everybody they got their hands on—raping the women first, of course—and burned houses and crops, all according to plan.

The Anguillans retreated slowly all day long, dragging with them their few small cannon, and finally took their last stand at Sandy Hill, ten miles from the original beachhead and almost at the opposite end of their small and narrow island. After running out of cannon balls they melted down the lead weights from their fishing nets to make new ones and fired *them* at the French. And Benjamin Gumbs displayed a certain grasp of military basics when he told his men, "I'll tell ye what, I know nothing about marching and countermarching, but my advice to you is to wait till the enemy comes close, and then fire and load and fire again like the devil."

At last, low on ammunition and high on despair, the Anguillans decided they had only one move left: counterattack. They came down off Sandy Hill with such fury and desperation that they drove the French back, and back, and finally all the way back across the island to their original beachhead at Rendezvous Bay.

As the French were scrambling off the island, having had more than enough of the Anguillans for one day, there appeared offshore the British frigate H.M.S. *Lapwing,* Captain Robert Barton commanding. The cutter that had gone for help had met up with *Lapwing* at Antigua. Now, between the crazy Anguillans on shore and the twenty-six-gun *Lapwing* out at sea, the end of the day was not a happy one for the French. And thus ended the second invasion.

The third military invasion of Anguilla took place on March 19, 1969, when the British sent in their 315 Red Devil paratroopers, who had been transported by frigate and who were supported by helicopters, the Royal Navy, the Royal Air Force, and a stand-by detachment of London policemen waiting on Antigua. This time the Anguillans put up absolutely no resistance of any land, and yet they defeated their invaders once again. The instant the first paratrooper boot touched the sand at Crocus Bay the Anguillans had won what is possibly their most glorious victory of all.

2

England does not love coalitions.

—Benjamin Disraeli

It may not be true that Christopher Columbus was the first European to set eyes, if not foot, on the empty and obscure West Indian island of Anguilla. If he did, it was during his second voyage to the New World in 1493. And if so, it is possible he named it, since he did name just about everything else round about. He may have done it in Spanish, *anguila* (eel), since he was on the road for Spain; or he may have done it in Italian, *anguilla* (eel), since he was Italian. Or he may not have named it at all, and he definitely didn't land there.

There was no particular reason to land. Anguilla was a small, dull and unpopulated bit of dusty turf, one of many low coral islands along the outer edge of the Caribbean Sea, far from the protection of the American continents and very exposed to the storms of the Atlantic Ocean. Fifteen miles long by two miles wide, the island possessed dozens of fine white beaches, several bays, no mountains, no natives, erratic rainfall and scrub vegetation. In the beginning there were some trees there, but most of them were cut down by early settlers for firewood or to build houses and ships, and the rest were swept away by droughts and hurricanes. One fat old mahogany tree still grows in the middle of the island; the Anguillans have put a picture of it on their stamps.

Even with all the trees intact the island wasn't particularly alluring to passers-by. The first recorded landing didn't come until seventy-one years after Columbus either did or did not open Anguilla's history. In 1564, Captain René Laudon-nière dropped in, and it could be that he was the one who named it, in French: *anguille* (eel). Whether he did or not, he didn't stay long; nor did the first Englishman to arrive, one Captain Harcourt, who merely stopped off for a minute in 1609 so he could afterward say, "I think never Englishmen disembogued before us." He also became possibly the first visitor who wasn't struck enough by the long, thin shape of the place to call it, in one language or another, Eel Island. Given that word "disembogued" it may be a pity he didn't try his hand at nomenclature after all.

Originally Anguilla had at least one other name, and possibly two. Before the Europeans came, the Caribbean had been populated by two different peoples: the Arawaks, a gentle, peaceful, delicate folk, and the Caribs, who used to eat them. ("Cannibal" is a Carib word.) If the Arawaks had a name for Anguilla it is now lost, but the Carib name for the island was Malliouhana—but wasn't Dorothy Lamour called that in one of the Road pictures?

Once it had a name, Anguilla was ready to start having a history, but unfortunately nothing happened for quite a while. Throughout the sixteenth century the nations of Europe, led by Spain, colonized and plundered and warred their way through the Caribbean, and nobody gave Anguilla a second look. The Arawaks and Caribs were subjugated and enslaved and exterminated; there are no Arawaks anymore, and only one last dwindling Carib reservation. Five million African slaves were imported to the West Indies in their stead to work on the plantations growing tobacco and sugar and cotton and bananas. The slaves survived, the islands produced wealth, and the wealth was exported. Still today the population in most Caribbean islands is divided between the white landowners, whose roots are still in Europe, and the black workers, whose roots are now in the West Indies.

Anguilla's story is different, and the difference is poverty. Having so little to offer by way of natural resources, Anguilla wasn't settled at all until 1650. "It was filled with alligators and other noxious animals," historian Thomas Southey said, not very encouragingly, "but the soil was good for raising tobacco and corn, and the cattle imported multiplied very fast. It was not colonized under any public encouragement; each planter labored for himself, and the island was frequently plundered by marauders." An inauspicious beginning that, apart from the alligators, pretty well set the tone.

These first arrivals were swelled in number sixteen years later by a group of English settlers who had just been driven from the island of St. Kitts by the French. At around the same time some shipwrecked Irishmen also arrived and stayed, and now and again in the next several years the white population was added to by deserters from one or another of the European navies constantly warring among themselves in the surrounding waters. And of course there was for a while an influx of black Africans, imported as slaves.

But a slave plantation economy on Anguilla never did become a roaring success; the island was just too poor in soil and rainfall to produce good plantation crops. Still, its poverty was a mixed curse; on Anguilla, slavery never became the deeply engrained life-style common to all the other Caribbean islands.

As V. S. Naipaul wrote in a London newspaper in 1969, "This feeling for their island, this sense of home, makes the Anguillans unusual among Caribbean peoples. The land has been theirs immemorially; no humiliation attaches to it." Or, as Lord Caradon, then chief British delegate to the United Nations and Minister of State for Foreign and Commonwealth Affairs, said to me in December of 1969, "For a number of strange and historical reasons the inhabitants of this island are passionately devoted to the spirit of independence. And this is, I think, the root of it all. It's not surprising, it's happened before in the world, and it's in many ways admirable."

Passionately devoted to the spirit of independence. Back when there *were* slaves, the white owners couldn't afford to feed them and so gave them four days off a week—Sunday for church, the other three to tend their own crops on their own lands. By the time slavery was officially ended in the British-controlled islands in 1834, every Anguillan family, white or black, owned its own home on its own plot of land, with its own chickens and goats. Many Anguillans had become craftsmen and tradesmen and fishermen, and Anguilla-built boats were already famous up and down the islands, as they still are today. White or black, slave or free, every last Anguillan was a property-owning middle-class petit bourgeois.

Which may be why Anguilla is the only populated Caribbean island that never had a slave rebellion.

It may also be why Anguilla is the only former colony ever to revolt *against* independence.

And it may be why the Anguillans are possibly the only rebels in history ever to have carried off a successful rebellion without killing anybody.

Politically, the history of Anguilla began twenty-five years before it had a population. For centuries, it didn't occur to Europeans
generally that anybody anywhere else in the world might have any
law or history of his own, rights or property or land or anything of
value that was already claimed. There were empires to be carved out
of the vast world beyond Europe's shores, and if that vast world already had a population living in it, "They should be," as Christopher
Columbus said of the Arawaks before the Spanish killed them all
off, "good servants of good skills." European kings tended to give
away whole continents to favorite nobles, without its ever crossing
the mind of either king or noble to check with the indigenous popu-
lations.

So it was with Anguilla, which became a political entity in
1625, while it was still an empty island, when it was given by the
English King Charles I, who didn't own it, to the Earl of Carlisle,
who did nothing with it. This was part of an offhand grant to the
Earl of Carlisle of *all* the Caribbean islands, including those with
Spaniards and other ferocious Europeans living on them, which
may explain why the Earl never dropped by to see his new property. This early political move, in which Anguilla was stuffed into
a package with several other more important items, set the tone for
the events of the centuries to come.

As the years went by, various political divisions were made in
the British Caribbean, with Anguilla always an odd-lot parcel in the
bottom of the bag, but none of this shuffling around ever had much
effect on the Anguillans' lives. They didn't pester the English administrators and the English administrators didn't pester them.

For example. In 1809 the Anguillans were ordered to build a
jail, but since they didn't have anyone to put in it they didn't do
it. Nine years later the Governor in St. Kitts got around to asking
about the jail and was told it hadn't been built because "the laws of
this island were lying dormant." It still didn't get built, and when
the Governor asked them four years later when they were going to
set up a civil court (something else he'd been wanting), they told
him "it was useless to erect themselves into a court of judicature for
want of a jail."

I mentioned the Governor in St. Kitts. Anguilla's connection
with St. Kitts began in 1822, when Anguilla was stripped flat by a

hurricane, then dried out by a drought, then swept bare by a gale, then decimated by famine. In response to all this, the English Secretary of State ordered the Governor of St. Kitts, through whom Great Britain more or less administered Anguilla, "to propose to the assembly of St. Christopher [the formal name of St. Kitts] that one representative should be received from the island of Anguilla which would enable the assembly to enact laws for the government of that colony." Laws, presumably, against hurricanes, droughts and gales.

The St. Kitts Governor proposed instead that Britain rule Anguilla direct, a suggestion that has come up more than once since that time. But England would have nothing to do with direct rule of such a microscopic entity as Anguilla, and forced the Governor of St. Kitts to take the smaller island under his wing whether he liked it or not.

The Anguillans disliked the arrangement as much as the Governor did. They sent a complaining letter to England, saying, "Can we indulge a hope that laws enacted particularly for this community, can or will be made with much regard to its interests, when they are to be passed by a body of men living in a distant and remote island, possessing no property of any kind here and having no connexion or relation whatever?" But the British blithely went ahead, setting up the legal framework in 1824, and the Anguillans obediently sent along somebody to St. Kitts to be present in the assembly every time St. Kitts planned to do something with, to, about or for Anguilla.

But all that was simply rigmarole to satisfy the English; it gave them a neat colonial administration, nice chain-of-command charts back home in London. On Anguilla, the islanders had their own government, the Vestry, which had eleven members elected by the people themselves. The Warden, the only official on the island from the St. Kitts Government, was invited to attend the meetings, and so was the Anglican rector, but neither of them could vote. The Vestry levied taxes, issued licenses, imposed export duties and generally ran the island.

This too was a pattern that would be followed throughout the island's history; one government, usually through St. Kitts and always under protest, to satisfy the constructionary minds of the English, and another government of Anguillans at home to get things done.

Fifty years later, in 1871, another political reshuffling took place, when the British created the Leeward Islands Federation, in which each island was to be its own presidency. Three years before, in 1868, phosphate had been found at Crocus Bay on Anguilla. It was being exported to Philadelphia, so the island was in one of its rare periods of financial well-being. The Anguillans appealed to Governor-General Sir Benjamin Pine, asking if they could be a separate presidency as long as things were being rearranged anyway, but when the dust had settled the combination of St. Kitts and Anguilla was *one* unit in the Federation.

What is this St. Kitts, that Anguilla keeps being stuck into paper states with it? Is it an island at all similar to Anguilla? No; it is volcanic where Anguilla is coral, mountainous where Anguilla is flat, rainy where Anguilla is dry, plantation-ridden and slave-oriented where Anguilla has always sheltered the independent poor.

Is it, then, the nearest island to Anguilla? No; the nearest populated island is St. Martin, three miles away; the next nearest is St. Barthélémy, twenty-five miles away; the next nearest is Saba, thirty miles away; the next nearest is St. Eustatius, fifty miles away. St. Kitts is seventy miles from Anguilla.

There is no geographical connection between St. Kitts and Anguilla of any kind, nor is there any social connection between them. St. Kitts's population is limited almost entirely to upper-class whites and lower-class blacks while Anguilla has a multiracial population limited almost entirely to poor middle-class property owners. (As an Anguillan said to me, "They call us poor, but you have to go to St. Kitts to see a filthy slum." I saw it, and it was filthy. The water supply is a communal curbside faucet every block, and the sewage disposal is a gutter down the middle of the street.)

There is only one connection between St. Kitts and Anguilla. On the maps and in the file drawers back in England, St. Kitts is the closest British colony to the British colony of Anguilla.

Two years after St. Kitts and Anguilla became one presidency in the Leeward Islands Federation, the Anguillans complained to England again, saying the Kittitians were "utter strangers to us" and "this legislative dependence on St. Kitts can in no sense be called a legislative union, it has operated and continues to operate most injuriously against us, and is mutually disliked."

That complaint went the way of the rest. In fact, when another administrative change was made nine years later (governments never last very long in the Caribbean), the paper linkage was formed even more tightly by combining the two islands with a third island, Nevis (which *is* the closest island to St. Kitts, which *does* have somewhat similar geography, and which *does* have a somewhat similar population), under a single presidency. But the portents were even worse than the action; the legal name for the combination of Anguilla and St. Kitts and Nevis was *St. Christopher-Nevis.* Not until seventy years later, in 1951, was the word *Anguilla* added to the name of the colony into which the island of Anguilla had willy-nilly been forced.

By the end of the Second World War, the British held several hundred islands in the Caribbean, most of them small and unpopulated, all of them grouped into fourteen separate political entities. There were also two small colonies on the mainlands of South and Central America (British Guiana and British Honduras) and the islands of Bermuda off the North American coast.

In 1958, the British Government attempted to unload practically all its Caribbean holdings, ten island colonies stuffed together into something resembling a loosely packed snowball thrown at a passing bus. This casserole was called the West Indies Federation, and it included Antigua, Barbados, Dominica, Grenada, Jamaica (with the Cayman Islands and the Turks & Caicos Islands), Montserrat, St. Christopher-Nevis-Anguilla, St. Lucia, St. Vincent and Trinidad-Tobago. It also included a lot of water, since the Federation was spread out over an expanse of Caribbean Sea 1,600 miles wide and 800 miles long. Jamaica and the Cayman Islands were a full thousand miles from the rest of the Federation, separated from the others not only by all that water but also by such trivia as Haiti, the Dominican Republic, Puerto Rico and the U.S. Virgin Islands. The Turks & Caicos Islands were a little north of everybody else, the other side of Puerto Rico and Cuba. Spotted amid the remaining nine were a half dozen colonies of France and Holland and the United States. Between Jamaica and Trinidad lay fifteen hundred miles of open water, with nothing in it at all.

This wasn't the first federation dreamed up by the British Colonial Office, but it was certainly the biggest. The Colonial Office loved the idea of neat packages, and federations make a charmingly neat package on paper. As Lord Caradon told me, "They've not done so well, federations, so far. I think they'll do better in future. I don't write off the federation idea." Lord Caradon, then Sir Hugh Foot, was Governor of Jamaica while the West Indies Federation was being organized and is generally considered a chief architect of the Nigerian Federation; his faith does seem to die pretty hard. Particularly since, of the half-dozen federations put together by the British since the end of the Second World War, not one has remained intact.

The West Indies Federation began, as federations do, with a conference, this one held at Montego Bay in 1947. A Standing Closer Association Committee was formed to study the idea of mixing and matching all these islands and to work up a constitution for the result.

It may be appropriate here to mention the old description of a camel as a horse designed by a committee, and to suggest that perhaps a federation is a country designed by a committee.

The conference eventually came up with a report saying the federation idea was a good one, and the report was submitted to a second conference, this one in London in 1953. The second conference was pleased with the first conference's report, and in turn submitted it to the island governments involved. Jamaica, by a unanimous vote in both houses, was the first to accept the recommendation, and all the other islands promptly followed suit.

(The two mainland colonies, British Honduras and British Guiana, the latter now Guyana, were also invited in but declined, for private reasons of their own, not because the Federation struck them as an unworkable idea. There is a complex racial balance in those two lands, particularly in Guyana; federation would mean unrestricted immigration of blacks from the overcrowded islands, which would destroy the balance forever. A tie to the mainland had been put forward as one of the primary advantages of federation. This tie was now proved to be impossible, but the Federation lunged forward anyway.)

A third conference took place, in London again, in 1956, and at this conference the irrevocable decision to federate took place.

Now a year passes, in which everybody argues about where the capital should be. A full year. Finally, after enough bitterness and squabbling to convince anybody but a conference that these people are never going to live together, it is decided to build the capital in Trinidad. No reason why not.

Princess Margaret officiated at the first session of the West Indies Parliament on April 22, 1958. It was planned that for the next four years the new nation would be half-free and half-colony, with Mother Britain keeping one hand on the reins while the boys got used to running things themselves. As of May 31, 1962, the West Indies Federation would be a completely independent nation, and Great Britain would have rid itself of ten colonies at one fell swoop.

But it didn't turn out that way. The first thing that happened, there was trouble about the capital. Chaguaramas, the site on Trinidad they'd finally chosen, was leased to the United States for a naval base and the United States wouldn't vacate. So after all that bickering about the capital, and finally coming to a decision, everybody had to go back and start all over again.

Then, on September 19, 1961, Jamaica had a referendum; should it stay in the Federation or get out? The decision was strongly to get out, which Jamaica promptly did. The first island in became the first island out.

Trinidad was the second, early in 1962. And on May 31, 1962, the date originally planned as Independence Day, the West Indies Federation was dissolved.

And they never did find a site for the capital.

The West Indies Federation wasn't a total loss, however. The practice had been good for the bigger islands, and in August of 1962 both Jamaica and Trinidad-Tobago became independent. So the British had at least managed to cut their colonial responsibilities by two.

But that was a far cry from the ten they'd been trying for, so the British came right back in again, with a *new* idea—a federation.

This time the federation would be composed of the "Little Eight"—Antigua, Barbados, Dominica, Grenada, Montserrat, St. Christopher-Nevis-Anguilla, St. Lucia and St. Vincent. Conferences were held, of course, both on Barbados and in London, and on November 1, 1964, a cheerful announcement was made that a new improved West Indies Federation would appear some time in 1965.

It didn't, though, and on November 30, 1966, Barbados went off by itself and became an independent nation, and then there were seven.

Back in 1960, during the half-life of the West Indies Federation, the Anguillans had asked through their elected member of the St. Kitts Legislative Council if they could please be separated from St. Kitts; they were ignored. On January 22, 1965, while the "Little Eight" conferences were going on, seventeen leading citizens of Anguilla signed a request that their island "remain outside the proposed Federation of the Eastern Caribbean and be administered from the Colonial Office"; they were ignored.

The requests from Anguilla for political separation from St. Kitts had never stopped since 1822, but from 1958 on they became ever more frequent, more urgent and more plaintive. General independence was in the air, and the Anguillans knew it and did not want independence from Great Britain if it meant they would remain under the authority of St. Kitts. And the reason for that was mostly a man named Robert Llewellyn Bradshaw.

Robert Bradshaw is a Kittitian, born in 1916 and destined to be a cane cutter on the plantations like the generations before him. In a special report on the Leeward and Windward islands in October of 1968, the London *Times* gave the background that altered Robert Bradshaw's destiny:

> A fairly consistent pattern can be seen in the islands. Political awareness began in the late 1930s, when depression in world commodity prices, particularly sugar, hit the whole West Indies hard. With the help of the British Labour Party and trade unions the workers came together. For the first time there was a basis for popular power. Mr. Bradshaw, of St. Kitts—the doyen of island politicians—and Mr. Bird, of Antigua, rose in this manner. They were union organizers and spoke for labour—the cane cutters, the dock workers and public employees. This became general in the islands, and today most of the ruling parties have Labour somewhere in their title.

Bradshaw's first job was in the St. Kitts sugar factory, where he formed the island's first union. He came to real prominence in 1948, when he was thirty-two years old and led the first major sugar workers' strike anywhere in the Caribbean. It blossomed into sixteen weeks of rioting and ended with some small concessions gained from the plantation owners. With universal suffrage on all the islands, union men were moving into government, and in 1952 Bradshaw became St. Kitts's Minister of Trade and Production. In 1956 he ran for Premier, got all the sugar-worker votes, and won.

There are, however, no sugar workers on Anguilla, which may be one of the reasons Bradshaw got practically no votes from Anguilla. This move may have been both democratic and honest on the Anguillans' part, but it wasn't very healthy.

Bradshaw was a strong supporter of the West Indies Federation. In 1958, at its inception, he won a seat in the Federal Parliament, turning over the reins of Kittitian government to his Deputy Premier, Caleb Azariah Paul Southwell, a burly man who is not a Kittitian by birth, but a Dominican. Bradshaw became Federal Minister of Finance and a vice-president of the West Indies Federal Labour Party, but when the West Indies Federation crumpled he returned to St. Kitts and eventually took his old job back, with Paul Southwell reverting to the Number Two spot.

The key to Robert Bradshaw may simply be that he wants to be loved. A small and slender man, with a huge moustache that he seems to have rented from Groucho Marx, Bradshaw likes to dress up in ways that have been called "outlandish," "odd" and "quaint." He has been known to appear in public in gaiters, in buckle shoes, in wing collars, in powdered wigs. He will take any opportunity to slap on a top hat. He wears uniforms the envy of every doorman along Central and Hyde parks, though according to the London *Daily Express* he also "delights in donning British military khaki and strutting around the indoor lily pond at Government Headquarters with pistol and peaked cap." Wearing one or another of his costumes, he likes to drive around his domain in his canary-yellow 1935 Rolls-Royce, occasionally tending his moustache with its special golden brush. For years he had on his office wall a cartoon showing John Foster Dulles on the toilet, with the caption: "The only man in Washington who knows what he is doing."

Bradshaw sees himself as a father to his people, a stern and knowing and loving father who knows best for his children. The violent aspects of paternalism are strong in him; when St. Kitts became semi-independent in 1967, he reintroduced flogging for criminal offenses.

There is nothing a father likes less than being rejected by one of his children, and Robert Bradshaw has felt like a spurned father in re Anguilla ever since 1956. "I will not rest," he was quoted as saying, shortly after the election, "until I have reduced that place to a desert." He said this at a speech in Basseterre's Pall Mall Square, at one time the largest slave market in the West Indies. He always makes this sort of remark in public, either in speeches at open meetings or over St. Kitts's Government-controlled radio station ZIZ; but then afterward, when he's feeling calmer, he denies he said any such thing. His political opposition on St. Kitts has taken to tape-recording his announcements—but that's all right, he denies them anyway.

He denies, for instance, that he ever said of the Anguillans, "I will put salt in their coffee, bones in their rice and sand in their sugar." Or that he varied the formula slightly on another occasion by saying, "I will put bones in their rice and pepper in their soup." Or that his suggestion for Anguilla's future development was that "they will have to suck each other's bones."

None of these statements, despite the subsequent denials, encouraged the Anguillans much. The London *Sunday Times* remarked in 1969, "The culmination of Bradshaw's increasingly idiosyncratic rule has been his boast that he is the spiritual descendant of Henri Christophe, the 19th century dictator of Haiti. Since Christophe achieved, even in that country's bloodstained annals, a unique notoriety for his cruelty, he is not perhaps the most reassuring hero."

How did it affect the Anguillans, over the years, having Robert Bradshaw as their Premier? Well, for example, the British had installed a telephone system on Anguilla shortly after the First World War—fourteen phones, hand-cranked. When Hurricane Donna flattened the island in 1960, all the poles were knocked down. The St. Kitts Government sent up some repairmen, but instead of fixing the poles they took away the central-office equipment. Anguilla went without telephones for twelve years.

Then there was the pier. Anguilla has never had a cargo pier where seagoing vessels could be off-loaded; everything delivered to the island—and everything except weeds has to be delivered—had to be brought in by small boat from ships anchored offshore. As the

Anguillans tell it, they asked Canada for aid money to build a pier. The money was sent to the central Government on St. Kitts, and the pier was built—on St. Kitts. It was named Anguilla Pier.

While on St. Kitts in 1970, I visited Anguilla Pier, which wasn't all that easy to do. It's at Sandy Point, on the opposite side of the island from the capital of Basseterre and all the shipping. There are no storage sheds, there is no industry in the area, there isn't even a town there. I couldn't swear to it, but the crane didn't look operable; my impression was that it had rusted into place. Some young boys were playing around the pier and the ocean was empty as far as the eye could see.

Pier, phones; the list goes on. No general electricity. Three hundred and fifty children in a one-room schoolhouse. Less than a mile and a half of paved road. Medical facilities that frequently had operations performed by the light of a hurricane lamp, and that gave funds to transport a maximum of two emergency patients a year to an off-island hospital.

The Anguillans could complain, but all communication with Britain had to go through the St. Kitts Government and complaints seemed to lose their force and urgency in transition.

But even though the Anguillans couldn't officially speak directly to Great Britain, they were soothed somewhat by the knowledge that at least Great Britain was there. Bradshaw might stick his thumb in Anguilla's eye every once in a while, but so long as St. Kitts-Nevis-Anguilla was a part of the British colonial structure, Bradshaw had to be at least somewhat restrained.

Then came independence.

3

"Hurrah! hurrah! we bring the Jubilee!
Hurrah! hurrah! the flag that makes you free!"
—Henry Clay Work,
"Marching Through Georgia"

As of 1966 the British had, for the moment, given up the idea of a federation in the West Indies. But only for the moment. Dr. Eric Williams, Prime Minister of Trinidad-Tobago, was quoted as recently as 1969 as hoping to see a new West Indies Federation in effect by 1975; it is known he has British support in his dream. But back in 1966 the British were temporarily weary of West Indies Federations, and as a result they began to cast about for some new way to cast off all those islands.

The new idea they came up with was something they dubbed an Associated State.

Generally speaking, the idea of an Associated State is that the nation's internal affairs are to be handled by itself, while its external affairs are handled by Great Britain. Financial aid for development schemes also continues to flow to the Associated State from Britain, and the plan is that Associated Statehood is a temporary way station on the road to complete independence.

Associated Statehood was offered to all the flotsam still floating after the capsize of the West Indies Federation, and six of the seven survivors agreed to it, only Montserrat choosing to remain a colony.

An Associated State bears one ominous similarity to a federation; it is preceded by a conference. In London in May of 1966, a Constitutional Conference took place to consider the Associated State of St. Christopher-Nevis-Anguilla. February 27, 1967, was the target date for Statehood Day, so there wasn't very much time to make sure the suit fit. The conference delegates included Robert Bradshaw, Paul Southwell and Basil Dias from St. Kitts, Eugene

Walwyn from Nevis and Peter Adams from Anguilla. Walwyn was one of the two Nevisian members of the Legislative Council on St. Kitts, and Adams was the Anguillan member of the Legislative Council. Remember the hurricane, the drought, the gale and the famine back in 1822? Remember the politicians' response to it all? They'd established an Anguillan representative in the St. Kitts assembly. As of 1966 that Anguillan representative was Peter Adams.

The conference produced proposals for a constitution and all the delegates agreed the proposals were good and thereby signed the report, including Peter Adams. Later on, the British and Kittitians were to claim that Peter Adams, speaking for all Anguillans everywhere, had agreed to anything Robert Bradshaw might think up, but Adams himself insisted that he had merely signed a Conference Report that said that such-and-such proposals were worth looking into. And in fact, the Anguillans asked for direct administration from Great Britain *twice* in 1966, in June and October; they were ignored.

The conference was followed by an election. In St. Kitts there are two political parties: the Labour Party, which Bradshaw leads and which is supported mainly by the black work force, and the People's Action Movement (PAM), which is supported mainly by the merchant middle class, the professional class and the fifteen or so rich white famines who own almost all the land on the island. (For the most part, the natives live around the fringe of the island, in the narrow border between the road and the sea; nearly everything else is owned by the whites and is mostly given over to sugar.)

On Nevis, there is no Labour Party, but there is the United National Movement, led by Eugene Walwyn, one of the London conference delegates, who declared after the election that he would support Bradshaw and the Labour Party in the Legislative Council. PAM put up a man to oppose him, and the division of support for UNM and PAM on Nevis was about the same as for Labour and PAM on St. Kitts.

If St. Christopher-Nevis-Anguilla were really the unitary state it's supposed to be, the same general political breakdown should exist on Anguilla as on the other two. There should be something like PAM for the middle and upper classes and something like the Labour Party for the workers. But it doesn't work that way. Anguilla has never had any political parties at all; everybody runs for everything as an independent. That's Anguilla all over, that absolutely sums up the place. Everybody runs for everything as an independent. Shortly before the 1966 election Peter Adams did declare he'd joined PAM, but that meant very little on Anguilla.

The elections didn't change much. The Labour Party had St. Kitts's seven seats on the Legislative Council before the election and still had them after. Eugene Walwyn was re-elected to one of the two Nevisian seats, and a PAM candidate, Fred Parris, won the other. And Peter Adams beat out two independents (two *other* independents, that is) for the Anguilla seat.

Now we have something strange. PAM is primarily a Kittitian political party, led by a Kittitian named Dr. William Herbert. But Dr. Herbert didn't win a seat on the Legislative Council, nor did any other PAM candidate from St. Kitts, so by default the position of Leader of the Opposition fell to Peter Adams, the man from Anguilla, who had joined the party about two months before, had always been an independent, and had aligned himself with PAM only because of short-range considerations concerning the proposed constitution and independence. Still, it gave the British a reassuring feeling of familiarity to know that the St. Christopher-Nevis-Anguilla Legislative Council had a Leader of the Opposition; it showed that the concept of British democracy and parliamentary rule had taken root in this exotic soil.

The Anguillans had been unhappy for 144 years about being governed from St. Kitts, and the Nevisians were themselves a little leery of the Kittitians' concern for their future. Therefore they were pleased that one of the proposals from the Constitutional Conference had been the establishment of some sort of local-government Councils for both Anguilla and Nevis, to operate in addition to the Legislative Council and the central Government on St. Kitts.

The British had promised to send to the islands a "local government expert" to help set up the two new Councils. Since the British were going to send this man all the way across the Atlantic the St. Kitts Government decided he ought to have somebody to talk to, so on October 22, 1966, five months after the conference, a committee was appointed to talk to him.

The 1970 Report of the Commission of Inquiry into the problem of Anguilla (called the Wooding Report) gives the most succinct description of what did and did not happen next:

> No meeting of the committee having been convened for some time, Mr. Adams enquired of the Chief Minister (Robert Bradshaw) about the establishment of local government in Nevis and Anguilla. Later, when it became known that the local government expert would be arriving in January the committee was summoned to meet on 23 December, 1966. We were told in evidence that the meeting was called at short notice and, because Mr. Adams was then in Anguilla, he was not notified.

On January 7, 1967, fifteen days after that meeting, the committee sent Peter Adams a copy of the minutes, along with a letter explaining why he hadn't been invited. Adams had copies of the minutes made up and circulated around Anguilla, the people took a look at the token suggestions for local government they contained, and at that point the smoothly running railroad began to break down. A group of Anguillans went to PAM headquarters on St. Kitts and warned Dr. Herbert and the other PAM executives that if local government didn't become a hell of a lot more local than this committee had in mind, Anguilla would quit its association with St. Kitts and that would be the end of it. The people from PAM said they would see what they could do.

PAM's role in all this is just slightly murky. The party was started by Dr. Herbert, a tall young man with a narrow beard who looks and moves like a professional basketball player and who talks faster than an encyclopedia salesman. Everybody who knows him at all calls him Billy, and the Dr. in front of his name simply means he has a university education complete with doctorate, not that he's a medical doctor. Billy Herbert is a lawyer, officially Dr. William V. Herbert, L.L.B., Ph.D., a graduate of London University and the Institute for Advanced Legal Studies. His father, owner but not editor of St. Kitts's only opposition newspaper, was a prominent union mediator for years, which on an island like St. Kitts means that he carried the white folks' words to the black folks. Since the man carrying the black folks' words to the white folks was for many years the labor leader Robert Bradshaw, it's no surprise that a certain antipathy developed between Bradshaw and Herbert *père*. Given the personality of Bradshaw, it is also no surprise that he would carry that antipathy into the next generation. When Billy Herbert came back from London and offered his services to Bradshaw and the Labour Government, Bradshaw in effect told him to go jump in Potatoe Bay. Instead of which, Herbert started PAM.

Some other members of PAM are, like Billy Herbert, people who have been frozen out of politics by personal whims of Bradshaw and who want to see a governmental structure a little less autocratic and more diverse. Some middle-class members of PAM would like to see participatory democracy in which more than the sugar workers participate. And the rich whites want PAM in because it's the only alternative to the Labour Party, and they want the Labour Party out because—Bradshaw's idiosyncrasies aside—it is a *Labour* Party; that is, socialist. Creeping socialism threatens the landed class throughout the Caribbean, particularly when combined with local independence (a total parallel with the situation several years ago throughout Africa).

But if PAM itself is slightly ambiguous, there has been nothing ambiguous about Robert Bradshaw's reaction to his Opposition's existence. The only radio station in St. Kitts is Z1Z, which is owned and operated by the Government; PAM has not been permitted use of the station. (There was no television station on St. Kitts, but the islanders could pick up three channels from other islands if they had television sets; unfortunately, the Government prohibited them from having television sets.) PAM was forbidden to hold public meetings without first getting the approval of Bradshaw's chief of police, which wasn't all that easy to do.

If Bradshaw was determined to reduce Anguilla to a desert, he seemed determined to reduce PAM to something less than a desert; possibly because it drew 35 per cent of the vote its first time out, in the 1966 election, as opposed to Bradshaw's Labour Party vote of 44 per cent. Bradshaw was operating with less than a majority and resented it.

Few Anguillan events directly affect any of the goals desired by the St. Kitts political party called PAM. But indirectly they can have quite an effect. That is, if disturbances on Anguilla were eventually to sour Great Britain on Robert Bradshaw personally, and if they were sufficiently to embarrass his Labour Party among its own rank and file, it just might do PAM some good in the next elections. And in any event, if Bradshaw could be kept distracted by Anguilla, it might be possible to delay a bit longer some of that creeping socialism.

Which is not to say that PAM is anti-socialist, though some of its supporters certainly are. Nor is it to say that PAM cynically fanned the flames of discontent on Anguilla, though it's unlikely that PAM or any other political party on earth doesn't contain at least a few cynics. Besides, whether PAM fanned the flames or not is essentially irrelevant. PAM's existence had nothing to do with the fact of Anguilla's rebellion; Anguilla had had enough no matter what interior squabbling went on in St. Kitts. PAM's leaders could have made agitative speeches nonstop for a month and it wouldn't have had as much influence on the Anguillans as Robert Bradshaw saying, just once, "I will not rest until I have reduced that place to a desert."

Anyway, by the time the local-government expert arrived from England, the third week in January 1967, it was a little too late to discuss the issue. The trouble in the air wasn't something that could be straightened out by adjusting some phrases in a constitution.

The expert, a man named Peter Johnston, was scheduled to visit Anguilla on January 27. The day before, the Anguillans had some public meetings to talk things over, and to decide they didn't like any of the options offered to them. Peter Adams was off with the local-government committee, and two of the leaders of these meetings on Anguilla were men who would become increasingly prominent in the affair: Ronald Webster and Atlin Harrigan.

Atlin Harrigan, young, slender and serious, left school at fourteen to earn his way in the world. He was a tailor, a fisherman, a carpenter and a deck hand before leaving home, in the traditional way of Anguillans, to seek greener pastures elsewhere. He lived in England for a while but didn't like the English winters and returned to the West Indies, where he became a skilled electrician on the American island of St. Thomas. When trouble flared up at home, Harrigan went back to Anguilla and has lived there ever since, frequently in the forefront of resistance to St. Kitts. He speaks mildly, with a combination of humor and despair best summed up in his remark at a public meeting in 1968: "If I told half what I know, the British would never give us self-government."

With the local Anglican minister, an Englishman named Canon Guy Carleton, Harrigan founded *The Beacon*, Anguilla's only newspaper, a weekly, in September of 1967. The editorial in the first issue, over Harrigan's signature, began:

> For the first time in the history of Anguilla, we have found it possible to publish a newspaper, THE BEACON, whereby the people of Anguilla and the world outside Anguilla can learn what is happening on the island, and whereby they can voice their opinions.

A little later in the same editorial he explained the new paper's name:

> I have chosen the name THE BEACON, because all the big ships passing to the north of Anguilla are grateful to Anguilla for her beacon at Sombrero to guide them to their destination. So, too, many people all over the world are grateful to Anguilla for the stand she has made for freedom and democracy. Like the BEACON may this paper be a help to guide Anguillans to pick out the good from the bad, so that they may have nothing less than the best.

Ronald Webster, not quite forty-one years of age at the point he enters our story, was born on Anguilla March 2, 1926, the son of a fisherman. He had an elementary school education and then emigrated to the nearby island of St. Martin, where he spent his youth as gardener and then farm foreman for a Dutch couple who were so taken with him they later named him prominently in their will, leaving him money and land sufficient to make him the richest of all Anguillans. Returning home, he opened a general store and bought some land, gradually increasing his wealth. Although he is probably not a millionaire, he likely doesn't miss by much.

A short and slender man, with long-fingered hands, Ronald Webster gives an impression of wiry strength under rigid control. In photographs he looks mild and meek, and some interviewers have come away describing him as shy; neither the photographs nor the interviewers are wrong, but they are incomplete. Webster *is* mild, with a soft-speaking voice and a sudden gentle laugh, and some manners of personal shyness, but there is an element in him that photographs never seem to catch. He seldom looks directly at the person he's talking to—that's the shyness, not guile—but when he does, everything changes. His eyes are deep-set and intense and very dark, and they gleam out like unwinking black stars. He has a thin face, the milk-chocolate skin taut over prominent bones, and what rays out from that face is an absolute and total sense of conviction. Ronald Webster is altogether certain of his own destiny.

A part of this is ordinary self-assurance, but another part is tied in with Webster's religious beliefs. He has changed his religion twice, most recently becoming a Seventh-Day Adventist at the age of thirty-four, conversions that suggest a restless yet thoughtful mind, and he has embraced each of his religions in turn with the same intensity. Throughout the Anguillan rebellion he was to read from his Bible every day and continue to do no work from sundown Friday till sundown Saturday.

Webster had spent his first four decades as a silent, personal man, concerned only with his religion, his business, his family—he had a wife and five children—but he would soon find a more public use for his qualities of self-conviction and intensity.

In the meetings led by Webster and Harrigan and one or two other Anguillans on January 26, 1967 (the day before the local-government expert, Peter Johnston, was due to visit the island), a broad vista of complaint was gradually winnowed into nine sections, as given in the 1970 Wooding Report:

> (1) Between 1948 and 1967 membership of the Legislative Council had increased from 3 to 7 for St. Kitts, from 1 to 2 for Nevis, but for Anguilla it had remained at 1: [Seats on the Legislative Council were apportioned by population, and the population of Anguilla remains fairly constant at around 6,000, with the excess leaving to find work and advancement in other parts of the world. It has been said that Anguilla's principal export is Anguillans; since most of the expatriates send money back to help support their relations at home, John Updike has written, "Fundamentally the economy runs by remittance."]
>
> (2) St. Kitts had made progress—she had a radio station, a cigarette factory and a "beer factory," but Anguilla still had one doctor and a Warden-Magistrate;'
>
> (3) Kittitians did not like Anguillans, so affiliation with them would

be to invite oppression and bloodshed;

(4) The Government in St. Kitts was restricting the free entry of foreigners, and this was already affecting Anguillans abroad; [The Anguillans feared that Kittitian restrictions against noncitizens traveling into the state would lead to reprisals by other islands against citizens of St. Christopher-Nevis-Anguilla. Anguillans, more than any other islanders in the area, travel and work in foreign lands; impose travel restrictions and what would happen to the remittances?]

(5) Anguilla was ignored generally—her name did not even appear on the number plates of vehicles; by contrast the term "Electricity Department of St. Kitts-Nevis-Anguilla" was a misnomer, since there was no public electricity in Anguilla; [There *is* no electricity on Anguilla. The Kittitian Government studied the problem at one time and decided it wasn't feasible to give Anguilla electricity because the houses were too far apart—no slums—to run an electric company at a profit. A government that refuses to furnish its citizens electricity unless it can do so at a profit is a strange government indeed.]

(6) Mr. Bradshaw the Chief Minister had threatened that Anguillans would have to eat one another's bones and that he would turn Anguilla into a desert;

(7) Anguilla would be subject to heavy taxation if she went into Statehood with St. Kitts; Anguilla should seek to join Montserrat or Tortola and remain with England as a Crown Colony; England would be bound to keep Anguilla as a colony since Anguilla was unwilling to associate with St. Kitts in Statehood: [The first part of this is a little ingenuous, since taxation in Anguilla is mostly import duties and Anguillans are known to be the premier smugglers of the Caribbean, practically nobody ever paying import duty for anything. The second part is the beginning of what would become a long string of alternate suggestions for Anguilla's future; Anguillans don't particularly crave association with either Montserrat or Tortola, but just about anything seemed better than Mr. Bradshaw's St. Kitts. As to the final clause, about England being bound to keep Anguilla since Anguilla didn't want to associate with St. Kitts, this was at least naïve and showed an appalling lack of historical awareness; Anguilla hadn't wanted to associate with St. Kitts since 1822 and England had never given a damn at all.]

(8) The signing of the Report of the Constitutional Conference by Mr. Peter Adams did not indicate agreement with Statehood, but only gave

members of the delegation "permission to negotiate for Statehood";

(9) The Chief Minister had held a committee meeting secretly for the purpose of negotiating local government with Mr. Johnston. [In other words, before the local-government expert ever even arrived in the Caribbean, the St. Kitts Government had managed to compromise him and condemn him to ineffectiveness by holding its committee meeting behind Peter Adams' back. This ineptitude is the Kittitian Government's only saving grace and has been the Anguillans' secret weapon from the very beginning.]

On January 27, 1967, Peter Johnston arrived in Anguilla, innocently expecting to talk about local government. They met him with everything but a rope.

Four hundred people were at the airport—a dirt strip with a shack to one side—and most of them were carrying signs. "We want no Statehood," one sign read, getting right down to business, and another one amplified, "We don't want Bradshaw and his Statehood." A long sign amplified the amplification: "Could we be united with Bradshaw who said he will turn Anguilla into a desert?" And another one, with simple but all-encompassing dignity, said, "No association with St. Kitts."

Johnston had a lot to read while getting off the plane. "No Trinity No Premier No Statehood," for instance.

Well, if they didn't want statehood or Bradshaw or the Trinity of St. Christopher-Nevis-Anguilla, what *did* they want? Other signs were glad you asked that question: "We want to be free," one of them said. "We don't want Statehood we want England," another said, and this was seconded by a sign reading, "No statehood for Anguilla seeking care of England." "God save the Queen," said yet another, to reassure Johnston that things were still all right between Anguilla on the one hand and the United Kingdom of Great Britain and Northern Ireland on the other. "We will continue to be united Trinity with our Mother Country, England," announced another, using the word "Trinity" in a way I don't entirely understand; but the one that made the ultimate summation of the situation went as follows: *"Seeking the choice of Mother's care."*

Upon arrival, Peter Johnston, the inadvertent representative of Mother, went first to Government House and then on to the Court

House, where it was his intention to meet with the people—most of whom were following him, waving their signs—and talk about local government. "There," says the Wooding Report, "a group of Anguillans who acted as spokesmen showed a total disinclination to discuss local government. Instead, they took the opportunity to express views against Statehood." A dozen troublemakers took the lead in this, including Ronald Webster and Atlin Harrigan.

But Peter Johnston wasn't the man to talk to, as he tried to explain. However, he was the only one available, so they kept at him until finally he left, with dissatisfaction on both sides. He had not managed to communicate to them effectively about local government, and they had not managed to communicate to him effectively about their growing fear of the local Government at St. Kitts.

Four days later, on January 31, some people from PAM came to Anguilla to make speeches praising the Anguillans for their anti-statehood stand. Billy Herbert came and so did two of his party's executives. They held meetings at three spots on the island and were very enthusiastically received. The Anguillans had decided on their path already, but they found it nice to hear there was somebody else on their side.

Though not exactly. PAM and the Anguillans were united in opposition to Bradshaw, but the Anguillans had already gone a giant step beyond PAM, as those signs had demonstrated a week before. PAM wanted a broader range of local government in the separate units of the state; Anguilla wanted to get out of the state entirely. In fact, the only thing all Anguillans have ever agreed on, agree on now, or are likely to agree on in the future, is that they want nothing to do with Robert Bradshaw or the state he leads.

Well, almost all. Peter Adams, the only Anguillan actually plugged in to the Government in St. Kitts, continued to believe much longer than most other Anguillans that some sort of compromise could be worked out. PAM and Peter Adams were the moderates in this dispute, with Bradshaw and the St. Kitts Government and the British Government the extremists frozen on the one side and the mass of the Anguillan people the extremists frozen on the other side. As in most situations where passions really run high, it was ultimately the moderates who got the worst of it.

Two days after the PAM leaders went to Anguilla to declare

solidarity with the Anguillans—even though the Anguillans had somewhat different goals from those of PAM—a letter was sent by PAM to Robert Bradshaw, listing the party's Nine-Point Plan for local government and demanding that Bradshaw implement it all. The letter was dated February 2, 1967, and so was Bradshaw's reply. This reply was brief, it was to the point, and it covered the territory.

DEAR SIR,

Reference is made to a letter of instant date addressed to me and signed by yourself as "(Secretary, PAM)," "P. E. Adams MLC for Anguilla of PAM" and "William Herbert, President PAM" referring to "proposals as to the composition and functions of the proposed local government under our new Constitution." There are no "proposals" before my Government.

Yours faithfully,
ROBERT L. BRADSHAW
Chief Minister

Nothing could be plainer than that. Herbert and Adams went at once to talk to the Governor, Sir Fred Phillips. He told them there really wasn't very much he could do, nor did he see any reason for them to be so alarmed. He told them he'd received a report from Peter Johnston, the local-government expert, which had led him to believe that things either were basically all right now or very soon would be basically all right, and not to worry.

Herbert and Adams told Sir Fred they intended to go to London to try and persuade the British Government to delay Statehood Day until this mess could be straightened out. He told them he didn't think there was any need for them to go to London, but if they insisted he would be more than happy to warn the Secretary of State that they were on the way.

Meanwhile, back on Anguilla, the first *incident* was about to take place. Up till now, there had been no end of speeches and demonstrations and meetings, but no real trouble had yet occurred. Then, on February 4, things suddenly turned ugly.

It was perhaps inevitable on Anguilla that if things were to turn ugly it would happen at a beauty contest. St. Kitts, in a lunatic attempt to build enthusiasm among the populace for the fast-approaching Statehood Day, had created a beauty contest to choose a Statehood Queen—or Miss Associated State, nobody was quite clear about the title—with contestants from the three islands. Beauties from Nevis and St. Kitts were flown to Anguilla on February 4 to compete with local girls at The Valley Secondary School. The very mention of the word "statehood" by this point so inflamed some Anguillans—even when the word was used in conjunction with a beauty contest—that while the show was going on in the school building, a demonstration began to form outside. The demonstrators decided to abort the beauty contest by shutting down the generator supplying the school's electricity, which they did, and which brought the cops down on their heads.

(An interpolation. Government employees on Anguilla tended almost exclusively to be Kittitians, and that definitely included the police. The seventeen-man Anguilla Police Force, at this time, contained no Anguillans.)

The police decided to disperse the demonstrators with tear gas, without first checking to see which way the wind was blowing. It was blowing toward the school. The tear gas dispersed the demonstrators and then drifted over to the school and dispersed the audience and then drifted up on stage and dispersed the beauty queens. End of beauty contest. End of first incident, with beauty queens diving headfirst out windows.

The next day, the police went out to the east end of the island and picked up three of the men they thought had taken part in the anti-beauty-contest demonstration, intending to bring them back to headquarters. On the drive back to the center of the island, some other cars joined the police car, everybody stopped, a rational discussion ensued, and the police agreed they didn't feel like arresting these three fellows after all. End of arrest. Second end of incident. But not the last.

After the attempted arrest, Ronald Webster and Atlin Harrigan took to sleeping out in the bush, and after a while they went over to St. Martin and sent a telegram to the Commonwealth Relations Office: WE ARE BEING HUNTED DOWN BY THE POLICE AND FIVE THOUSAND PEOPLE IN ANGUILLA ARE DEMONSTRATING. There was no reply.

A week after the second ending of the beauty-contest incident, British Marines landed on Anguilla. This isn't the big invasion; that won't happen for another two years. This is a small quiet landing; so quiet, in fact, that no announcement was made of it at the time, and when the question was first brought up, the British Government denied it had ever happened.

But it did. After the second act of the beauty-contest incident, the Kittitian police on Anguilla asked the central Government on St. Kitts to send reinforcements. Fortunately, there turned out to be no particular urgency about being reinforced since it took the extra police a week to get there. It is one of the minor absurdities of this affair that all of the ships and planes in the nation of St. Kitts-Nevis-Anguilla were owned by Anguillans. As of February 1967, there were two Anguillan-owned airlines and many motor-driven fishing boats and launches. The St. Kitts Government had no airplanes at all, and only two non-sail ships: the Revenue Cutter and the *Christiana*, a lumbering tub on a regular ferry service to Nevis. (The *Christiana* eventually sank on one of her two-mile runs to Nevis, killing a hundred people.)

After a week of looking around for some vehicle that would take reinforcements from St. Kitts to Anguilla, Bradshaw at last convinced the British to help. They laid on a warship, H.M.S. *Salisbury* (the same name as the capital of Rhodesia), which brought the reinforcements—variously reported as numbering forty, seventy and one hundred—to Anguilla. They landed at Island Harbour, an out-of-the-way corner of the island not too far from where some of the alleged demonstrators lived. The Kittitian police were escorted ashore by a detachment of Royal Marines wearing steel helmets and carrying rifles—they had been led by their superiors to expect trouble.

(Those in authority on the British side consistently failed to understand that the Anguillans *like* the English; it's Bradshaw they don't like. The British perhaps *have* reduced Anguilla to a desert, but they never said they would; Bradshaw said he would.)

The Kittitian police and British Royal Marines were met on the beach by people living in the area, who had come down to find out what that big ship was all about. They ignored the Kittitians but greeted the Marines with big smiles of welcome, plus candy bars. Yes, the natives gave the soldiers candy bars.

The Marines took their rifles and helmets back to the *Salisbury*, picked up some candy bars of their own to give the Anguillans, and returned for a swim with the local citizens, while the Kittitians poked around the scrub, looking for Ronald Webster and Atlin Harrigan and the other beauty-contest troublemakers, who weren't there. The police did find a shotgun in one house and confiscated it. (A later news report would say, "Illicit arms were found on the island.")

Finally the Kittitians gave up. They went off to join the regular police detachment and the Marines got back into their boats, and as they set off toward the *Salisbury* the Anguillans stood on the beach behind them and sang out a chorus of "God Save the Queen."

Now, *that's* an invasion.

Meanwhile, on the thirteenth of February, despite the British Administrator's assurances that everything was really all right, Billy Herbert and Peter Adams left for London. Statehood was due to arrive in exactly two weeks, and Herbert and Adams were desperate to have it held off. From their manner when they arrived in London, they seemed more like men trying to get a stay of execution than delay national independence.

In London, they spoke to Mrs. Judith Hart, then Minister of State for Commonwealth Relations, who promised them something would be done very quickly about local government. They also spoke with reporters, and the result was another first: Anguilla made the headlines. In the London *Times* of February 18, 1967, under the headline "POLICE LANDED ON ANGUILLA BY FRIGATE," appeared an item in two distinct parts. The first part, which announced the *Salisbury*'s deposit of Kittitian police, missed accuracy on a few points; the British landing wasn't mentioned, the Kittitian force was reduced to four men, and Anguilla was placed in the Windward Islands instead of the Leeward Islands. The final sentence of this part was, if nothing else, extremely hopeful: "The Commonwealth Office announced yesterday that the situation in Anguilla was now normal."

The second part of the item told about Billy Herbert's meeting with Mrs. Hart, said that PAM was "discontented," and failed to mention the man from Anguilla, Peter Adams, at all.

Back at the Commonwealth Office, Statehood Day had taken on the inexorability of the birth of Christ. There was no possibility in

British minds that it could be delayed past its prophesied arrival.

The Labour Party was then in power in Great Britain, so Herbert and Adams turned to the Conservatives for help. They had entree via various Englishmen who had connections in Nevis, principally old Etonian James Milnes Gaskell, owner of that island's Montpelier Hotel.

The natural ally of middle- and upper-class PAM was the middle- and upper-class Conservative Party, just as the natural ally of Bradshaw's Labour Party was Harold Wilson's Labour Party. Circumstances would eventually alter these cases to some extent, but the natural political flow was Labour to Labour and PAM to Conservative.

The result was, on February 14, Lord Jellicoe raised in the House of Lords the question of whether or not it was a bad idea to give independence to a nation simultaneous with its breaking apart. Speaking in reply for the Government, Lord Beswick said he understood things were really all right, the necessary legislation for local councils on Nevis and Anguilla had already been drafted. This answer combined vagueness with inaccuracy in perfect proportions to stifle the discussion.

However, Mrs. Hart, either wanting to make a token gesture to please Herbert and Adams or else belatedly worried that perhaps they were right, sent out an Under-Secretary, Mr. Henry Hall, to look things over. Hall arrived in St. Kitts on February 20, one week before Statehood Day, talked with some people in the Government, and the next day left to visit Anguilla. When he arrived, there was some shouting and perhaps some jostling. The last Englishman the Anguillans had been able to talk to, Mr. Peter Johnston, the local-government expert, had so far as they could tell left without having heard a word they'd said, so they raised their voices a bit while talking to Mr. Hall.

Much later, in a letter to the London *Times*, James Milnes Gaskell described that situation, and some of what had led up to it, and wrote:

Mrs. Hart sent Mr. Henry Hall to Anguilla to explain Statehood. On February 23 Mrs. Hart issued a press release saying: "I am told that there is a very much calmer atmosphere in Anguilla. My official has toured the

whole island and he tells me that his reception has been most friendly."
But on February 22 I had received a cable from St. Kitts saying that Hall
had been booed in Anguilla, demonstrated against and shot at.

On the same day that Henry Hall was failing to hear himself
be booed, demonstrated against and shot at, the beauty-contest incident was moving into a new stage. Sir Fred Phillips, Governor of
St. Kitts-Nevis-Anguilla (a primarily ceremonial position), himself
a West Indian, had gone to Anguilla to talk quietly with Atlin Harrigan and Ronald Webster. He was the only Kittitian official they
would agree to meet. They had a secret meeting in the bush, and
Phillips promised them they would only be fined, not given jail
terms, if they surrendered in re the beauty contest. They surrendered
at once, were tried in a court on Anguilla, and both were charged
with throwing stones. Harrigan was also charged with indecent language. They pleaded guilty and were fined and that was that.

On February 22, the day following his ambivalent meeting with
the Anguillans, Henry Hall went back to St. Kitts to talk things over
with Bradshaw and some other people, and the day after that he
went back to Anguilla with eight statements from the central Government. These statements narrow in on the Anguillans' specific
complaints much more than anything that had happened before in
the 317 years of British rule.

The first two were simple reassurances concerning local political structures, but the next four all referred to the island's development:

3. Projects for Anguilla had been included in the Development Plan, including road improvements and the construction of a jetty, and they would
be carried out accordingly.

4. A consultant having advised that due to the wide dispersal of
housing it would be uneconomic to set up an electricity undertaking in Anguilla, the law would be amended to permit any person to supply power
to his neighbors, and the Government would give five to ten years' notice before withdrawing such permission if it should thereafter propose to
provide a public supply. [Electricity wouldn't be profitable for the Government, so they'll turn it over to private industry!]

5. Work had already begun under contract with Cable and Wireless

to provide a telephone service, but delay had been occasioned due solely to the United Kingdom equipment manufacturers failing to keep their promised delivery dates; every effort would however be made to speed up delivery.

   6. Canadian aid had been sought and promised for providing a supply of pipe-borne water, but distribution problems remained to be resolved—again because of the wide dispersal of housing.

   Number seven explained why St. Kitts couldn't afford to do any more for Anguilla financially, and Number Eight would be baffling if I weren't prepared to explain it, which I am:

   8. Policy reasons did not permit applications for licenses under the Aliens Landholding Ordinance to be dealt with otherwise than by the State Government, but any such applications would be given prompt attention.

   The Aliens Landholding Ordinance said, in effect, that Anguillans could sell their land to one another all they wanted, but if they wished to sell land to an off-islander—a retired American pilot, for instance, or an English hotel builder—they had to get approval from the central Government on St. Kitts. The idea of this was that the central Government would have a chance to keep "undesirable elements"—such as the Mafia—from buying land on any of the three islands. However, the Anguillans claimed the Kittitian Government stalled *forever* in making decisions about applications, and that Kittitians attempted to dissuade prospective buyers from their Anguillan choices in order to sell them Kittitian land instead. The result was that sales to rich foreigners of homesites were well below the Caribbean average. The Anguillans suffered a loss of revenue not only in the immediate sale but also in the ongoing process of having a rich foreigner build a house and then live in it. For an island that had damn little to sell foreigners *except* land, this was a source of irritation, about which the Bradshaw Government proposed to do nothing except speed up the red tape in the applications. (The phrase "policy reasons" leads me to believe that British insistence on the status quo was back of this one, and that British distrust and dislike and envy of Americans was back of the insistence.)

   The day after Mr. Hall brought these eight statements to Anguilla, the Anguillans held another meeting. Thirty-five people showed up and they decided they didn't care for the eight proposals.

The same day, just three days from statehood, Mr. Arthur Bottomley, the British Minister for Overseas Development, arrived in St. Kitts to join in the independence festivities. Two days later, he and his party, plus Paul Southwell, Bradshaw's Deputy Premier, all went to visit Anguilla and have a big Statehood Day celebration there. Bottomley, like Hall before him and Johnston before *him,* went smiling to Anguilla, expecting happy islanders and a jolly celebration.

Bottomley was met by the usual demonstrators with the usual signs. Being British, he personally was cheered as he stepped from the plane. Southwell, however, was roundly booed. Bottomley took this ill, and took up a loud-hailer to tell the Anguillans he intended to tour the island. They cheered. He said he intended to tour the island with Paul Southwell. They booed. He said he was *going to* tour the island with Paul Southwell. They booed louder.

Bottomley and Southwell got into a car together and proceeded to tour the island, and a group of young men trotted along on both sides of the car, banging on the roof. Because years of British neglect and Kittitian animosity had resulted in incredibly potholed and unfinished roads, the chauffeur couldn't drive fast enough to get away from the young men—a charming incident of biter-bit. The car toured the entire island, accompanied throughout by young men thumping on the roof. As one group tired of trotting along, another group would take over. The tour ended at the airport. Bottomley and Southwell and party gathered their dignity about themselves and left Anguilla.

The next day was February 27—Statehood Day. At four in the morning, Vincent Byron, the Warden—the St. Kitts Government representative on Anguilla—raised the new state flag *in secret* at his house, guarded by police officers. He was wearing pajamas at the time, and after hoisting the flag he yawned and went into the house for breakfast.

Independence had arrived.

4

They never would hear,
But turn the deaf ear,
As a matter they had no concern in.
                    —Jonathan Swift, "Dingley and Brent"

Governor Sir Fred Phillips had received a report from the local-government expert, Peter Johnston, saying there had been no serious trouble on Anguilla. Mr. Henry Hall, sent to the colony by Mrs. Judith Hart two weeks later, where he was shouted at, shoved around and perhaps shot at, returned to England to claim there had been no disturbances. And now Mr. Arthur Bottomley, the British Minister for Overseas Development, having gone to Anguilla to help the islanders "celebrate" Statehood Day, and having received a variant on the same treatment as his predecessors, also returned home to insist that nothing had happened.

The *Commonwealth European and Overseas Review,* a publication of the Conservative Party, stated in July 1967, "Mr. Bottomley went to the islands for the Independence celebrations, and perhaps unwisely visited Anguilla where he was booed and jostled by a large crowd, but on his return to London refused to admit there was any trouble."

Driving around an island accompanied by relays of young men thumping on the roof of the car doesn't constitute trouble.

There is an old story about a man who owned a very stubborn donkey, and who was told that in a nearby town there lived a famous donkey trainer whose work was guaranteed. The owner got in touch with the donkey trainer, who arrived the next day at the owner's farm, took a baseball bat from the trunk of his car, stepped in front of the donkey, and began to lambaste the animal backward and forward about the head. "For God's sake, stop!" the owner cried. "You'll kill him! What are you trying to do?"

"I am trying," the donkey trainer said, "to attract his attention."

On February 27, 1967, statehood had come to the former colony of St. Kitts-Nevis-Anguilla, and on Anguilla the new state flag had been raised in a guarded secret ceremony by the Warden, Vincent Byron, in his pajamas. He was in his pajamas once more on the night of March 8 when his official residence burned to the ground and he leaped out an upstairs window just in the nick of time. He left Anguilla the next day, and things were fairly quiet until the night of March 20, when shots were fired into the police station, manned as usual by the police from St. Kitts.

On the twenty-first of March, in London, Mr. George Thomas, speaking as Minister of State at the Commonwealth Office, and replying in the House of Commons to questions raised by the Conservative Opposition, said, "I am not aware that any difficulties have arisen since the inauguration of statehood."

He was perhaps also not aware of difficulties that had arisen shortly before the inauguration of statehood, when Robert Bradshaw had cut off Anguilla's mail and medical supplies in an effort to soften the islanders' resistance. The mail, containing so much of the islanders' income, was a serious enough problem, but holding back medical supplies was even worse.

On the twenty-fifth of March, the police station on Anguilla was fired at again. And on the eleventh of April somebody shot at it a third time.

According to the *Commonwealth European and Overseas Review*, "Between February and the end of May, the Conservative Opposition asked a number of Questions in the House of Commons and Mr. Wood, the Conservative Front Bench spokesman, wrote a number of letters to Mrs. Hart. The Government refused to admit that there was any tension on the island."

On the fifteenth of April, Peter Adams wrote a letter to Robert Bradshaw, which said:

SIR,

It is with regret that I have to bring to you a matter which is of prime importance and not without some justification:

(1) People of Anguilla have no confidence in the Government of St. Kitts;

(2) Anguilla is treated like a very distant poor relation and is in effect a neglected Colony of St. Kitts;

(3) Anguilla has not been given proper Local Government to suit her geographical position seventy miles away from St. Kitts with several French and Dutch territories between them;

(4) The Constitution is not being followed in the letter nor in the spirit;

(5) Complaints to the Government of St. Kitts and to the Government of Britain have not improved conditions and divorce seems imminent.

The majority of Anguillans think that the only course open now is to work towards secession from St. Kitts for it appears that Nature herself did not design them to be together; they want to be able to decide their own future.

Will you please take some action to rectify these matters?

I have the honour to be,

Sir,

Your obedient servant,

P. E. ADAMS, J P,

Member of Council for Anguilla

No response.

On April 20, six shots were fired at the small hotel owned by Mr. David Lloyd, one of the half dozen or so statehood supporters on the island. As the Wooding Report describes him, "Mr. Lloyd is a member of the St. Kitts-Nevis-Anguilla Labour Party and was once the elected member for Anguilla in the Legislative Council and later a member for the State with Mr. Bradshaw in The West Indies Federal Parliament."

Throughout April and May, gunfire was sporadic over the island, including another attack on the police station, and culminating on the twenty-seventh of May when more than fifty rounds of ammunition were fired into Mr. Lloyd's hotel. An Acting Warden, replacing Mr. Vincent Byron, was staying in the hotel that night, but the next morning he left and went back to St. Kitts.

Meanwhile, no medicine was getting through. The only doctor on the island, a Welshman, Dr. Jeffrey Hyde, wrote to the St. Kitts Government repeatedly throughout the winter and spring of 1967, warning of dwindling medical supplies and asking for the new shipment, and never got either the medicine or an answer. The only message he had from St. Kitts was a brisk note demanding to know why he was serving white sugar in the little local hospital instead of less expensive brown sugar. He wrote back and said he could buy white sugar cheaper in Puerto Rico than brown sugar in St. Kitts, and where are the medical supplies? No answer.

Things were obviously building to a climax. Obvious in Anguilla, that is; not so obvious in London, where the Government was still pleased to report that everything was just fine. Hundreds of shots had been fired but—possibly because no one had been killed—the British Government hadn't heard a one of them. How would Anguilla manage to fire her shot heard round the world?

The boom came on May 29. After the customs building was shot up, Peter Adams called a meeting at which it was decided to order the Kittitian police off the island.

It seems not to have occurred to anybody at this point—passions were high—that in throwing the police off the island they were doing anything *more* than throwing the police off the island; that is, that they were mounting a rebellion. They were still operating from the donkey-trainer theory: *something* is going to attract the British Government's attention.

The entire crowd of three hundred people from the meeting in the park went over in a body to the police station to tell the police their services were no longer required. They found Acting Assistant Superintendent Edgings, the officer in charge, and told him their decision. Edgings, understandably edgy, said anything that was all right with the Anguillans was all right with him. They gave him till ten in the morning to vacate the premises. Fine, he said. Fine.

By seven the next morning, a lot of Anguillans were waiting outside the police station to wish the Kittitians a brisk farewell. Nothing happened, no policemen emerged, and after a while two or three Anguillans began to take pot shots at the wall of the station.

At nine-fifteen, Acting Assistant Superintendent Edgings emerged to talk things over with Peter Adams and Ronald Webster. He told them he was waiting for a plane to land from St. Kitts to take himself and his sixteen men away. The Anguillans, not wanting to be disturbed by any more police from St. Kitts while getting rid of the ones they already had, said No to that. They'd already blocked the airport's one runway by parking cars and oil drums on it.

A plane was at that time circling the island, trying to land. It contained Kittitian policemen, but it is no longer possible to say for sure how many or exactly who they were. One report stated it was a "planeload" of policemen, intended as reinforcements. Another said there was only one policeman, John Lynch-Wade, the Kittitian chief of police, who had decided to come up by himself to find out what was going on.

The plane never got to land. Instead, Ronald Webster went to the airport and more or less commandeered a small plane to take the policemen off the island. Over the rest of the daylight hours, the police departed in dribs and drabs.

Leaving their weapons. They had originally planned on taking their armament with them, but the Anguillans told them, "No guns at all, they belong to us." As the Wooding Report puts it, "The policemen were surrounded by armed men who took away all the arms and ammunition, including an automatic rifle, and forced them to enter the plane under duress."

All the police eventually left, but not before dismantling the radio at the police station. This radio was not only Anguilla's only means of contacting the outside world, but was also the outside world's only means of contacting Anguilla. It was also the only means of contacting the lighthouse up on Sombrero Island. Under the circumstances, the reasoning of the Kittitian police seems obscure.

Now the Anguillans had the island to themselves. A group of them who had formed a Peacekeeping Committee put Ronald Webster in charge of island defense, since he had at one time been a corporal in the Netherlands Antilles Army. Webster posted guards at the airport, where the runway was blocked by cars and oil drums and grazing goats, and also set guards to patrolling the coast at night. Most of them were armed with conch shells with which to sound a warning if necessary; conch shells have been used for this purpose on Anguilla since the earliest settlement. A few of the guards also had walkie-talkies, of the kind found in toy stores, with which to make contact directly with Ronald Webster at his command post in the police station.

With the Kittitians gone and guards posted, the Anguillans settled back to see what would happen next. This was the same day, May 30, 1967, that Biafra declared her own independence from the Federation of Nigeria.

The following day, Robert Bradshaw sent telegrams to the Prime Ministers of Barbados, Guyana, Jamaica and Trinidad-Tobago asking for the loan of armed forces—and ships to transport them in—so he could put down the insurrection on Anguilla. He also made the same request of Great Britain. Everyone regretfully refused to take part in the affair.

But Bradshaw's actions weren't confined to asking everybody else for help; he also counterattacked. Mail delivery to Anguilla had virtually ceased back at the beginning of the year, but now Bradshaw ordered that all mail of any kind addressed to Anguilla should be held in the Basseterre Post Office. He froze all Anguillan accounts in St. Kitts banks and declared an embargo on all financial transactions with Anguillans—no selling, no buying, no lending.

Finally—all this on the thirtieth of May—Bradshaw declared a state of emergency; not on Anguilla, on *St. Kitts*. The declaration gave him many extraordinary powers, the most unusual of which permitted burial without inquest or autopsy of anyone dying during the time of the emergency, which is to say, during the period that the Emergency Regulations were in force. All the Emergency Regulations would be found useful by the St. Kitts Government in the days ahead—including this one.

Meanwhile, the Anguillans were gradually beginning to understand that the last swing of the bat had killed the donkey. Throwing the Kittitian police off the island had not after all been a simple difference in degree from shooting up the police station; it was a difference in kind. Bradshaw's actions of May 30 demonstrated this in Anguillan eyes much more than their own actions of the day before.

Anguilla, without thinking about it or planning it, had stumbled into open revolt.

5

But in spite of all temptations
To belong to other nations,
He remains an Englishman!
>   —W. S. Gilbert *H.M.S. Pinafore*

The day after the Anguillans realized they'd rebelled—which is to say, two days after the rebellion—Peter Adams sent a telegram to U Thant at the United Nations. It outlined the problem and asked the "United Nations and men of goodwill everywhere for help."

Never has a rebellion turned so consistently *to* authority rather than *from* it. The rebel flag, flying at the airport and all over the island, was Great Britain's flag, the Union Jack.

Adams followed his message to U Thant with a personal visit, at the head of a delegation of four, to Robert Bradshaw. They met with Bradshaw, Paul Southwell and Eugene Walwyn, Bradshaw's Nevisian supporter who was now the Kittitian Attorney General. Adams handed over a memorandum stating the current Anguillan position—it said, among other things, "Anguillans are not prepared to accept NO for an answer"—after which he and his delegation went back home.

The Kittitian Government replied in a Cabinet Statement on June 1. Since the Statement began by saying "that this is the very first occasion on which an approach of this sort concerning the wishes of the people of Anguilla has been made to the Government," it came as no surprise to the Anguillans that the rest of it was also obtuse. The Statement presented the standard argument that since Peter Adams had been behaving himself in the Legislative Council all these years, and had signed the report of the Constitutional Conference, the Anguillans didn't have the right to a capricious change of mind. It also said there were constitutional ways to do this sort of thing, without explaining what they were, and finished by ordering the Anguillans to give back the guns to the policemen and start behaving.

As the Wooding Report says of this Statement: "It held out no promise to the Anguillans. If it was intended as a call to the Anguillans to surrender it failed because it misjudged the tempo of feeling on the island and the fact that, if not world opinion, certainly the Press in Britain and in the Caribbean as well as the Caribbean Bar Association was on the side of the Anguillans."

(Actually, the last part of that quote isn't entirely accurate. Nobody was on the side of the Anguillans yet—it was still too early as of June 1, 1967, for anybody to have picked sides at all—though a little later everybody *would* be on Anguilla's side, when the affair had been blown up into an international incident. At two days of age, however, the rebellion was still small potatoes. In fact, the press in Britain hadn't as yet even reported its existence, though the press in New York would do so the next day; *The New York Times* for June 2, 1967, under the headline "BRITISH HELP REQUESTED TO END ANGUILLA REVOLT," gave a brief six-paragraph summary of the events, in which each fact was just slightly off, like a color television set improperly tuned. The item took no sides.)

The Anguillan delegation had already returned home when the Cabinet produced its Statement, so a British journalist named David Smithers carried the Statement from St. Kitts to Anguilla. Smithers also carried a letter he'd been given by the St. Kitts Government, which he'd been told was a note from Bradshaw to Peter Adams; but when he landed in Anguilla the envelope turned out to contain a copy of the Emergency Regulations, which in effect promulgated the regulations on Anguilla and made them legally effective there. Bradshaw had risked Smithers' neck in conning him this way (had the Anguillans been a bit less civilized or more irritated, they might have killed the messenger in the time-honored tradition), and as a result Smithers did take Anguilla's side, and he did so with great enthusiasm, one unfortunate result of which would be to create embarrassment for a couple of other journalists two years later. In the October 1967 issue of *Venture,* a British magazine published by the Fabian Society, Smithers did a pro-Anguilla piece that included the following paragraph: "In March Premier Bradshaw imported from Britain a yellow Rolls-Royce. His deputy, Paul Southwell, ordered a Bentley. The Anguillans—not least the sick ones—despaired." Partisanship leads to a certain selectivity of the eye; inadvertently or not, Smithers had left out the fact that the Rolls was vintage 1935 and had cost £700 ($1,680). By the time the Rolls-Royce item had passed through the hands of several other journalists, it had blossomed into a lovely work of fiction. The London *Sunday Times* of March 23, 1969, reported that Bradshaw "drives a canary yellow Rolls Royce which cost £8,000—the finance minister who oversaw the purchase drives a Bentley."

Actually, the spirit of the *Sunday Times* piece was accurate, even if the facts were a little off. The annual per capita income in St. Kitts is £77 ($184.40) and the Rolls-Royce cost £700, which is either one man's salary for nine years or nine men's salary for one year. Adjusting the figures to an average Englishman's income, £8,000 is dirt-cheap.

Let us return, however, to the beginning of June 1967 and the beginning of the Anguillan rebellion. The Cabinet Statement from St. Kitts did not have its intended effect; that is, the Anguillans did not give the police back their guns, and they did not decide to behave themselves. Peter Adams did, however, get in touch with the Kittitian Government again, hoping to keep some sort of diplomatic relationship alive. The result was a tentative agreement in early June that he and Deputy Premier Paul Southwell would meet for general talks on the neutral island of St. Martin. But when the Lieutenant Governor of Dutch St. Martin thought it over, he withdrew permission for the meeting. St. Martin is half French and half Dutch, and the Governor saw no reason to be dragged into a squabble between two islands belonging to the British.

The next event took place on June 6, and at first it didn't seem to have anything to do with the Anguillan rebellion at all. Bradshaw's Government emptied its main prison facilities on Cayon Street in Basseterre, shifting the prisoners to other locations and even sending some of them over to Nevis. For the first time in well over a hundred years, the cells of the Cayon Street prison were all empty. It seemed an odd thing to do, without much point or meaning.

But then came the night of June 9. As *The New York Times* reported under the headline "REBELS ON ST. KITTS ATTACK THE POLICE":

Gunmen attacked police headquarters here before dawn today with small-arms fire 11 days after Premier Robert Bradshaw's Government had proclaimed a state of emergency. Policemen and members of the volunteer defense force rushed to guard government offices and installations. Police chief John Lynch-Wade reported that one defense force member had been wounded and at least two men had been detained.

By the time the dust settled, many more than two men had been detained. On the morning after the attack, the Bradshaw Government arrested all the leaders of PAM, including Billy Herbert. In addition, two Britons were also arrested: James Milnes Gaskell, the young owner of the Montpelier Hotel over in Nevis, who had served as entree for Billy Herbert to the Conservative Party in England, and Miss Diana Prior-Palmer, then a guest at another Nevisian hotel.

Milnes Gaskell had come over the previous night from Nevis and was planning to take a morning flight from St. Kitts to return to his home in England. A journalist at the hotel, a Reuters man named Ronald Batchelor, told Milnes Gaskell there had been trouble the night before and suggested that Milnes Gaskell could expect to be detained, since he was known to be a friend of Billy Herbert's and the rest of the PAM leadership. Milnes Gaskell thought not; at the worst, he expected to be deported, which he didn't mind since he'd been planning to leave anyway.

Two Kittitian lawyer friends of Milnes Gaskell's accompanied him to the airport; one of these was named Robert McKenzie Crawford and he has a further role to play a little later.

St. Kitts is serviced by Leeward Island Air Transport, generally known as LIAT, and the LIAT personnel at the airport knew Milnes Gaskell since he was a frequent traveler in and out of the island. This morning they looked at him oddly when he arrived, and the clerk on duty told him, "You can't travel today."

'Why not?"

The clerk, a friendly and peaceable man, was embarrassed but adamant. "I can't say. You just can't travel today."

Outside, Milnes Gaskell saw a plane landing. He said to the clerk, "You mean to tell me, if I went out there and got on that plane, you'd stop me?"

"No," said the clerk.

However, there was a police corporal standing guard at the outer door, and more police were anticipated momentarily; so, rather than make a mad dash for the plane on the runway, Milnes Gaskell walked instead to a telephone, called Ronald Batchelor at the hotel, and said, "It looks as though I'm to be arrested."

"Fine," Batchelor said, "I'll just add your name to this list here that I'm about to send out."

At that point a Land Rover arrived at the airport, full of police, led by one Sergeant Edgings. This was the same Acting Assistant Superintendent Edgings whom we last met at the airport on Anguilla, when he was being sent away. Now, back to his permanent rank of Sergeant, he had come out to Golden Rock Airport to apprehend Milnes Gaskell. He and his four men were all armed with rifles, which was not standard, and they were wearing tin helmets, which were also an innovation. Edgings knew Milnes Gaskell and seemed uncomfortable about this morning's duty. His four men took up positions around Milnes Gaskell, and the Sergeant said, "I'm sorry, sir, but I have to arrest you."

Milnes Gaskell, a slender, quiet-spoken young man of impeccable manners, said he quite understood. He accompanied the Sergeant and his men in the Land Rover back to Basseterre.

At the Cayon Street prison he was put through a long complexity of red tape and bureaucratic maundering. One young officer checked his height and weight, but seemed as baffled as Milnes Gaskell as to just why he was doing it. At another stop in the processing, an officer became irritable and impatient, and Milnes Gaskell told him, "I'm sorry, but I'm not familiar with the procedure." He might have been speaking for them all.

Finally he was taken to his cell, which was actually the prison chapel. There were five others in it with him, plus eight more in a large cell across the way and another eight in a third cell. As Milnes Gaskell told me much later, "We were all detainees, rather than prisoners, and St. Kitts had never had any detainees before and didn't quite know what to do with us." None of the people in the cells had been charged with anything. Twenty-two detainees, aged between seventeen and seventy-one, none of them charged with any specific crime, all packed into three cells that had coincidentally been cleared of their regular prisoners just four days before.

There have been several theories about the events of the night of June 9-10, but basically they sift down to three: (1) PAM tried to overthrow the Bradshaw Government by shooting bullets into the Basseterre police station; (2) Anguillans came over from their island and shot up the police station; (3) the Kittitian Government staged the whole thing itself as an excuse to arrest the PAM leadership and deport some troublous foreigners.

The first theory, that PAM tried to overthrow Bradshaw by shooting at the police station, is absurd on the face of it. Though it was the Government's official theory it's doubtful that even Bradshaw ever believed it. Billy Herbert and PAM's other legal whiz kids and the families who own the plantations are very sophisticated people; if they were going to pull a *coup d'état,* they would probably behave a little more effectively than the gunmen of June 9.

The second theory, that Anguillans came down to St. Kitts to do some plinking, also has some problems with it, principally the fact that there wasn't any reason for them to do so. However, Trinidadian author V. S. Naipaul has reported this theory as fact in the London *Sunday Times* saying, "... the Anguillans raided St. Kitts and shot up the police station and Defence Force headquarters. The raid, by 12 men, was openly planned; people went down to the wharf in the afternoon to wave as the 50-foot cutter left for St. Kitts. Five and a half hours later the cutter tied up, quite simply, at the main pier in St. Kitts. Then the Anguillans discovered they hadn't thought about motorcars. They had intended to kidnap Bradshaw; they had to be content with scaring him."

The third theory, that the attack was staged, certainly *sounds* like something the St. Kitts Government might do. And there are those cells so conveniently emptied three days ahead of time. And when I was on St. Kitts and went to the police station in Basseterre, I noticed that none of the bullet pocks in the wall were less than nine feet up from the floor; either the attackers thought they were shooting at giants or they didn't really want to hit anybody.

However, the fact is, theory number two should stand up, because it's the truth. The Naipaul account is pretty accurate, except that it wasn't motorcars the Anguillans couldn't find; it was Bradshaw.

A dozen of them, including three raffish young Americans, decided to kidnap Bradshaw and hold him for ransom. The ransom was to be Great Britain's acknowledgment of Anguilla's secession from St. Kitts. (They were still, of course, trying to attract the donkey's attention, and this was one time the burning-sticks-on-sheets-of-powder contingent got their way.)

They sailed to St. Kitts, landed at Basseterre, and went roaming around town, a dozen men with rifles. They claim to have stopped a policeman at one point and asked him where Bradshaw was, but he insisted he didn't know.

They never did find Bradshaw. In the old days, on hot nights when they had nothing to do but think about their aggravations, the boys on Anguilla used to go over and shoot up the police station, full of its uniformed foreigners from St. Kitts. Now in Basseterre, with time on their hands, they reverted to form, and before leaving gave Sergeant Edgings a nostalgic salute.

(That wasn't all the shooting done that night. In addition to the police station and the Defence Force building and the electricity plant—one can empathize with electricityless Anguillans pumping a couple of bullets into the Kittitian electricity plant—there were shots fired at two dances. Did the Anguillans open fire on dances? Or did somebody else do some shooting that night, too, for reasons of his own?)

And what of the jeep found blazing away in a cane field north of town near the dead body that had been buried there apparently for some months? And what about the boat stolen at Heldens Bay?

The jeep and body have never been successfully explained, but the Heldens Bay boat was stolen by part of the group from Anguilla that had become separated from the rest. While the main party returned in the cutter they'd traveled down in, this second group, including the three Americans, stole the boat and lit out for the Dutch island of St. Eustatius, with the St. Kitts Revenue Cutter in hot pursuit. It failed to catch up. The Dutch authorities wouldn't permit Kittitian police to make arrests on Dutch soil, so Group Two took a plane to St. Thomas, where they did enough blabbermouthing for the St. Thomas *Daily News* to be able to print the names of the three Americans in its issue of June 16.

But what about those fortuitously empty cells? The answer, I think, is that Bradshaw knew his opponents and anticipated that sooner or later the Anguillans would do something that would give him the opportunity to clap PAM in the clink. I doubt he anticipated that PAM would do anything; the Anguillans would act, and PAM would pay the consequences. And so it was.

An additional result of the spree of June 10 was that Bradshaw once again asked all his neighbors, plus Britain, for armed help to put down the Anguillan rebellion. Once again he got a series of polite refusals, and from the British the first indication that the donkey might be listening; Bradshaw was told by the British Government that "unless some firm understanding could be reached with the Anguillans about their problems it is difficult to see how far a military operation could solve the situation."

Closer to home, the Prime Minister of Jamaica offered to set up a "Caribbean Fact Finding Mission" to try to find out what was wrong between St. Kitts and Anguilla, or, as the Mission put it, "initiate discussions between Mr. Bradshaw and leaders of opposition factions in an endeavour to find a basis for an amicable settlement to the dispute."

But Bradshaw said no thank you to fact-finding missions; what he wanted was men and guns and ships.

He was having trouble about the ships, but the other two he was getting, one way and another. He already had an army, called the Defence Force and consisting of seventy men; Bradshaw now declared himself a colonel in charge of this army, put on a khaki uniform complete with Sam Browne belt and holstered pistol, got a rather stout lady with a rifle to be his bodyguard, and went out in his Rolls-Royce to watch his army pass in review. (In the American Army, by way of contrast, seventy men is slightly larger than one platoon, usually led by a lieutenant.)

Then there were the police. Great Britain, before the Anguilla rebellion, had agreed to replace the old arms of the St. Kitts police with new weapons, and now these started coming in. The police force numbers 110 men, and the British sent along guns enough for the entire crew, plus the Defence Force. Colonel Bradshaw promptly invented a new militia called the Special Volunteer Constabulary, found 162 volunteers, and gave them the old Lee-Enfield .303 rifles that the police and army had been using until the new guns had arrived from England. This Special Volunteer Constabulary was a very scruffy group of men, built around the nucleus of a street gang called The Breadfruit Tree Boys, who had been credited with much rape and burglary in the Basseterre area before blossoming into constables. (One Kittitian police inspector stated in court, under oath, that some of the volunteers would have been facing criminal charges if they weren't in the Constabulary.)

Meanwhile, back on Anguilla, an uneasy week followed the invasion of St. Kitts. Boys and men patrolled the beaches at night, armed with conch shells and toy walkie-talkies. By day the Peacekeeping Committee, led by Walter Hodge, a local builder who was later to emerge as the island's financial wizard, gradually altered itself from an emergency organization into a government. Rebellion or no rebellion, life had to go on. The schools had to run, the airport had to be maintained, customs duties had to be collected (whenever possible), and the general public operations of society had to continue without interruption. Almost all the members of the Civil Service had chosen to stay at their jobs, so what the Peacekeeping Committee did was move naturally into the vacuum left by the removal of St. Kitts's authority.

But Anguilla couldn't go it alone. The Anguillans really did want to get back somehow with Mother Britain; they were rebelling, after all, under the British flag. But the English apparently wanted nothing to do with them. And so, reluctantly, the Peacekeeping Committee turned elsewhere.

On June 16, just a week after the foray into Basseterre, Peter Adams flew again to San Juan, Puerto Rico, to send some more telegrams. One went to U Thant at the United Nations, asking for "guidance" in the current troubling situation. Another went to President Lyndon Johnson, asking the United States to accept Anguilla as an American territory in a status similar to that of the American Virgin Islands. While on Puerto Rico, Adams also made an attempt to round up some medical supplies, which by now were nearly half a year overdue on Anguilla.

U Thant didn't answer this telegram either, but Adams did get an answer from the United States Government. That is, he got it if he read *The New York Times* for June 17, 1967, which reported, "Officials said today that the United States would never negotiate directly with Anguilla on the question of association. Britain still handles Anguilla's foreign policy 'as far as we are concerned,' Government sources said, adding: 'If Anguilla is serious, the request must be handled through the United Kingdom.'"

It's no surprise, really, that the United States was the nation to produce *Catch-22*. Great Britain wouldn't talk to Anguilla unless the words came through St. Kitts, and now the United States wouldn't talk to Anguilla unless the words came through Great Britain.

However, with the Anguillans sending out all those telegrams and giving so many statements to reporters, it isn't unlikely that various governments began talking among themselves, suggesting to one another that something be done to quiet things down. Whatever was or wasn't said, Colonel Bradshaw suddenly reconsidered the question of the Fact Finding Mission and decided he'd appreciate their efforts after all. The Fact Finding Mission was forthwith assembled and turned out to be composed of four government officials and one university professor, all from various West Indian islands. It was the sort of group whose equivalent members in the United States would be on a committee to raise funds for a community cultural center.

The Mission arrived in St. Kitts in late June, at around the same time that something very mysterious was happening on Anguilla. On the night of June 23, two young men patrolling the beach at Limestone Bay saw a ship without lights stopped beyond the reef. Three rowboats were moving toward shore. Limestone Bay is perhaps the most remote corner of the entire island, with neither a road nor a footpath leading to it. The two boys hid in the brush and watched the rowboats land and counted the men who came ashore; they were thirty.

While one of the boys kept watch, the other took off through the brush until he was close enough to the police station for his walkie-talkie message to be picked up. Truckloads of Anguillans immediately set out, but the trucks had to be left behind on the nearest road while the men ran across the rough ground toward the bay. The noise of their approach alerted the invaders, who immediately got back into their rowboats and headed away from shore again. That is, most of them did; five stayed behind on the island, drifting away into the darkness. When the Anguillans finally thundered down onto the beach, the boats were gone and so were the men; all that was left was one policeman's boot.

In his as yet unpublished book *Anguilla: Island in Revolt,* British journalist Colin Rickards mentions this incident and adds, "At noon the following day I happened to see the St. Kitts Revenue Cutter entering Basseterre roadstead towing three rowing boats, but thought nothing of it." When he heard about the previous night's invasion, however, Rickards began to look into things at the St. Kitts end. "My own careful investigation in St. Kitts," he says, "pinpointed five men, all known to be Government loyalists, and all of them crack shots, who were missing from their homes and various places of work."

The next evening, Colonel Bradshaw got on his radio station, ZIZ, and denied everything. "We sent no one to Anguilla," he said, "and if the island was in fact raided or invaded it must have been done by Anguillans living in Anguilla who are fed up with the terrible state to which Adams and Company have brought their island." He also said that some of the Anguillan rebels were "known to be Communists," which was pretty well news to everybody.

Meanwhile, the Fact Finding Mission, five men of a different ilk, had arrived on St. Kitts. They talked with Colonel Bradshaw and other officials, and they talked with the detainees. On the twenty-ninth of June, they went to Anguilla to talk to the Peace-keeping Committee. The other five were still on the island then, occasionally showing up at remote houses and stealing food at gunpoint, and these two groups of five show the range of potential solutions being considered for the Anguilla problem.

The Peacekeeping Committee would have liked to talk to the five men in the bush, but they couldn't find them. However, they were also pleased to talk to the Fact Finding Mission and agreed to send a delegation to St. Kitts to chat with the Government there if three conditions were met: first, they required safe-conduct; second, the British must have somebody present at the meeting; and third, the Governor, Sir Fred Phillips, should preside at the meeting instead of Colonel Bradshaw.

Everything was arranged, and the next day the delegation of five went off to St. Kitts, led by Peter Adams and including a man named Jeremiah Gumbs, a businessman who hadn't actually lived

on the island for thirty years but who was soon to become more famous and more important in the ongoing Anguilla crisis than any of
his fellow delegates.

In the history of *The New York Times,* only two Anguillans have
ever made its "Man in the News" column; the second was Ronald
Webster, but the first was Jerry Gumbs. A big bearish man, with
a strainingly sincere expression of face and a deep, mellow, slow-
moving voice, Jerry Gumbs is perhaps the most middle-class of all
the middle-class Anguillans. Born on February 18, 1913, the son of
a fisherman, he received primary school education on Anguilla and
in his youth became a tailor. "Some people are still wearing suits I
made for them," he claims, which says as much for the economy of
Anguilla as it does for Jerry Gumbs's tailoring.

Two of Gumbs's sisters had already emigrated to the United
States. When he was twenty-five he followed them. This was 1938
and America was still in the grip of the Depression, but it nevertheless offered far more opportunity to an industrious young man than
did Anguilla. Jerry Gumbs stayed in Brooklyn with one of his sisters and enrolled in the Metropolitan Vocational High School to get
caught up on his education. Finishing there, he won a scholarship
to City College of New York, but immediately after Pearl Harbor,
in 1941, he quit college and joined the Army. After six months'
service he had the right to become an American citizen, which he
did, and after the war he got married and went to college on the
GI Bill to learn furnace installation. He's a hard worker, and he's
smart about money, and it wasn't long before he had his own fuel-
oil delivery business in Edison, New Jersey. (In January of 1968,
the Anguilla *Beacon* ran what it called an "Alphabet of Anguillan
Personalities," and when it got to "J" it went: "*J* is for *Jerry,* named
after the Prophet: If profit's his motive, he gets plenty of it.")

I talked with Jerry Gumbs late in 1969, and never have I met a
man who so totally combined the sincere with the humbug. In fact,
he's even sincere *about* the humbug. For instance, over the years he
has been responsible for much charitable fund raising for Anguilla,
and he says, "I gave Anguilla secondary education. I gave them a
library. I gave them an operating light. I gave them an X-ray. I gave
them encyclopedias in every school. I gave them a Community Center. I gave them medical supplies of all kinds; in the hospital now

there's a frigidaire there; in the health center there's a freezer. And any man who works with his hands as hard as I've worked and do this for a people could not be doing it for personal gain."

Well, yes and no. The truth is slightly more complicated than that. There are now more than a thousand Anguillans living in the general area of Edison and Perth Amboy, New Jersey, and several years ago Jerry Gumbs founded an Anguilla Improvement Association to raise money to give things like libraries and operating lights to the people back home. It is true that Jerry Gumbs founded the Association, that he has been its leader more years than not, that he has contributed his own money and a great deal of his own time and effort, but to say that he alone is responsible for the Association's good works is not 100 per cent accurate.

Jerry Gumbs is reminiscent in some ways of a particular kind of forceful movie director—the sort of man who, if a picture turns out well, begins to believe he alone made up the story, wrote the dialogue, worked the camera, designed the sets and composed the music.

A man like that makes enemies, and Jerry Gumbs has as many detractors as Orson Welles. He is accused mostly of being money-hungry and a sharp practitioner, but that's far too simplistic a reading of the man. Listen to him talk about the house he built in Edison: "I built this house with my own hands. I wasn't taught to be a carpenter, but I had to build a home, and I lived in a community where our people, black people, were nobody. And I had to come into a community where there were no black people and do something so people could see. Not by fighting and clubs and marching, but by definitely struggling in a society, the way others have struggled whether they're white or not, to show people that what they're trying to say is not true. I think they got the message. Because right here in this community this was the only ranch-style house built here in 1952. And people moved around it, you look around, you see a piece of land, they built ranch-type homes around it. There was change in the pattern of thinking."

Did *no* other pair of hands do any of the work on the house? If so, their contributions have been swallowed within Jerry Gumbs's own pride of accomplishment. "The only reason," he says, "why perhaps I have accomplished what I have accomplished even in building this house is because I was blessed with a body with tremendous strength, and maybe a mind to understand. Two things going together. Now, most people are not that way."

He gestures across his long, neat living room full of bric-a-brac. "When this was built, there's a steel beam across it, and that piece of steel, I couldn't get it here, although I paid for it. The union would not deliver it. And I had to deliver it, on a little truck that I had, and I did it. And I had to put it up without a crane, and I put it up with my shoulders." All this trouble because he was a black man, of course, building in a white neighborhood. He *will* be the strongest man around, and he will never stop finding arenas in which to test his strength.

"You build a house, now," he says, "and at night people are gonna gather and lack it down. They're gonna back up the truck, they're gonna take your lumber, you gotta bring it back tomorrow. It's not easy. And you don't go and make a public scene. Inspectors won't give you a license. You run around for months trying to get somebody to sign a document which is already documented and signed. You dig open a hole to put a sewer in; they tell you you can't put that type of pipe in it, you must put a certain type, and that certain type does not exist in the state." But the house got built.

Other things got built, too. The fuel-oil business; the Anguilla Improvement Association; a family with four children, all of them college-bound; and back on Anguilla two things, a small air ferry service called Anguilla Airways and the Rendezvous Hotel, a motel-type operation on Rendezvous Bay, where the French dried their powder in 1796. The most modern hotel on the island, it is still a bit more primitive than an Iowa tourist cabin in the twenties. Still, it does have electricity—until nine-thirty at night, when the generator is turned off and the guests convert to kerosene lamps. And it has running water, a trickle, icy cold, from cisterns that catch the infrequent rain. And it has a restaurant, half a dozen tables, with meals prepared by Aunt B, Jerry Gumbs's sister, who runs the place for him. And it also has a beautiful white-sand beach, and if tourism ever does become a major industry on Anguilla, Jerry Gumbs has the jump on the trade and can be relied on to drive himself to stay ahead of the competition. Not entirely for money; to be *first*, and proud of it.

When trouble started on Anguilla, Jerry Gumbs couldn't possibly stay out of it. He flew down to the island—the last leg, on his own airplane—joined the Peacekeeping Committee, and bulled his way into prominence as naturally and unmaliciously as if he were building his own house.

Jerry Gumbs and the Anguillan delegation met with the St. Kitts Government on June 30, 1967. Whether pressure had been exerted on Colonel Bradshaw by outside forces it's impossible to say, but he was more inclined toward compromise than usual. He offered to appoint a new Warden for Anguilla who would not only be Anguillan (Wardens had almost always been Kittitian before this) but somebody acceptable to the people of Anguilla. He also promised to restore mail deliveries once the Warden had been appointed and to arrange for the payment of Government salaries and pensions that had been held up by the rebellion. The delegation said they'd talk it over with the folks back home and let the St. Kitts Government know in a few days.

The only true comparison with the governmental form on Anguilla is Athenian democracy. Whenever a problem comes up, the entire population gathers at Burrowes Park, everybody shouts at everybody else, a couple of fistfights are dealt with, speeches are made, the Bible is quoted from, God's assistance is invoked, and gradually everybody comes around to the same general point of view. The general point of view that everybody came around to on the first of July, 1967, was that Colonel Bradshaw's offer wasn't good enough. Nothing had been said about an Island Council, nor medical supplies, nor an amnesty. There was no reason to suppose the Colonel would remain even this mellow once the spotlight of publicity had been turned off. And those five mysterious invaders were still roaming the countryside, stealing food from poor people at gunpoint. Besides, Anguilla had already declared her independence from St. Kitts, which was what they all wanted; why turn around and go back?

On Monday, July 3, two cables were sent by the Peacekeeping Committee to St. Kitts from Puerto Rico. One to Sir Fred Phillips, the Governor, said: GOVERNOR MAY COME AND BRING THE MAIL. CAN BE ESCORTED BY MR. WADE, CHIEF OF POLICE. The other one was addressed to Mr. Urban C. Hodge, a retired Anguillan Civil

Servant living on St. Kitts, who had been suggested by Colonel Bradshaw as the new Warden; it said: HAPPY TO HAVE YOU IN ANGUILLA BUT NOT AS REPRESENTATIVE OF THE CENTRAL GOVERNMENT.

The Fact Finding Mission was understandably distressed that all its work had come to nothing. They went away from St. Kitts and wrote a report that criticized the British for playing at Watchmaker God while turning out lousy watches. They criticized the Government of St. Kitts for any number of things, including its refusal to offer the Anguillans an amnesty as a first step in negotiations. Exit the five men of the Fact Finding Mission.

Exit also the other five. After ten days of terrorizing old people and children for food, the five mysterious invaders left Anguilla, at night, by rowboat, out to a ship with a silhouette not unlike that of the St. Kitts Revenue Cutter. They were seen to leave, but a force large enough to capture them didn't arrive in time. "The following morning," Colin Rickards writes in *Anguilla: Island in Revolt,* "my five 'missing men' were back at their various jobs in St. Kitts."

(During the time the five were on Anguilla they very nearly got Jerry Gumbs, though only by indirection. Armed patrols were spending every day searching for the five invaders, and one afternoon two of these patrols spotted each other across Burrowes Park, mistook one another for the enemy, and both opened fire, though without hitting anything. Jerry Gumbs and reporter David Smithers were at the airport nearby, and both went running toward the sounds of shooting. It was late in the day, and both were wearing white shirts; they quickly became the most visible moving objects in the park, and both patrols at once started shooting at *them.* Gumbs and Smithers jumped behind a tree until passions cooled and they could identify themselves.)

With the several five-man missions having proved impossible, the Anguillans decided to hold a referendum on the independence they'd already declared. They aimed to prove it was really a popular rebellion, and to counter Colonel Bradshaw's charges that Anguilla was being terrorized by gunmen on the Peacekeeping Committee. (Considering what had happened to Jerry Gumbs, the truth was just the other way around.)

Walter Hodge, Chairman of the Peacekeeping Committee, explained the referendum, saying, "We are breaking away from St. Kitts because we must. And through this act we know that we are technically breaking away from Britain. But by doing so—and becoming Independent—we hope to show the British Government that we mean business. Then maybe Mrs. Judith Hart will take some notice of us and perhaps we will get what we are asking for, and have asked for all along. Our Independence will, we hope, be our currency and we will have something with which to negotiate."

Independence, in other words, wasn't really independence at all, but was simply an effort to switch sovereignties from poor and hated St. Kitts to wealthy and well-liked Great Britain.

The referendum was announced for July 11, and a proclamation was issued four days earlier to acquaint the people with what was going on. There would be two questions on the referendum, both to be answered either Yes or No:

"(1) Are you in favour of secession from St. Kitts?

"(2) Are you in favour of setting up the interim Government?"

The second one meant that the Peacekeeping Committee didn't look upon itself as a government but would be prepared to organize one if the people did vote for independence. "Interim," of course, meant until such time as Great Britain would take over or regular elections could take place.

Although Anguilla has 75 per cent literacy—high for the West Indies—symbols were used on the ballots in addition to the printed words "Yes" and "No"; a picture of a hat stood for "Yes," a boot stood for "No." I don't know why they chose the hat to represent secession, but when I think of that lone policeman's boot found on the beach at Limestone Bay I think I know why they chose a boot to symbolize a continued link with St. Kitts.

The regular Electoral Roll of qualified voters from the last legal election was used to determine eligibility, and just about every registered voter turned out. The results: 1,813 hats, 5 boots.

Although Paul Southwell had claimed over ZIZ the night before that "terrorized" Anguillans would be "forced to vote at gunpoint," it was probably the most thoroughly observed and uncorrupted election in modern times. Reporters were there from the major wire services and two British papers. In addition, a British television unit from Granada's *World in Action* was in the area and spent the day on Anguilla filming the voting; the film was shown on British television the following week, under the title "Duel in the Sun." A duel without guns, however; none of the reporters present saw any voters being terrorized. What they mostly saw was voters standing in line at the five polling places, smiling happily in the hot sunshine and singing a new calypso that started, "Papa Bradshaw, run you run." Never was a father so cheerfully disowned by his children.

In addition to all the newsmen who had shown up for the referendum, there were other outsiders present, principally Roger Fisher, a professor of international law at Harvard. Jerry Gumbs, through his eldest son, had met Fisher a couple of years earlier, in New York, and before flying down to Anguilla at the end of June, he had called Fisher in Boston and asked him to become the island's legal representative. Fisher had agreed and had followed Jerry Gumbs to the island.

On the evening of July 11, 1967, referendum day, while the votes were being counted in the Administrative Building at the Valley, Roger Fisher was next door composing a Declaration of Independence on a portable typewriter, with a pistol on the chair beside him. Confusion now exists as to whose original idea it was to have a Declaration of Independence, or how much help Professor Fisher might have had from various Anguillans in putting it together, but the bulk of the Declaration is probably attributable to Fisher. It was written in haste, to be done in time to be read to the people massed outside waiting to hear the results of the voting.

The vote count—also filmed by the television people—wasn't finished until one in the morning, at which time Peter Adams went outside to announce the tally, accompanied by Walter Hodge, who was carrying the Declaration of Independence. Adams told the crowd the numbers and 1,813 people cheered, while five presumably remained silent.

In a display of independence and personal bravery rare even among the brave and hardy Anguillans, those five naysayers had voted their consciences even though everyone was sure to know who they were. Three boots were stomped in the same election district, and everybody knew the Bradshaw supporters in that neighborhood; it had to be David Lloyd, owner of Lloyd's Hotel, which had been shot up so badly the night the replacement Warden was staying there back in May, plus his wife and son. David Lloyd, a barrel-chested, booming-voiced man of fifty-seven, whose second wife had presented him with his most recent child just three years before, had known Robert Bradshaw in his youth; in fact, he and Bradshaw had roomed together at one time. "In the evenings," he told me, "I'd take a girl or two and go dancing. Robert, he pick pick pick at all his books." Lloyd has a deep admiration for Bradshaw, the sort of admiration felt for him by the cane cutters on St. Kitts, and despite the events of the last several years he could never believe that Robert Bradshaw would set out purposefully to do wrong. When the time came to vote whether or not to reject Bradshaw, Lloyd could do nothing but vote the way he felt. "What they gonna do to me?" he cried when I talked to him in the spring of 1971. "I lived my life, I already *lived* my life, I had a *good* life. What they gonna do to me?"

Nothing, as it turned out.

After the cheering and the singing, Walter Hodge stepped forward and made a brief speech, followed by a reading of the Declaration of Independence, which began, "We stand before the Queen in the greatest humility, with the desire in our hearts to be faithful subjects to her." It went on from that self-destruct opening to a recountal of the wrongs done Anguilla by St. Kitts and ended on a high note of nobility, poetry and confusion: "We pledge our lives and hearts to create a true democratic government, however small. If, for financial want, we must suffer, then let us suffer in silence."

However small? A true democratic government, *however small*? What does that mean? It seems to work from the premise that the larger the government, the more democratic, an assumption that anyone who has ever dealt with the bureaucracies of the United States or Great Britain will regard with a certain skepticism. As to the final sentence about suffering financial want in silence, that was precisely what the Anguillans were *not* doing.

The Declaration of Independence was met with rousing cheers, and the next day telegrams were sent to Great Britain and the United States and various Commonwealth countries, saying, OVERWHELM-ING REFERENDUM CONFIRMS ABSOLUTE AND FINAL INDEPENDENCE OF ANGUILLA FROM THE FEDERATION OF ST. KITTS, NEVIS, AN-GUILLA. THIS LEAVES NO LEGAL TIES WITH CROWN. WE WISH TO EX-

PLORE STATUS OF ASSOCIATED STATE OR OTHER ARRANGEMENT OF
FREEDOM AND LOCAL AUTONOMY WITHIN THE COMMONWEALTH.

No more shilly-shallying. Anguilla had firmly declared that she
was/wasn't dependent/independent, had made an irrevocable decision and was willing to talk it over. And that's definite.

6

A man cannot be too careful in the choice of his enemies.

—Oscar Wilde, *Picture of Dorian Cray*

The middle of July 1967. The Caribbean, as usual, was sunny and hot. On Anguilla, Peter Adams was trying to figure out some way to attract the attention of the British Government. Walter Hodge was in charge of the day-to-day running of the island. Ronald Webster was keeping his patrols moving around the beaches. Seated on a bench in Burrowes Park was Roger Fisher, tapping away in the sunlight at his portable typewriter; he was writing Anguilla a constitution.

Seventy miles away on St. Kitts, the Cayon Street prison was hot and muggy and foul-smelling. The twenty-two detainees were still detained. Colonel Bradshaw was in the process of writing a little booklet, *The Present Crisis in the State of St. Christopher-Nevis-Anguilla*, which would be published in September and in which he would reveal a plot against his government worthy of a segment of Beowulf: "The plan," he was writing, "involved the killing of the Premier, Deputy Premier, Attorney General and the Minister for Education, Health and Welfare, as well as the mutilation of the Head of the Civil Service, Mr. Ira Walwyn, and the Cabinet Secretary, Mr. Probyn Inniss, by chopping off their hands."

To save the hands of the Head of the Civil Service from being chopped off at the hands of the heads of the plot, Colonel Bradshaw had been reluctantly forced to take action. The action had included pushing those Emergency Regulations through the legislature, detaining the twenty-two detainees, and deporting some other people.

One such deportee was Miss Diana Prior-Palmer, British-born but a naturalized American citizen. Miss Prior-Palmer was arrested at the same time as the twenty-two men, her property was searched, and her diary was confiscated. After two days she was deported, but Colonel Bradshaw kept her diary. Over ZIZ he announced several times that the diary was "juicy" and that it would play a key role in the upcoming trials of the twenty-two detainees. He also gave private readings in his office to journalists of passages he claimed to be excerpts from the diary. If Colonel Bradshaw is to be believed, Miss Prior-Palmer was a diarist in the modern manner; however, there's no way to be sure since the promised publication of the diary during the trials never did take place.

Other deportations followed. The manager of the local Coca-Cola bottling plant was deported to his birthplace, Barbados. Other West Indians were deported to their birthplaces, including one man who'd lived on St. Kitts since the age of four. A couple of Englishmen were deported, one unsuccessfully. Peter Keller, his name is; he was deported to Sint Maarten (the Dutch half of St. Martin), and the Dutch wouldn't accept delivery and sent him back.

Meanwhile, the detainees sat in jail. Stuart Roberts, the chief representative of Great Britain on St. Kitts, visited the prison almost every day because one of the detainees, James Milnes Gaskell, was a British subject. Milnes Gaskell gradually got the idea that the British Government preferred him to remain in detention, since it gave Roberts an excuse to come in, count heads and make sure nothing really drastic was being done to any of the detainees; Milnes Gaskell's attitude about this was, understandably, ambivalent.

There is a story that at one point in the course of the summer Colonel Bradshaw told Stuart Roberts that he would release Milnes Gaskell if Milnes Gaskell would promise not to make any statements to the press. Roberts brought this offer to Milnes Gaskell, according to the story, and Milnes Gaskell refused, which appeared to both please and relieve Roberts. However, when Milnes Gaskell asked Roberts, a year later, to verify that offer in writing, Roberts said he would have to check with the British Government first, and then returned to say that Milnes Gaskell must be mistaken about his facts, the offer was never made, none of it ever happened …

The Emergency Regulations under which the detainees had been detained required that they be told the reason for their detention within two weeks, and that they appear before a magistrate for review within one month. The reasons appeared within the time period and were very broad-ranging. One young attorney was charged with having written two published letters critical of the Government.

On the twenty-eighth of June, ten of the detainees appeared in Supreme Court on habeas corpus proceedings; but they had barely gotten started when they were adjourned, without explanation. When they resumed again several days later, the chief defense attorney, a Dominican, told the judge that his work permit for St. Kitts was up that day and the Government wouldn't renew it, which meant he couldn't defend his clients, which in turn meant they were being denied counsel of their choice. The judge responded with another adjournment.

Finally, on July 3, a habeas corpus hearing was actually completed on three of the detainees, and the judge ordered their release. (The judges, above the level of magistrate, are not Kittitians, nor are they responsible to the Government of St. Kitts; they work a circuit through the Associated States.) The three men were released, and the next morning they were arrested again and put back with their friends in the Cayon Street prison; this time, it was "*preventive* detention."

July seemed to be National Adjournment Month on St. Kitts, with much backing and filling in the law courts; it wasn't until August 11 that the Appeal Court decided that the detention orders weren't any good because the legislature hadn't properly enacted the Emergency Regulations.

It was a technicality, but a technicality is sometimes as good as a home run. Fifteen of the detainees were immediately released; five of them were just as immediately arrested again on different charges. One of the ten freed was Milnes Gaskell, who was at last deported, without protest. The remaining nine included Billy Herbert.

On August 13 six more of the detainees were supposed to be released on bail. The court proceeding began but was interrupted when the judge was called away to the phone. When he returned to the bench he had become extremely nervous. "I have just received a telephone call," he announced to the court, "from a voice I recognized, telling me that if I release these men I will be shot." So he didn't release them; he adjourned the hearing instead. And when an English reporter later asked him who had called, he would say only, "A member of the Cabinet."

That was Saturday. On Monday the fifteenth, Colonel Bradshaw whipped some new legislation through the House of Assembly to correct the flaws in the first batch of Emergency Regulations. Armed with the new Regulations he had six more of the freed men, including Billy Herbert, clapped back into prison.

Defense attorneys were being harassed in a variety of ways. Some had trouble getting to see their clients, some had trouble about work permits, all had trouble with the local radio station. But one had the worst trouble of all; he died.

Robert McKenzie Crawford, one of the two attorneys who had been with Milnes Gaskell out at Golden Rock Airport the day of his first arrest, was one morning suddenly rushed to the hospital. It happened to be a day when his wife was off the island, and it is said that nurses at the hospital heard Crawford loudly refusing to be operated on until someone could get in touch with his wife. Nevertheless, a stomach operation was prepared for and apparently took place. That night Crawford died. Because the Emergency Regulations waived inquests and autopsies, it was afterward impossible to tell what complaint had brought Crawford to the hospital or exactly of what he had died. The other defense attorneys knew that legally Crawford had died of natural causes. They were, nevertheless, not totally reassured.

By late August there were thirteen men left in prison—not an encouraging number—still waiting for the trials to start.

While the legal war struggled along, Colonel Bradshaw's Government was trying to get another kind of war off the ground. The 70-man Defence Force and 110-man police force had been armed with new guns by the British, and the old guns had gone to the newly created 162-man Special Volunteer Constabulary. This gave Bradshaw 342 men more or less under arms, ranged against a people who were known to have the weapons they'd taken from seventeen policemen, plus a dozen or so shotguns. (Later the Anguillans would go out and buy some rifles of their own, but as of the summer of 1967 they were ill prepared to defend themselves.)

Which Robert Bradshaw didn't know. Every time Peter Adams

or any other Anguillan leader got close enough to a reporter to make a statement, the statement always included some boast about the island's defenses. At one time they claimed to have bought an American Navy surplus PT boat, and at another time they announced they now possessed an antiaircraft gun. Every bit of this was moonshine. There was no PT boat, there was no antiaircraft gun.

The capstone of the actual Anguillan arsenal was a cannon left over from the Napoleonic Wars. Not the whole cannon, actually; not the wheels and carriage; just the barrel, lying on the sand. The Anguillans tucked some more sand under the front of the barrel to give it a better trajectory, found an old cannon ball, opened some shotgun shells for powder, and had artillery practice. They'd load the cannon and fire, and then trot down the beach to pick up the ball and bring it back and fire it again.

But one cannon is not a barrage. All the declarations of strength were bluff, and every journalist visiting Anguilla knew it; yet all the bluffs were reported as undoubted facts.

One newsman told me why. "I went around the island," he said, "and visited a beach with only one house on it. Two eighty-year-old ladies, retired schoolteachers, lived there. I asked them what they would do if Bradshaw's soldiers landed on their beach, and they showed me cane-cutting knives they had behind the door. 'We'll chop their heads off,' they said, and I knew they meant it. Any soldiers landing there would have had to kill those two old ladies. No choice. That, or get their heads chopped off."

Knowing the defenselessness of the Anguillans, and their determination, the reporters to a man went along with the bluffs and did their own small bit to discourage a Kittitian invasion. And it worked. Bradshaw, who at that time could probably have swept the island clean with ten determined men, hung back to build up his strength.

First he sent Paul Southwell to London to ask the British for more guns. The British looked at their files, saw they'd just given St. Kitts full armament for its regular uniformed forces, and decided not to overburden Basseterre's storage facilities.

Next, Southwell flew to Washington to ask for rifles, machine guns, ammunition and, please, *two* PT boats. The United States also said No, and it began to look as though St. Kitts was going to have to struggle along with just the weapons it had.

But then the Kittitian luck changed. A contact was made with some people in Fort Lauderdale, Florida, who would be more than happy to supply guns and ammunition, though no PT boat.

The group in Fort Lauderdale assembled the arms in Miami and put them in crates marked "Intransit, Excess Baggage for the Government of St. Kitts," a declaration that made them immune from customs inspection at any point in then-travels. The crates were then put on regular Pan Am passenger flights and flown to Coolidge Airport in Antigua. If you traveled from Miami to Antigua during the month of July 1967, the odds are good that you flew with hand grenades.

And you thought you had nothing to worry about but hijackers.

Once on Antigua, the crates of guns and ammunition were loaded after dark onto a plane belonging to a non-scheduled cargo carrier. This plane was then flown to St. Kitts.

At St. Kitts, security was very tight, but not very bright. Every evening for a week, at just about the same hour, a security lid was clamped on the airport, all civilians were excluded, the place was all lit up, and armed guards were everywhere. Into the middle of this movie set would stream the plane, settling down amid guns and lights. Mysterious crates would be taken off the plane and stacked in a waiting truck and then the truck, itself under heavy guard, would be driven out of the airport and down into the town of Basseterre and into the Defence Force headquarters compound.

The Anguillans, of course, learned about these shipments early in the game. Some of the more imaginative among them suggested they fly one of their own planes over to Antigua one night, claim to be the parcel service to St. Kitts, collect the mysterious crates, and bring them home to Anguilla instead. (Throwing burning sticks on sheets of powder again.) More gentlemanly heads, however, once more prevailed.

And so, over the long summer, the detainees of St. Kitts danced an endless quadrille with the courts and jailers, while Colonel Bradshaw assembled his armed might, read excerpts of Diane Prior-Palmer's diary to visiting journalists, and wished there was some place he could get hold of just *one* PT boat.

7

Speak not of my debts unless you mean to pay them.
——George Herbert, *Outlandish Proverbs*

The publicity attendant on Anguilla's declaration of independence had attracted a flow of outsiders, most of whom were a little strange. There was the kilt-wearing, cigar-smoking Jewish Chinaman from the United States who wanted land for some sort of ill-defined "thousand-year-old European religious sect," which the Anguillans decided translated into "free-love farm plus abortion clinic." There was the young American hippie couple who appeared on the island one day with nothing but a tent and a shotgun and began cadging food from the natives. There was the American in a business suit who seemed impervious to heat and who promised to solve all the island's economic problems in two weeks if he were simply given a free hand and the title "Economics Minister."

Another American offered twenty-five thousand dollars a month for an indefinite period if the Anguillans would mortgage the island to him for security. Another businessman said he was buying a floating hotel from Montreal's Expo 67 and wanted permission to moor the thing offshore. An Englishman wanted to dump his freeloading brother-in-law on Anguilla, and a Canadian offered to build the islanders a radio station if they would give him a couple of beaches. A man named Dino Cellini, said to be a representative of Meyer Lansky, who in turn was said to be the head of the Mafia in Florida, dropped by either to chat about gambling casinos or just to get a tan.

A doctor from America wanted land on which to build a clinic for the machine he'd invented that cures all diseases. A group from America—they were coming over in flocks after a while—wanted the Anguillans to join them in a partnership to make gold from sea water. Yet another American wrote a letter saying he represented Aristotle Onassis, who was prepared to offer a million dollars a year for the use of the island as a flag of convenience for his shipping, in the style of Panama and Liberia.

The kilt-smoking Chinaman was gently escorted to the airport. The hippies, minus their shotgun but with their tent, were bundled into a boat and taken to St. Barthélémy to bother the French. The would-be "Economics Minister" was thanked for his interest and asked to provide details; he disappeared instead. The Englishman with the ne'er-do-well brother-in-law was told to go on being his brother's keeper. Dino Cellini got his tan, but nothing else. As to the doctor with the miraculous machine, Jerry Gumbs had gotten involved with him and had high hopes of helping him build his "Center for Physical Medicine," but the trouble was, as Jerry Gumbs said worriedly, "Will I get my people to understand it? Or will they object to it like the American Medical Association?" They objected to it, just like the American Medical Association.

As to the other businessmen, with floating hotels and gold from sea water and radio stations and flags of convenience, the Anguillans subscribed to the business credit checking agency, Dun & Bradstreet, and began sorting out this bag of mixed nuts. They also wrote back to the man who claimed to represent Onassis, politely requesting further details. He never replied, and some time later the Onassis office denied any connection with the original offer.

But another little covey of outsiders had also shown up, with nothing to sell and nothing to offer but their talents and good wishes. For the next few months they took an active role in the history of Anguilla. They came to be known on the island as the San Francisco Group, and their contribution could be described as making sea water from gold.

The San Francisco members of the San Francisco Group were Mr. Scott Newhall, managing editor of the San Francisco *Chronicle*; Mr. Howard Gossage, an advertising man; Dr. Gerald Feigen, a surgeon and a member of the board of directors of *Ramparts* magazine; and Mr. Lawrence Wade, a onetime promotion manager on the *Chronicle*. But they were merely the satellites for the central figure of the San Francisco Group, Dr. Leopold Kohr, a man whose connection with San Francisco—in fact, with the planet Earth—is tenuous at best.

Dr. Leopold Kohr, a professor of economics specializing in the economic viability of small states, was born in Oberndorf, Austria, the town where "Silent Night" was composed, but he later became a naturalized American citizen and in 1967 was teaching at the University of Puerto Rico. At the beginning of 1967, he had visited San Francisco to conduct a seminar on city-states sponsored by Scott Newhall's newspaper. The idea was to consider the possibility of turning San Francisco into an independent city-state. At the time of the seminar all those who would later be part of the San Francisco Group thought it an excellent idea.

Since the Group had initially come together to ponder the secession of San Francisco, it was a pretty sure thing that any help they chose to offer Anguilla would be a trifle odd. It was.

One of Dr. Kohr's first suggestions was that the Anguillans give up automobiles, not only because of air pollution but also because of the bad balance of trade caused by the necessity of importing gasoline and oil and spare parts. In place of automobiles, he suggested horses. In addition to their not using gasoline, horses make a nice source of natural fertilizer, and Dr. Kohr is death on artificial fertilizer. Unfortunately, there are no horses on Anguilla, and barely enough water to go around as it is without a lot of thirsty horses forever at the trough, but theoretically it was a nice idea.

The assembling of the San Francisco Group was, however, only partly caused by a shared passion for city-states and natural fertilizer. The rest was chance. It began when Dr. Kohr arrived on Anguilla in the middle of June 1967 toting a briefcase bulging with books and articles he had done on small states. He met with the Peacekeeping Committee and began to outline his theories. As he later explained to reporters, "When Anguilla broke loose, it animated me. At last I could put my theories to the test."

Dr. Kohr's theories boiled down to a suggestion that Anguilla, having removed itself from St. Kitts, should now remove itself from the twentieth century. Dr. Kohr is a fervent admirer of the Pennsylvania Amish; what he had in mind for Anguilla combined an Amish forswearing of machinery with a sort of feudalism-*sans*-barons. He had no desire to make a profit out of the Anguillans—no, he wanted them to make a prophet out of him—which made him different from most of the other people the Peacekeeping Committee met around that time. They listened carefully to his suggestions before declining them with thanks. Untroubled, Dr. Kohr went away to regroup his arguments and returned about a week later to start all over again.

At about the same time, Scott Newhall, the *Chronicle* man, also showed up on Anguilla. Later he reported in *Scanlan's Monthly,* "Having a week I could spare for a first-hand excursion into a revolution, I decided to accompany George Draper, the *Chronicle* reporter I immediately assigned to Anguilla."

Newhall and Dr. Kohr bumped into each other in the corridor of Lloyd's Hotel. Astonishment and pleasure on both sides; they hadn't met since they'd freed San Francisco. As Newhall later reported their dialogue, Dr. Kohr speaks like a minor character in one of Shakespeare's history plays: "We have a chance to prove, at last," Newhall says Kohr said, "my theory that the Athenian city-state will work and is the answer to the future. I just know it! And seeing you here, I am convinced that this will be the beginning of a new social organization. I will get hold of Howard Gossage and Dr. Feigen, and two or three other people, the doctor that takes care of Vice-President Humphrey and some other very important men, and we shall make here a magnificent society!"

When Dr. Kohr next went to see Peter Adams, Scott Newhall went with him, and the result was a certain general misunderstanding all around. Newhall tells us that Dr. Kohr told Peter Adams, "We will put together a committee that will help you and see through to the end of your success in setting up your city-state that will rival, one day, the glories of ancient Greece." What Peter Adams thought they were saying was that they would help Anguilla solve its financial crisis—incoming mail, Government salaries and off-island bank accounts had been frozen for several months—and so he expressed definite interest.

When Newhall returned to San Francisco, he met with Howard Gossage and Dr. Feigen. They had dinner at Trader Vic's—there's something awry in the picture of revolutionary theorists having their first meeting at Trader Vic's—and agreed to band together to help Dr. Kohr. (What they told each other was that they were banding together to help Anguilla.)

On Puerto Rico, Dr. Kohr was collecting more people to participate in his Anguilla scheme. They included an architect named Henry Klumb, and Dr. Edgar Berman, who was Hubert Humphrey's personal physician.

Dr. Gerald Feigen flew from San Francisco to Anguilla on referendum day, the eleventh of July. He had dinner at the home of the local bank manager, who told him the bank had advanced all of its funds to the Anguillans, could get no more, and the island desperately needed around twenty-five thousand dollars right away, just to keep going. Dr. Feigen said that was what he was there for.

That evening he waited at the Administrative Building till after the results of the vote were announced and then buttonholed Peter Adams and said, "Look, it's very important that you come to Puerto Rico to a meeting of people who want to help you without any thought of personal profit, because they believe in Professor Kohr's theories."

Adams wasn't entirely convinced, but he agreed to go and listen, mostly because of the island's financial problems. He talked it over with the rest of the Peacekeeping Committee, and it was decided that Jerry Gumbs should go along with him. Peter Adams is not a businessman; Jerry Gumbs, being not only a businessman but also a fellow who'd been living among Americans for thirty years, could serve as a sort of interpreter.

The breakdown in communication between the Anguillans and the San Francisco Group was total from the beginning and remains total to this day. The Anguillans understood two kinds of outsiders; profiteers and philanthropists. They had met both and they could tell them apart. The San Francisco Group clearly weren't profiteers, so the Anguillans concluded for a while that they must be the other thing: philanthropists.

But they weren't. Profiteers work at a profit, and philanthropists work at a loss, but the San Francisco Group was performing in the service of a theory, and all they asked was that they break even. This was the unstated corollary to their offers to help the Anguillans raise money, and it was to cause some bad feeling all around a little later.

So Peter Adams and Jerry Gumbs went to Puerto Rico to get some money. They were given theory instead. The meeting took place at night in the jungle home of architect Henry Klumb; the Group members there included Dr. Kohr, Dr. Feigen, Dr. Edgar

Berman and Howard Gossage. As Gossage described it all much later in *Scanlan's Monthly,* "It was a lovely tropical house surrounded by a verandah and trees. It had no real walls, and the wind went right on through. This makes for wonderful tropical living, but that night it was rather windy and we could hardly hear each other talk."

Jerry Gumbs described the setting to me this way: "We were met at the airport and taken to some place in Puerto Rico like in the Bohemian Mountains, to a luxurious home, a nice home set among trees like bamboo, with record players set on the outside so the music sounds, is played around the house, and all kinds of fantasy."

Not all the fantasy was architectural. Howard Gossage reported, "Leopold Kohr was more or less chairman of the evening and we addressed ourselves to figuring out some solutions for Anguilla's financial crisis." The idea of selling coins and stamps was discussed. Gossage again: "I tried to hedge those suggestions with a good round maybe, but Kohr would have no maybes. He had an unlimited and, it seemed to me, unwarranted faith in our ability to solve all the problems of this tiny principality. 'Why, Mr. Gossage here will solve your problems with a wave of his hand,' he told the Anguillan leaders. I tried to hold Leopold down, but there was no way of stopping him."

Jerry Gumbs has a slightly different memory of that night: "We listened to Professor Kohr exhort all type of smallness, and small nations, how they could be independent. It went on till maybe one, two o'clock in the morning after we heard all that. And there was a man there supposedly from the United States State Department, by the name of Doctor Berman. He was supposed to be close to Humphrey at the time, had pictures of himself and Humphrey. And at that time they said they had the resources to assist the people of Anguilla and were willing to finance any scheme that we had. But at no time that I asked them for a substantial sum of money did anybody say how they would come up with this money."

The confusions and misreadings here are almost endless; and the vision of Dr. Berman, in the middle of it all, impressing the Anguillans with pictures of himself with Hubert Humphrey, is very sad.

Jerry Gumbs really did think the San Francisco Group would

"finance any scheme that we had." And on the other side Scott Newhall is being straightforward when he says of a meeting between Peter Adams and Dr. Kohr, "He and the professor had a long talk, and the professor brought out books and theses to explain himself and his theories of the small city-state. Adams heard him loud and clear." But all Adams heard loud and clear was that the professor knew some philanthropists.

After all, it was on the night of the referendum that Dr. Feigen invited Peter Adams to Puerto Rico in the first place. Dr. Feigen had been right there to listen to Walter Hodge read a Declaration of Independence that began, "We stand before the Queen in the greatest humility ..." And at the conclusion of his brief speech just before reading the Declaration of Independence, Hodge had said, "We humbly beg our Queen and the people of Britain to talk to us about sharing the future." Feigen and Newhall and Kohr had all landed at Wall Blake Airport on Anguilla; had none of them noticed that the rebel flag flying over the airport shed was the Union Jack? Peter Adams had been sending telegrams and making statements to reporters all through the summer insisting that what Anguilla wanted was a connection with some power other than St. Kitts, preferably a direct link with Great Britain (but they had also considered joining up with Canada, the United States, the Virgin Islands, St. Martin and several of the other British islands in the Caribbean). Economic isolation in total independence was the last thing the Anguillans wanted. The San Francisco Group could never see, and still can't see, that theories about Athenian city-states are just as irrelevant to Anguilla as they are to San Francisco.

But everybody concerned with the summit conference in Puerto Rico came away convinced that a great and lasting understanding had been reached. As Dr. Feigen wrote, also in *Scanlan's Monthly,* "Howard and Leopold and I worked on Mr. Adams to the point where he understood we were really trying to help. He agreed in principle with making us the island's agent, so to speak, and told us to go ahead with some of our ideas. We thought we could work out a way to raise some money for him."

The ideas expressed in this house of fantasy were not all on the mundane level of stamps and coins. One idea, for instance, was for an Anguillan schooner to voyage sixteen hundred miles to New

York, where it would sail dramatically into New York Harbor with the entire Peacekeeping Committee aboard. Then they would make a direct appeal to the United Nations.

Can't you see that as a television commercial? Haven't you seen it as a television commercial?

Unfortunately, the Anguillans couldn't see it at all. Aside from the hazards of the journey and the fact that nobody would be left to mind the store, they objected to the very idea of the idea; the Anguillans have a natural dignity that some of their friends have perhaps on occasion lacked.

A few days after the Puerto Rico meeting, Peter Adams and Jerry Gumbs left Anguilla again, this time heading for New York. A rally in a church had been planned by the Anguilla Improvement Association, to raise money for the island, and Adams had been invited to come up and speak. He intended, while in New York, to try for some discussions at the United Nations and to do some public agitating in another attempt to catch the ear of Great Britain.

Also in New York was Dr. Feigen of the San Francisco Group. Feigen had arranged for a not inexpensive suite at the Lombardy Hotel and had set up a press conference, which had to be delayed twenty-four hours when it was upstaged by race riots in Newark, New Jersey. Adams and Gumbs accepted what they took to be Feigen's hospitality at the Lombardy; Gumbs brought up a relative or two from New Jersey; and they all began calling room service.

Dr. Feigen complained about this episode later, saying, "Through most of Sunday and Monday the Anguillans, between interviews, were ordering lamb chops from room service—I couldn't believe anyone could eat so many lamb chops. And every few minutes Gumbs would pick up the phone and call St. Thomas or St. Martin or someplace. The hotel's bill for one day included $137 for lamb chops. I think they thought we were millionaires."

How close to the truth. The Anguillans thought the San Francisco Group were not profiteers. They thought the San Francisco Group were the other thing: philanthropists. Philanthropists, generally speaking, are millionaires. Yes, it would be fair to say that the Anguillans thought the San Francisco Group were millionaires. But what did the San Francisco Group think the Anguillans were?

Howard Gossage reported that he told Scott Newhall at this

point, "Obviously we can't chase everybody around the world with a butterfly net. Why the hell don't we bring them out to San Francisco where we can control the situation, and work out the plan to get Anguilla some money?"

Control the situation. In the eyes of the San Francisco Group, *they* were the heroes of the story and the Anguillans were spear carriers, and damn lucky to be allowed on stage at all. In a Foreword to the San Francisco Group's reminiscences in *Scanlan's Monthly,* American novelist Herbert Gold (well, why not?) had this to say: "The San Francisco heroes, Dons Quixote de la Pan Am, lances tipped with metaphysics, who gave nerve and fancy to the idea of Anguilla, are about to tell their story."

So they controlled the situation. Adams and Gumbs were invited to San Francisco. They understood money was going to be found for Anguilla, so they agreed to go. And Scott Newhall whipped into action. To begin with, he designed an Anguillan flag; he reports that when he showed it to an artist who called it horrible, he answered, "No, it's beautiful. It's not Picasso or Pollock, it's Anguillan."

Anguillan: two Caucasian mermaids, one holding a spear and the other an olive branch, and both leaning on some sort of sea shell. Their hair, fortunately, is long enough to keep Anguilla from having the first national flag with nipples, but that is absolutely the only concession to taste.

But Newhall isn't finished. He is a nation-builder, and a nation needs more than a flag. It also—as Adams and Gumbs have been pointing out—needs money. Newhall invents money.

"My son Tony," he wrote, "had recently bought 1,500 Peruvian soles, which are dollar-sized, or crown-sized, coins. All we would have to do was counterstamp them ... I ordered a die made that would say 'Anguilla Liberty Dollar' around the rim, and in the center 'June 11, 1967'—their Independence Day." (Actually, they said "July 11, 1967," which was referendum day.)

Money, a flag. What else does a nation need? Letterhead stationery! Newhall gets some of that, too.

Then he turns his attention to the imminent arrival of the delegation from Anguilla. He reserves a suite at the St. Francis, which like the Lombardy back in New York is not a cheap hotel. And whenever the representative of a foreign nation is in residence at the St. Francis—definitely not a cheap hotel—that nation's flag is flown over the entrance. Would the St. Francis please fly Scott Newhall's Anguilla flag, if it could be finished in time? That's the managing editor of the *Chronicle* asking, and he designed the flag himself, and it will get space in the paper. The St. Francis flew the flag.

Newhall: "The Mayor was out of town, but the acting Mayor, enjoying the idea, agreed to meet President Peter Adams at the airport with his limousine. We invited people to a reception, as many people as the suite would hold, and Howard's secretary did a beautiful job of arranging for bordelaise snails, crab legs, and a tape recorder."

City limousines—maybe San Francisco *should* secede—carried the Anguillans to the St. Francis Hotel. "The reception went off swimmingly," said Newhall. "One guest jumped up and pledged $1,000 to Anguilla, and Peter Adams made a very moving speech."

Once again Jerry Gumbs had a slightly different memory of the affair: "We went to San Francisco," he told me, "and we were met by the city fathers at the airport and had a big parade and there were flags, a flag of Anguilla with mermaids in it. All the city limousines, and a big party was thrown. Then we went to the St. Francis Hotel and there was a big suite, and all the people, ranchers and everybody, were there. They had a big thing, all types of food, and everything. And all this big display. And people then started donating thousands and thousands of dollars toward the Anguillan situation, all promoted by Scott Newhall. To date, we have never seen a dollar from the money that those people promised to give."

After the reception and the pledges of money, Newhall and Feigen showed Peter Adams three or four coins they'd run off on their die press and explained the deal to him. He said he'd think it over.

Oh, yes, the deal. The San Francisco Group wasn't going to *give* these "Anguilla Liberty Dollars" to the Anguillans, not at all; the San Francisco Group aren't millionaires. The idea was that the San Francisco Group would buy ten thousand silver-dollar-sized coins, which would cost one dollar each, and then counterstamp them all, which would cost another dollar each, making two dollars. Then the San Francisco Group would sell the ten thousand coins to the Anguillans at cost, that is, two dollars each, or twenty thousand dollars. Then the Anguillans, now legal owners of the coins, would declare them legal tender of Anguilla and sell them *back* to the San Francisco Group at *ten* dollars each, for a clear profit of eight dollars on each and every coin.

Adams said he'd think it over. It seemed a roundabout way to donate eighty thousand dollars, but that was the pitch, and he'd think it over.

But that night reality intruded, delaying things a bit for the San Francisco Group. The governments of the English-speaking Caribbean nations had been working in concert with Great Britain to find a way to calm this increasingly public and increasingly embarrassing problem of the Anguillan secession. Finally they had decided on holding a full-scale conference. It would meet on Barbados, it would have representatives from everywhere, and it would be charged with straightening out the mess once and for all. The Anguilla delegation to this conference would be headed by Peter Adams.

8

No doubt but ye are the People.
　　　　　—Rudyard Kipling, *The Islanders*

The Barbados Conference was announced by Mrs. Judith Hart, Minister of State for Commonwealth Relations, on July 18. When the Conference got under way a week later, Mrs. Hart wasn't the Minister anymore; her job had been taken from her the day before by Prime Minister Harold Wilson and given to a man named Lord Shepherd.

Well, this is what the telephone company does all the time. You call and call and get the name of the individual responsible for your exchange and talk to that individual day after day after day, and just at the point when you've finally made yourself understood, they have a reshuffling down at the phone company and you find yourself listening to a brand-new voice that says, "Well, now, what's the problem?"

Having at last attracted Mrs. Judith Hart's attention, the Anguillan delegation arrived in Barbados to discover they had to start all over again. And from farther back than before; whereas Mrs. Hart had simply spent a long time ignoring Anguilla, Lord Shepherd apparently arrived in Barbados convinced that he already knew everything about Anguilla it would ever be necessary to know. It proved very hard for the Anguillans to get new words into a head that was already full.

The Anguillan delegation to the Conference originally consisted of five men, led by Peter Adams. The other four were Walter Hodge, Chairman of the Peacekeeping Committee, and three Committee members.

In addition to the British delegation led by Lord Shepherd, and the Anguillan delegation accompanied by its Barbadian attorney, and a Kittitian delegation composed of Colonel Bradshaw and

Eugene Walwyn, there were delegations to the Conference from Jamaica, Trinidad-Tobago, Guyana and the host island, Barbados. The main meeting of the Conference was planned for July 29, but in the days prior to that all sorts of small informal meetings were held, with everybody being very low-key and earnest and concerned about getting this problem solved to everybody's satisfaction.

Almost everybody, that is; Colonel Bradshaw gave an interview to a local newspaper in his usual style, full of storm clouds and rolls of thunder. The editor of the paper was persuaded by some of the conferees to expurgate the interview before publication, but Colonel Bradshaw's voice comes through all filters, and the Anguillans began to feel their hackles rise.

Then there was the pressure. Afterward, the Anguillans were to claim that the pressure on them had been continuous from the very beginning of the Conference and had grown more intense with every day. The threats, like Salome, lost their veils as time went along and became blunter and harsher every day.

Some Anguillan delegates claim the British threatened an embargo if they failed to agree to return to St. Kitts; for an island like Anguilla, which imports practically everything it uses, an embargo could be a fearful thing. There was already that Kittitian/British embargo on mail deliveries, cutting off the remittances by which the island kept itself healthy and alive, as well as the embargo on medical supplies, so a broader embargo was certainly a possibility.

The reason for the pressure was the Anguillan delegation's insistence that they couldn't sign anything until the people back home had had a chance to look it over. As the Wooding Report put it, one of the "factors which contributed to the failure of the Barbados Conference" was "the apparent practice in Anguilla that all important issues must be resolved by reference to the people." Which sounds very much like a definition of democracy.

Whatever it sounds like, the British didn't like the sound of it. Like the San Francisco Group, they wanted the Anguillans handy so they could control the situation. Pressuring five men in a hotel room was one thing; pressuring six thousand people on their own island would be something else again.

After several days of informal diplomacy, the Conference had its first formal session on July 29. The Anguillans were still saying they couldn't make any binding commitments until they talked it over with the people at home. Everybody else leaned very hard, and finally the Anguillans asked for a postponement until they could bring up some more delegates.

Three Anguillans flew home. They had some meetings, and flew back with five reinforcements, which brought the full Anguillan strength up to ten men, plus the Barbadian attorney. This was greater than any other delegation, but ten men is still only .0017 per cent of a population of six thousand.

The new men contained some not-so-new faces. Anguillan defense chief Ronald Webster and editor Atlin Harrigan were there, and so was Jerry Gumbs, and the team was rounded out by two more Peacekeeping Committee members, Alfred Webster and John Rogers. Only Ronald Webster and John Rogers were considered full delegates, the others being along in an observer capacity. Rogers is a cabdriver, usually to be found down by the airport when he doesn't have a fare. He is a tall, well-built man, with a square face and the look of a boxer about him, and he is a firm believer in the politics of conspiracy. Still, when it comes to immediate practical political questions he has a fast intuitive mind, and he has been connected with most post-rebellion Anguillan governments.

The Conference had its next session on July 30. The Anguillans, perhaps feeling safety in their new numbers, began to get snappish. They'd been leaned on for a week, they hadn't had enough sleep, they'd been threatened in ugly ways, and nobody seemed to care that what they had back home on Anguilla was a democracy and not a republic. They couldn't sign for everybody because they *weren't* everybody.

Lord Shepherd wouldn't accept that. "A failure of your representatives to accept the very favourable terms worked out in these talks, and to return to constitutional rule," he told them, "is an exceedingly grave step."

The "very favourable terms" gave some very minor concessions to the Anguillans, brought out the local-council proposition in its usual vague and dateless way, and arranged for a "peacekeeping team" of policemen from Jamaica, Trinidad-Tobago, Barbados and Guyana to be stationed for an indefinite period on Anguilla. Whether these police were supposed to protect Bradshaw from the

Anguillans, the Anguillans from Bradshaw, or the Anguillans from one another wasn't spelled out.

Finally the Anguillans agreed to sign the Conference report, but only to acknowledge the existence of the proposals, not to consider the report binding. Great Britain and St. Kitts and the others would sign the report and *would* consider it binding.

Of the seven Anguillans classed as full-fledged delegates, only four actually signed the report. These were the most "political" and the most moderate of the delegates: Peter Adams, Walter Hodge, Emile Gumbs and John Rogers. But in the middle of the signing, there was a small gesture, and the history of Anguilla pivots upon that gesture; there was everything before it was made, and there was everything else after it was made.

The scene was this: The Conference report was a bundle of papers, a thick stack of documents, and it was being carefully passed from hand to hand as each delegate from each nation signed his name to it. The bundle was placed before Ronald Webster. Without pausing, Webster picked it up and casually tossed it to the next man, Attorney General S. S. Ramphal of Guyana, as though it were wastepaper for baling.

In that small gesture, Anguilla found her hero.

9

When constabulary duty's to be done, to be done,
The policeman's lot is not a happy one.
—W. S. Gilbert, *The Pirates of Penzance*

Ronald Webster and the other dissidents got home from Barbados a full day before Peter Adams and the other signers of the Conference report. Webster called a public meeting to announce the Conference decision. The enraged reaction was immediate and general and not unexpected: Foreign policemen on Anguillan soil? *Back* to Bradshaw after finally getting away from him, with practically nothing changed? No, No, six thousand times No.

Bradshaw himself had also rushed home before the Conference finished its closing formalities. He made a speech over ZIZ in which he announced that Anguilla had "surrendered." It sometimes seems Colonel Bradshaw must have an Anguillan for a speech writer. He couldn't possibly make all those tactical and tactless errors without help.

The four Anguillan signers stayed till the end of the Conference, returned home, and found a group of very irritable people waiting for them at the airport. Ronald Webster showed up before tempers got too thoroughly frayed and explained that the signatures had committed Anguilla to nothing but an agreement to look the proposals over. Everybody went away to decide what to do next, and gradually they came to the conclusion it was time for a change in leadership.

Up till then, there had been four leaders in the island. Peter Adams had been in charge of external affairs, maintaining contacts with the outside world. Walter Hodge had been in charge of internal affairs, running the domestic side of government. And Ronald Webster and Atlin Harrigan had together composed a kind of informal leadership of activists, whose pushing and prodding had paved the way to rebellion, with Webster thereafter in charge of island defenses.

Now both of the primary political leaders, Peter Adams and Walter Hodge, had compromised themselves in the eyes of the people by signing the report of the Barbados Conference. Harrigan was too young, his fieriness not yet seasoned, and he had only been an observer at Barbados, not a full-fledged delegate. That left Ronald Webster, whose gesture at Barbados had been the first signal of what the true Anguillan response to the proposals was to be.

So now, two months after the bloodless rebellion began, there came about a bloodless change of leadership. In a very informal way, later ratified by the Peacekeeping Committee, the overwhelming majority of Anguillans chose Ronald Webster to take over the reins.

Their choice, as it turned out, was a wise one; Ronald Webster was rich, he was dedicated, he was tireless, he was uncompromised, he was determined, and he had guts.

The shifting of leadership was done smoothly and with no unnecessary loss of face. While Ronald Webster became the new Chairman of the Peacekeeping Committee, Walter Hodge became Finance Minister, a job he turned out to be very good at, and Peter Adams was appointed Magistrate. (There had been no legal judiciary on the island since the rebellion, and Adams couldn't sit for cases much more complex than drunk-and-disorderly. He couldn't settle land disputes, for example, without the strong possibility that his decision might someday be set aside by a recognized court after Anguilla's secession had come, one way or another, to an end. Still, so long as the rumshops were open, even a magistrate with limited powers was a good idea, and Adams, a careful and sympathetic man, was a good choice for the job.) Only Atlin Harrigan remained outside the political structure, as observer and critic, a role that would crystallize the next month with the founding of the *Beacon*.

Meanwhile, Anguilla was full of rumors and misunderstandings and apprehensions, all brought about by the Barbados Conference. To calm things down and get everybody back to an orderly condition, the Peacekeeping Committee published on August 7 a document titled *Statement to the People of Anguilla by Their Govern-*

ment. Roger Fisher, who had written the Declaration of Independence, was back on the island at this time and probably had a hand or two in the *Statement's* composition.

The *Statement* officially announced the changes in the leadership and went on to speak very gently and carefully about the Barbados Conference report. It explained that the report wasn't binding on Anguilla, that the signers had simply "believed that these were the best terms that could be obtained from that conference, and that they should be brought home for serious study by the people," and that the people hadn't had a chance to study them yet, so therefore couldn't be said yet to have either accepted or rejected them. It described the report as "a complex document of 21 pages with four appendices," and said that it "contains intricate proposals concerning a Commonwealth peacekeeping force, economic aid, local self-government and proposed legislation." It suggested that everybody study the proposals and then, "if the people are unwilling to accept them as they stand, we should come back with specific proposals of our own designed to provide adequate self-government for the people of Anguilla."

Ronald Webster then went over to St. Martin and phoned the Conference chairman on Barbados. He said the Anguillans were thinking about the proposals, would be happy to talk them over informally with anybody sent by Barbados or the other Governments involved, and that they definitely hadn't as yet come to a decision one way or the other.

The Governments of Barbados, Jamaica, Trinidad-Tobago and Guyana were having second thoughts themselves about this peacekeeping force they were supposed to be sending to Anguilla. The Anguillans were getting a reputation for not suffering fools gladly, and nobody likes to get a bloody nose in somebody else's fight. There were newspaper reports about Ronald Webster training a "defense force" of two hundred ten men, and the *Statement* had said that "a hasty use of force by any other island would be most unwise"; in the context of such a calm and rational document, that warning seemed very tough indeed. The British had a frigate, H.M.S. *Lynx,* waiting nearby to carry forty policemen from the four other Governments over to Anguilla, but all at once no one was in a hurry to go.

Instead, they called another conference in Barbados, this one on August 12, 1967. It was attended only by those four Caribbean Governments that had been left holding the baby. The stated purpose of the conference was to "iron out certain snags in the plan to send a Peacekeeping force to Anguilla."

Everybody agreed that things looked a little trickier now than at the first Barbados Conference. It was decided to take up Ronald Webster's offer, send a couple of Civil Servants to the island to have a chat, and wait a while with the forty policemen.

Hugh Shearer, Prime Minister of Jamaica, then announced that none of *his* police would be among the forty. "I have never liked the idea," he said. And the day after that, when two officials from Jamaica and Barbados did respond to Ronald Webster's invitation by going to Anguilla, they found that things were not as calm there as the *Statement* had suggested. Speaking of their visit, the Wooding Report says they "appear to have been discomfited by a large and noisy crowd." They took their discomfiture back to their respective Governments and suggested that Great Britain be left to pull her own chestnuts out of the fire.

Time for yet a third conference. This one was held in Kingston, Jamaica, with the four Caribbean Governments that were supposed to be doing the peacekeeping, plus Lord Shepherd, who'd organized it all.

Lord Shepherd made a speech in which he suggested gangsters had taken over in Anguilla—Colonel Bradshaw had been the only one to make this kind of remark up till now—and that the rebellion was supported by "hot money." He also talked about "fragmentation," that awful bugaboo that seems to take the place in official British minds that Communism does in official American minds; it refers to countries and areas that break into pieces too small to survive economically or politically or militarily on their own.

By this time, however, Jamaica was pretty much on Anguilla's side. The chief Jamaican delegate suggested maybe Anguilla did have the unilateral right to secede after all. He compared it to Jamaica's own decision in 1961 to secede from the West Indies Federation, which had also been done in conjunction with a referendum.

But Lord Shepherd wasn't of a mind to listen to arguments

that didn't aim at getting Anguilla back into the box where she belonged. And if Anguilla wouldn't go back, he threatened, then by thunder Great Britain would cut off all aid! (Considering the amount of aid that had been getting through to Anguilla when things were going good, this news didn't cause trembling in very many boots. As the *Trinidad Guardian* said, it was "about the most empty diplomatic threat in history.")

Colonel Bradshaw hadn't been invited to this particular conference, but he sent a telegram, in which he said that "gangster elements have taken charge in Auguilla" and that if the other Caribbean Governments didn't get his island back for him it would have "only the most shattering consequences for entire Leewards and Windwards who watch with interest."

Jamaica had been the first to say she wouldn't have anything to do with the peacekeeping force. Barbados was second and Trinidad-Tobago third. Guyana, which with Antigua represented about the only wholehearted support Colonel Bradshaw had in the Caribbean, said it was perfectly willing to take *part* in a peacekeeping force, but it wasn't about to *be* the peacekeeping force, and then there were none.

Lord Shepherd responded by suggesting Great Britain might send in troops of her own, but only if the four Governments made a formal request that she do it. Great Britain didn't intend to invade any part of the Caribbean without getting a commitment from the Commonwealth Caribbean first.

The Caribbean delegates visualized what their political futures at home would look like once it was learned they had asked a European colonial power to invade a brother Caribbean island. They chose not to take up Lord Shepherd's offer. Which meant that Great Britain, for the time being, abandoned the idea of invading Anguilla.

This third and final conference broke up on August 20, 1967, completely deadlocked. As the Wooding Report put it, "The Jamaica Conference achieved nothing." And a British Commonwealth Office statement explained that the idea of the peacekeeping force had "run up against local tensions and disagreements, about which we would rather not say too much."

Lord Shepherd didn't have quite the same attitude. On his way home he amplified his earlier comments about gangsters and hot money, saying that "outside organizations" were going to use the island as a base for "gambling and drugs," which is a nice combination and guaranteed to get a good response on both sides of the Atlantic. (What Communism is to the American Government and what fragmentation is to the British Government, the Mafia is to *both* Governments.)

It wasn't hard to believe, at that. Prime Minister Eric Williams of Trinidad-Tobago spoke for practically everybody when he said, "If the Mafia or any other sort of American crooks are not already in Anguilla, they soon will be. They are everywhere else in the Caribbean."

As it turns out, in this particular case there's Mafia and there's Mafia. Professor Roger Fisher had been trying to talk to Deputy Prime Minister Cameron Tudor of Barbados back in July, to ask his help in mediating the dispute between Anguilla and St. Kitts, and he had trouble reaching Tudor until he found out the British had warned Tudor that *Fisher* was from the Mafia and was a lawyer for gamblers in Miami. Fisher, whose background in international law is so sound and extensive that he doesn't even *need* to show pictures of himself with Hubert Humphrey, had no trouble convincing Tudor that the British had been selling gold-mine stock. But the same thing happened again a month later in New York, at the United Nations. People Fisher tried to talk to there had been told—by the British—that he was a dangerous man, a known agent of "Mafia-type" gangsters.

None of which is to say the Mafia is *not* in the Caribbean, only that it was not in Anguilla. The fact is, Eric Williams is right; the Mafia is everywhere in the Caribbean. Through either British indifference or British stupidity, the Mafia has taken over gambling in the Bahamas, for instance. And the American airline Pan Am, which owns three casinos on three islands in the area, found, when looking for managers to run them, that the Mafia were the people with the experience for the job. When Fidel Castro threw the Mafia out of Havana after the Cuban revolution, very few of the troops traveled all the way back to the States.

But with Mafiosi as common in the Caribbean as sand fleas, why would Lord Shepherd go out of his way to warn that a poverty-stricken little speck in the ocean with no electricity, no roads, no telephones, no hotels, damn little water and not one limbo dancer was about to be overrun by gangsters?

In any case, by the time he'd returned to Great Britain he'd eased back the throttle a bit and had something more vague and less ominous to say: "The island is wide open to strong-arm influences. There is no political organization and there are interested bodies, whose names I shall not mention now, who definitely feel that there is money to be made from these little islands."

Never mind skipping ahead; he never did mention their names.

10

Get money by fair means if you can; if not, get money.

—Horace, *Epistles*

But enough of real life! What about the San Francisco Group?

After Peter Adams departed for Barbados, the San Francisco Group was left with Jerry Gumbs, who was then calling himself Ambassador-at-Large. Scott Newhall and Howard Gossage and Dr. Gerald Feigen all sat down with Jerry Gumbs and gave him the Liberty Dollar pitch. He signed an agreement they'd drawn up, and they told him they'd be seeing him on Anguilla with the thousand silver coins. As Scott Newhall described it later, "Using these coins as a starter, Anguilla could get $80,000 without investing a penny. The risk would be ours. What we were getting out of it at the moment was the excitement of planning."

In the meantime, however, they didn't have ten thousand silver coins, they had fifteen hundred silver coins. They also didn't seem to have eighty thousand dollars. So they invented a company, the Anguilla Charter Company, and set about raising some cash for it. Newhall: "Gerry Feigen pledged to put up securities behind the company. He told the bank we would like to have $15,000—preferably in British West Indian currency." This, of course, is a bank in San Francisco, which incredibly enough didn't have fifteen thousand dollars in British West Indian currency. So they took the money—watch this, now—they took the money in one-dollar bills.

Why did they take the money in one-dollar bills? Think of it as though it were a movie, try to visualize it. Which would *play* better, a check for fifteen thousand dollars or a suitcase full of one-dollar bills?

Now the fourth San Franciscan in the San Francisco Group enters the picture. Newhall: "I called Larry Wade, a former promotion manager on the *Chronicle,* and asked him to help out ... So on Friday morning Larry went over to the bank and picked up this great canvas sack with 150 packages of $1 bills, 100 to the package. He came staggering in, looking as though he had a body in the sack."

Actually, the bills were divided into thousands. Each thousand was packed between wooden slats and wrapped around with iron straps, none of which made it any lighter. The Group removed the wood and iron, packed the paper in a case that had once held Eagle shirt samples, stowed the silver in six small canvas money sacks they'd had printed with a mermaid and the words "250 Anguilla Liberty Dollars"—God knows why; maybe to attract muggers—gave it all to Larry Wade, and headed for the airport.

At the airport Gossage bought two maroon Qantas canvas bags and put three of the moneybags in each. Gossage: "The redcap had to wheel the hand baggage—130 pounds of coins in two bags and the flat case with $15,000 in currency—onto the plane. At that moment, we turned and walked out of the place. The tension was over, and it was all so ridiculous, we began to laugh. We laughed all the way back to the fire-house." (Don't ask.)

Larry Wade and all the money had to change planes in New York, where people are less fun-loving than in San Francisco, and nobody would help him carry the money off the plane. So he found a wheelchair and wheeled it all to Pan Am.

Eventually, Wade and the money reached Anguilla, where he discovered he was supposed to go through customs. Rather than open the shirt case and display the fifteen thousand one-dollar bills, he opened his suitcase instead and distracted everybody by showing them Newhall's flag with the mermaids. Like bewitched mariners, the customs men gaped at the mermaids while Wade quickly scooted off to the only local bank, the Mid-Atlantic, and stowed the cash in the vault. Then he went looking for Peter Adams, to get him to sign the agreement Jerry Gumbs had already signed, but Adams was still on Barbados, at the first Barbados Conference.

The next day Adams came back to Anguilla to get reinforcements—Ronald Webster and John Rogers were now added to the delegation at Barbados—and Larry Wade tried to talk to him about the money, "but," as he later wrote, "they were so preoccupied with their political concerns, understandably, that they hardly heard me."

Preoccupied they might be, but Wade had all that money to think about, so the next day he followed Adams and the rest back to Barbados.

Wade bearded Adams in his hotel room. Wade: "I gave him a letter from Scott and the presentation coin set, and he said 'Thank you' rather abstractedly. He could talk about nothing but the great pressure he'd been under. He said he felt as if he were on top of a mountain with guns pointing at him from every side. He seemed exhausted and defeated. I left him the flag, as a memento of his visit to San Francisco, and was about to turn to the coinage agreement when the phone rang."

Wade left the coin agreement and came back the next day to ask if he'd signed it. He hadn't, but he *had* signed the Conference report. Wade: "I was stunned. I decided that my principal mission now was to get the money off Anguilla before the St. Kitts government could seize it."

Wade hitched a ride with Jerry Gumbs in one of his own Anguilla Airways planes. Back on Anguilla Wade and Gumbs headed together for the bank. (Gumbs had no intention of being anyplace where that money wasn't.) Wade: "Jerry Gumbs tried very hard to get me to deposit the money in his account so he could give it to the government of Anguilla. Mr. Rogers went to the vault, and there were the coins and the suitcase full of cash, just as I had left them. Gumbs wanted the money so badly that finally, as a last flourish, I opened the bag of dollar bills and gave him $100 for his expenses."

Wade is not only magnificent at distracting the opposition, he also knows precisely what to use in every situation. The customs men he mesmerized with mermaids, and now he clouds Jerry Gumbs's mind with one hundred dollars in one-dollar bills.

Leaving Jerry Gumbs struck to stone, Wade next carted his cash to the airport. Here he met Ronald Webster, who had just taken over the island leadership. Wade: "I told him I was going to leave with him a bag of 250 coins, if he wanted to put them in circulation, and $2,000 to cover their redemption."

(Now, I don't understand that. Either Wade *left* the coins or he *redeemed* them, but he couldn't very well do both. And if he redeemed them, he was supposed to pay twenty-five hundred dollars—ten dollars per coin—not two thousand. So what he says he did, he says he gave Webster one of his six bags of coins, paid him the wrong amount of money to get them back, and didn't ask for them back. Did the master mesmerist meet an even *more* master mesmerist?)

Now Wade went from the airport to Lloyd's Hotel, where he'd been staying, and, he says, "I paid my bill to [Mrs. Lloyd] in Anguilla Liberty Dollars, which pleased her." (Now, since this is the Mrs. Lloyd who was one of the five no votes at the referendum three weeks earlier, and since the hotel—in which she lived—had been shot up by the rebels at least twice, I truly doubt that the Anguilla Liberty Dollars pleased her. But the relationship between Anguilla and San Francisco is one long unrelieved saga of misunderstanding anyway.)

At last Wade left Anguilla, carrying with him 1,250 silver coins (less his hotel bill) and 12,900 one-dollar bills, all of which he stuffed in a hotel safe as soon as he reached St. Thomas, about two hundred miles away.

Wade stayed in St. Thomas two days, until Jerry Gumbs came to see him. His mind apparently had cleared, and he was back for more money. Wade: "He carried a letter from Ronald Webster—a plea to send back the rest of the money, since they now had a new government."

(A mark of their desperation for money by this point can be seen in the fact that they had just broken into the Warden's safe. For two months after the rebellion they didn't touch that safe. It was the Queen's property and not theirs. But at last they were in such desperate straits they were forced to do it, despite their qualms. Rebellion had been one thing; breaking into the Queen's safe was something else again.)

So Wade phoned Newhall, back home in San Francisco, and Newhall said sure, go ahead, give them the money. Wade promptly turned over all the dollar bills to Jerry Gumbs and went home to San Francisco with the five moneybags full of coins. He had just made a ten-thousand-mile journey, carrying 108 pounds of silver coins, and at last delivered them to the spot where he'd picked them up. Mission accomplished.

11

"Unimportant, of course, I meant," the King hastily said, and went on to himself in an undertone, "important—unimportant—unimportant—important—" as if he were trying which word sounded best.

—Lewis Carroll,
Alice's Adventures in Wonderland

The Anguillans, their rebellion already being fought on two fronts—the Caribbean and San Francisco—now opened a third front: the United Nations. This campaign didn't get into full swing until August, after Lord Shepherd had given up at the Jamaica Conference, but its first shot had been fired U.N.-ward back at the very beginning, two days after the Kittitian police were sent packing, when Peter Adams had gone to Puerto Rico and sent a telegram to U Thant. It had said, among other things, "Anguillans prefer death to the oppression of St. Kitts." Adams sent Thant a few more telegrams during his tenure, but Thant never replied.

In the middle of July, when Adams and Jerry Gumbs had traveled up to New York, Adams had announced his intention of going to the U.N., but the San Francisco Group had come along at that point with Howard Gossage's butterfly net and whisked the Anguillans away to be controlled in San Francisco. Then in August came the first real onslaught at the U.N.

Jerry Gumbs traveled to New York on August 5 (while the peacekeeping-force idea was still alive back in the Caribbean) intending to breach the U.N. and demand international assistance in his homeland's quest for freedom; he had been spending a lot of time with the San Francisco Croup recently and was therefore full of heady talk about independence. At first he got only as far as a telephone interview with a reporter from *The New York Times,* but he made the most of it. "I have been asked by the people of Anguilla to tell Secretary General Thant that they desire to be free," he announced. "After three hundred years of neglect as a British colony, the people feel they are able to take care of their own affairs, and that all they need to prosper is to be independent." He also made a pitch for the San Francisco Group's Anguilla Liberty Dollar while he was on the phone and explained just how independence was going to make Anguilla prosperous: "There are a lot of things a little island can do to raise money if it is free. We can sell flags."

Personal contact works better than telegrams with the U.N. Jerry Gumbs managed to set up an appointment with a U.N. official, Issoufou Djermakoye, Under-Secretary for Trusteeship and Non-Self-Governing Territories Affairs. They met on August 7, 1967. (This was the same date the *Statement* was being published on Anguilla.) Gumbs asked Djermakoye to ask Thant to send a fact-finding mission to Anguilla. Djermakoye said Thant couldn't do that without authorization from a "competent organ."

It turned out that a competent organ was a committee. In this case it was the Special Committee on Colonialism. This Committee was just then looking into the whole business of Associated States anyway; the Committee was under the impression that an Associated State was a colony and therefore the Committee's business, while Great Britain claimed it was an independent nation and therefore out of the Committee's jurisdiction.

Anguilla, by now, had become news. On the same day Jerry Gumbs was talking to Issoufou Djermakoye at the U.N. and the *Statement* was being published by the Peacekeeping Committee on Anguilla, *The New York Times* ran the first of the four editorials it would publish on the subject of Anguilla over the next two years. Under the heading "The Ins and Outs of Anguilla" ran copy that looked as though it had been written by Lord Shepherd. "The erratic procedure of recent days," said the third paragraph, "shows that there is no truly representative government to speak for the island. The man who was President until a week ago, Peter Adams, had a mandate to negotiate for Anguilla. When he did so and signed a pact that seemed fair to him and to delegations from a number of the islands and Britain, Mr. Adams was ousted." Compare that with Larry Wade's account of Peter Adams' feeling at Barbados that he was "on top of a mountain with guns pointing at him from every side."

Jerry Gumbs thanked Issoufou Djermakoye for his time and went in search of the Special Committee on Colonialism. Unfortunately, the Special Committee on Colonialism was in recess, but it had a Third Subcommittee that was sitting and that gave Gumbs an appointment for the next day.

A brief reminder here. Anguilla did *not* rebel against colonial rule; Anguilla rebelled against independence. After 317 years of neglect and mismanagement as a colony, Anguilla rebelled three months after being set free. Now of course this runs absolutely counter to the flow of contemporary history, and it was very hard for anybody to believe that a tiny group of six thousand people was fighting *against* independence and *for* colonialism.

In fact, it was sometimes hard for the Anguillans themselves to keep it straight. Revolutionary rhetoric is all geared in one direction, and it's hard to make yourself understood if you're trying to go the other way. What Anguilla wanted to be—with side trips into other possibilities—was a British colony. The statement of complaint given to Peter Johnston four months before the rebellion included this: "England would be bound to keep Anguilla as a colony since Anguilla was unwilling to associate with St. Kitts in Statehood." And when the first reporter reached Anguilla after the beginning of the rebellion, Peter Adams told him, "We would like to return to Crown Colony rule."

That's what Anguilla wanted. What the Third Subcommittee of the Special Committee on Colonialism wanted was freedom, baby; freedom *now*. The full Special Committee is weighted heavily toward anti-colonialism, with a majority of its twenty-four members coming from recently free nations, mostly in Africa and Asia. A few months earlier, when the Committee had started looking into these things called Associated States, Lord Caradon had reproached it with the following soaring sentence: "Are we to assume that the sponsors of this resolution wish to stipulate that all the remaining colonial territories, however small, poor or isolated, must be required to abandon their own freely expressed aims, and that they should be forced to walk the plank into independent isolation whether they wish it or not?" Or, as the London *Times* said in reporting Lord Caradon's address, "So far, there is no indication that Lord Caradon's arguments will carry conviction with the majority of the 24 committee members, who have in the past delighted in flogging the dead horse of colonialism. The committee has a built-in majority in favour of ideological extremism."

So on the one side we have Anguilla, which is independent and wants to be a colony, and on the other side we have the Third Subcommittee of the Special Committee on Colonialism, which wants every colony in the world set free by sundown.

Jerry Gumbs went to talk to the seven-member Subcommittee on August 8 and started off right away talking independence: "The desire of the people of Anguilla is to improve their situation, and all they need to do this is self-government." The Subcommittee listened attentively to Gumbs's rundown of Anguilla's run-down condition—the roads, the schools, the phones, the electricity. The only sour note of the day was sounded by a minority of one on the Subcommittee, Pedro Berro of Uruguay, who asked mildly whether an independent Anguilla would be economically viable, and suggested Anguilla might go directly from British colonialism to "neocolonialism under foreign capital." Still, despite Berro's interpolation, the day was generally considered satisfactory all around, and Gumbs was asked to come back the next day.

He did, bringing Roger Fisher, who had just come up from Anguilla with a copy of the *Statement* and who also wanted to speak to the Subcommittee.

The Subcommittee wasn't sure about that. Jerry Gumbs had presented himself to them as an Anguillan, representing the people of his home island. But Roger Fisher was an American, a professor of international law, and—according to the British—an agent of the Mafia. The Subcommittee wasn't sure it wanted to make the same accommodation of its rules for Fisher that it had made for Gumbs.

So, for the second day, Jerry Gumbs alone spoke to the Subcommittee, first reading them the *Statement* Since this was by far the most moderate declaration by anybody so far, full of reassurances that the Barbados proposals hadn't been rejected out of hand, the Subcommittee found its vision of Anguilla blurring a bit around the edges. Pedro Berro was probably speaking for everybody when he asked "who now is really authorized to speak for Anguilla." He assured Jerry Gumbs he wasn't questioning his good faith, but inquired, "When he says 'the people of Anguilla' have authorized him, how do we know what it means?"

Roger Fisher finally got to talk to the Subcommittee nearly a week later, and apparently he too talked "independence." Throughout this whole affair, it was very difficult for people to talk about what they were doing without getting the words wrong.

Whatever Fisher said, he said it at an informal meeting with Subcommittee members rather than at a formal session. As *The New York Times* explained, "Some committee members had objected that Mr. Fisher could not testify as a petitioner without clearance by a petitions subcommittee or the full Colonialism Committee." Nevertheless, he did get to talk to them, after which the Subcommittee retired to prepare a recommendation for the full Committee.

But then Great Britain got miffed about the whole thing. Sir Leslie Glass, acting head of the British delegation in Lord Caradon's absence, sent a note to the Subcommittee warning that it had no right to think about this "purported secession" of Anguilla since it was the internal affair of a sovereign state: St. Kitts-Nevis-Anguilla. It was a testy note, it also said Great Britain wouldn't "collaborate" with the full Committee any more in connection with the other Associated States, and it was pretty well guaranteed to raise hackles and to induce the Subcommittee to think about the purported secession twice as hard as before. Which they did.

But the irritable memo from Sir Leslie Glass didn't portray the full spectrum of British opinion. On August 21 the London *Times* contributed the first of the eight editorials it would do on the subject over the following three years. Under the headline "ISLANDERS IN REVOLT," it gave a much more comprehensive and compassionate summary of the Anguilla situation than its New York namesake had done two weeks earlier. After the mandatory brief mention of economic viability, it said, "But the principle for which they stand—the right not to be ruled by people they don't like, don't trust, and never agreed to live with—is no absurdity at all." This was followed by a nicely encapsulated history of events, finishing with, "Mr. Bradshaw's behaviour excuses the refusal of other states to use force on his behalf. He has rushed through draconian emergency legislation, gaoled his opponents, and adopted postures that worry everyone.

An armed move against Anguilla is unlikely."

Meanwhile, the Anguillan sally against the U.N. was changing its angle of attack slightly. On August 25, a week and a half after his first meeting with them, Roger Fisher went back before the Subcommittee again and suggested a new relationship between mini-states and the United Nations. Under Fisher's scheme, the mini-state would retain its independence, would *not* be a member of the U.N., but would be able to call on the U.N. for whatever help it might need—expertise, medical care, financial help and so on. He suggested that everybody "drop nineteenth-century ideas of sovereignty that required total self-sufficiency" and consider the fact that these mini-states were going to keep coming along whether anybody liked it or not. Anguilla could be the first of these U.N. babies, but it wouldn't be the last.

The chairman of the Subcommittee, Mohsen Sadigt Esfandiary of Iran, was a little doubtful at first. He thought Fisher meant some sort of trusteeship, which smacked of colonialism.

No, Fisher said, they'll be independent, they'll just be under U.N. *protection.* Esfandiary agreed the idea sounded interesting.

Apparently the Subcommittee's interest had been very strongly aroused because three days later it asked Great Britain to allow a mission from the U.N. to visit Anguilla and check the situation out. Unfortunately, the British were so annoyed with the Subcommittee, and so obtusely determined that Anguilla wasn't really a problem, that they said No. Great Britain's refusal had a lot of bad effects. It ended, at least temporarily, serious consideration of Roger Fisher's U.N. orphan idea, some variant of which just might solve the problems of fragmentation. And it meant that Great Britain's last opportunity to shift the responsibility of the Anguilla mess had just been missed.

12

"Myself, I never believed in taking any man's dollars unless I gave him something for it—something in the way of rolled gold jewelry, garden seeds, lumbago lotion, stock certificates, stove polish or a crack on the head to show for his money."
—O. Henry, The Gentle Grafter

The San Francisco Group has been keeping busy, you can be sure of that. As Newhall says, "We were firmly attached to Leopold Kohr's theory of the small city-state. Over meals at San Francisco restaurants we talked about things they could do."

The San Francisco members of the San Francisco Group are, if you will recall, a newspaper managing editor, an advertising executive, and a member of a magazine's board of directors. These three, having hitched their wagon to a fun star, having invented a nation and a flag and a people and letterhead stationery and cash money, are now looking for something to do next. What will they do next?

They will run an ad.

"Suddenly," Newhall says, "the whole matter of the advertisement became very pressing. On Wednesday, August 2, we heard that a British frigate was preparing to land on Anguilla the following week, or sooner, to force them to accept the Barbados agreement. We had no time to lose."

Is the pen mightier than the sword? Can a full-page ad in *The New York Times* stop a frigate?

Newhall: "Howard came bursting into the firehouse early Wednesday evening and said, 'I've got it! It's done! It's great!'"

What Gossage had that was done and was great was the ad. It was called "(The Anguilla White Paper)," parentheses theirs, and it was done as a response to the August 2 editorial in *The New York Times.* It was signed by Ronald Webster, but Newhall says Gossage wrote it. A bit later, when a dispute came up about the accuracy of the ad, Gossage told the *Times* he'd written it but said he'd sent an associate to Anguilla to show a copy to Ronald Webster. This associate and his trip are not mentioned by any of the participants in the reminiscence in *Scanlan's Monthly,* and Webster told *Times* reporter Henry Giniger that he had only been shown parts of the final ad.

Who's right? Well, let's look at some excerpts from the ad and see. We know, for instance, the Anguillan attitude about telephones; they'd had phones for forty years, Hurricane Donna knocked down the poles, Bradshaw took the central-office equipment away, and the Anguillans had been angry and telephoneless for seven years. The ad quoted the *Times* editorial as saying the islanders "lack such modern amenities as telephones," and replied, "This is a terrible indictment in New York eyes, we suppose, but do you know what one Anguillan does when he wants to telephone another Anguillan? He walks up the road and talks to him." The island is fifteen miles long. When you want to telephone somebody fifteen miles away, do you walk up the road and talk to him? If so, you'd better pack a lunch, because it will take you four hours to get there.

Then there's terminology. Peter Adams had been upset when newspapers called him "President" because it struck him as foolish and demeaning to claim a title he didn't deserve. There was no Anguillan President. Ronald Webster retained the same attitude, and the ad is signed with his proper title, "Chairman, the Anguilla Island Council," but in the body of the ad there is this sentence: "We would not think it either good or polite that so many visitors should be on the island at once that they couldn't at least have lunch with the President." There are other things wrong with that sentence, but for now let us all put our heads together and try to figure out just who we're supposed to be having lunch with.

As for the lunch itself, Ronald Webster was the leader of a rebellion, not the captain of a cruise ship; was he really planning to spend the rest of his days having lunch with schoolteachers from Boise, Idaho?

Another thing wrong with that sentence is its implication about the number of visitors the island wants. The preceding sentence reads, "In the first place, we have only 30 guest rooms on the entire island at the moment, with no plans to expand." Well, Jerry Gumbs was even at that moment busily adding ten rooms to his Rendezvous Hotel, and another Anguillan was industriously building a brand-new ten-room hotel that would open in less than four months, with an ad in the *Beacon* boasting of "hot and cold running water."

It was perfectly true, as the ad said, that the islanders didn't want their home to become the lobby of a new Hilton. But the notion that they didn't want to attract more tourists is just foolishness. And what of alien home builders? The Anguillans would love to see more Americans retire to Anguilla—a few already have—build themselves a house, move in, spend a little money; but there wasn't a word about this in the ad. In fact the ad would tend to discourage thinking along those lines by being so totally Anguilla-for-Anguillans.

On the other hand, Ronald Webster *was* leading a rebellion and he *did* need money. It's possible he might have agreed to the ad no matter what Howard Gossage had put in it, since the San Francisco Group had assured him the thing would make a pot of money. I don't know if that's what happened, or if Webster saw only a part of the ad, or if he saw the whole ad but was thinking about something else at the time—Robert Bradshaw's armed forces, for instance—and didn't quite follow what the thing said, but whatever happened, the result was that the honeymoon was over. "(The Anguilla White Paper)" was at one and the same time the San Francisco Group's biggest caper and ultimate smashup.

But here I've spent all this time talking about the ad and haven't even said what it was selling. Ads always do sell something, that's what they're for.

This ad was selling Anguilla; it was a pitch for money, contributions, charity. But in the best traditions of American hucksterism, the customer doesn't go away empty-handed: "First off ... we had better send you an autographed picture of the Island Council, a facsimile of the original handwritten version of our national anthem, and a small Anguillan flag."

But wait; there's more. "If you wish to help us with as much as $25.00, we'll also send you one of the Anguilla Liberty Dollars." Now, that one was a good deal. In January 1970 Jerry Gumbs told me, "The silver dollars are still being sold in Texas, by a man named Long; they're selling them for thirty-nine dollars and fifty cents."

That's a 60 per cent appreciation in less than three years; you don't hardly get a deal like that one.

Or this one: "Those sending $100 or more will become Honorary Citizens of Anguilla. They will receive a document in the form of an Anguillan passport, identical to that which we are issuing to Anguillans, except that it will have an Anguillan Dollar inlaid as shown in the picture. While Americans should not expect to use this passport for foreign travel, it will be good for entering Anguilla. In fact, *only* holders of this passport will be able to visit Anguilla as guests."

Yes, well, if you think the hundred-dollar deal is the one for you, take a tip: go for the twenty-five buck offer four times. The Honorary Citizen thing never had any reality outside Howard Gossage's head; there was no such legislation passed by the Island Council or drafted by the Island Council or even considered by the Island Council. As to the Anguillan passports, Anguillans much preferred to go on using their British passports. There are no Anguillan passports, except the mock-ups done for the ad in San Francisco. (Some others were made up later on to send to the people who sent in the money.) As to Anguilla's refusing admission to any tourist or other visitor who failed to have one of these passports, why don't you just think about that yourself for a minute?

The ad was scheduled to be run in *The New York Times* on Monday, August 14. That was the day Roger Fisher, dweller in a more mundane world, was making his first appearance before the Colonialism Subcommittee at the U.N. Fisher heard about the ad the day before and apparently thought it might do him some damage before the Subcommittee—it would put him in the position, more or less, of asking the U.N. to grant independence to a Hula-Hoop factory—so he phoned Newhall to get the thing stopped. Newhall quotes the conversation:

"He said, 'I hear there is an ad running and I want you to stop it for a day.'

"I said, 'I certainly will not.'

"He continued, 'I am going to call the *Times* and tell them not to run it.'

"'Be my guest,' I said. 'Be prepared to see me in court.'"

Newhall then explained to Fisher that the "timing was crucial" on the ad because of that British frigate. He doesn't seem to have been aware that the British frigate was going to be landing not British soldiers but Caribbean policemen. In any event, he reports Fisher at last giving up with the words, "I'm unhappy about this." If Fisher tried to explain anything about the U.N. and concepts of dignity and taste, Newhall doesn't mention it.

So the ad was run on August 14, 1967. That was a red-letter day for the Anguillans. They had a full-page ad in *The New York Times;* they had a Harvard professor pleading their case at the United Nations; the two Caribbean Civil Servants from the second Barbados Conference were on Anguilla itself, in the process of being discomfited by that large and noisy crowd; and Jerry Gumbs became the first Anguillan ever to be "Man in the News" in *The New York Times.* All on the same day. Not bad for six thousand people who for 145 years hadn't been able to get anybody to listen to them. Things were looking up.

But not for the San Francisco Group. Once they had put their ideas down on paper the game was up. The theories of Professor Kohr had glittered through the wording of "(The Anguilla White Paper)" like the gilt border on a Peruvian bronze-mine stock certificate.

On Friday, August 18, *The New York Times* ran an interview with Ronald Webster under the headline "ANGUILLAN LEADER SEEKS VISITORS AND HOTELS," and the subhead, "Disputes Ad Saying Island Will Attempt to Block Tourism." Webster was quoted as saying, "We cannot depend on rain any longer for produce. Tourism is the only source of money-making on the island." He was also quoted as saying he had no objection to resort hotels; it was only gambling casinos the Anguillans would refuse. But the harpoon that really struck "(The Anguilla White Paper)" in its vitals was Webster's comment on the passport gimmick: "It sounds so cheap," he said. He told the *Times* he hadn't known a thing about that part of it in advance.

All of this was both baffling and painful to the San Francisco Group. They must have felt like the ventriloquist whose dummy suddenly turns against him. Hadn't the Anguillans *wanted* a city-state that would rival, some day, the glories of Greece? Hadn't Peter Adams heard Leopold Kohr loud and clear? Hadn't the whole thing been both great fun and essentially *good?* Or had some sort of ghastly mistake been made somewhere along the line?

No. Scott Newhall discovered the true explanation: "I had rather expected this reaction from the *Times*—no newspaper will sit by passively and let itself be attacked in its advertising columns." And referring to the peacekeeping force—"the seeming imminence of a forcible landing on Anguilla" is the way he phrased it—he consoled himself with the thought that, "I still feel that the ad played a part in stopping precipitate action." But the second Barbados Conference, which had been called because of "snags in the plan to send a Peacekeeping Force," had taken place the weekend before the ad appeared.

The San Francisco Group soon had more pressing problems to think about than the betrayal by Ronald Webster of Leopold Kohr. The Chase Manhattan Bank office in St. Thomas, where the ad had told the customers to send their cash, refused to give them a bank account. Then the Virgin Islands National Bank did the same thing.

Absolutely nobody wanted to have *fun.* There were rumors that checks were coming in, checks were being sent back, checks were disappearing. Nobody knew precisely what was happening; the only clear fact they had was that their Congressman had talked to the people at the Post Office, who had checked with St. Thomas, and there wasn't any Anguilla mail in the St. Thomas Post Office.

And it was Howard Gossage's birthday. They were having a party, described by Newhall as "a glorious affair on a remodeled San Francisco Bay ferryboat." But it was impossible for the gang to really have fun at the party with all this mess hanging over their heads. For all they knew, they had giggled themselves into a mail-fraud rap. As Newhall says, "All our fun, our good intentions, had somehow turned to a horror."

At least they didn't lose their sense of humor. They decided the only thing to do was go down to Anguilla themselves, and Gossage describes the trip: "It was hilarious enough. We were all so tired and this whole venture had become so disastrous that there was nothing to do but laugh."

They didn't laugh to the firehouse this time; they laughed to the Caravan Hotel on St. Thomas. Gossage again: "A lot of people had gathered for this meeting. Ronald Webster was there, the banker

Clifford Rogers, and a few other assorted Anguillans. Leopold Kohr was there, too, talking about Andorra and Liechtenstein. A little later Roger Fisher arrived with another lawyer. We had engaged a corner suite for the meeting, and it was pretty full."

Of *course* they'd engaged a corner suite.

Henry Giniger, *The New York Times* reporter who had interviewed Ronald Webster, was also present in St. Thomas, and they met at the airport. Gossage says, "I patiently explained to Henry how all our frustrating efforts on Anguilla's behalf were made because we believed in Leopold Kohr's theory of smallness, which the Anguillans believed in, too." Giniger suggested that maybe the Anguillans *didn't* share this belief in the glories of minuscule isolation, and suggested further that Gossage ask Webster about it, since Webster was at that moment nearby. Gossage did, and reports his brush with the truth this way:

"'Hey, Ronald, Henry Giniger here thinks that you want hotels or a shipping port or something big like that on the island. Tell him what you really think about remaining small.'

"Webster looked up at me and smiled. 'Well, now, Howard,' he said, 'I've been thinking it over, and maybe it wouldn't be all that bad an idea to have just maybe one hotel or so ...'"

After that, the downhill plunge was steep and bumpy. But there was no great enlightenment on either side. The shift was merely to a new set of misapprehensions. Anguilla had seceded from St. Kitts *in order to be reunited with Great Britain,* a fact too non-romantic for the San Francisco Group ever to understand. Their first misapprehension was that Anguilla had rebelled against the onset of twentieth-century civilization and was both spiritually and intellectually united with Leopold Kohr's craving for a return of feudalism. Once that notion had exploded itself, all they could see was that the Anguillans had prostituted themselves, had succumbed to the lure of modernism, and had betrayed both the ideals of Leopold Kohr and the selfless activities of the San Francisco Group.

As to the Anguillans, they had started by believing the San Francisco Croup were philanthropists. When that idea fizzled, some Anguillans decided they must have been the other thing after all—profiteers. So far as I have been able to determine not one Anguillan has ever understood that the San Francisco Group was neither.

The bitterness came first to Howard Gossage. After his climactic exchange with Ronald Webster at the airport he went back to the hotel and "they were still talking and drinking. I blew up, I said that we had financed the whole damned enterprise; we brought their missions to the United States; we paid the bills for the Ambassador-at-Large and sent a man to help him out. And what had they done? Discredited us. After my speech they handed me the bar check to sign, for $32."

Gossage was feeling so betrayed that he slipped into bad language. He says that when one of the people in the hotel suite asked what he was going to do next he replied, "I'm going to get a big boat and tow your fucking island out to sea and watch it sink." At least he knew it was *their* fucking island.

The checks in response to the ad were found in the St. Thomas Post Office after all—never believe your Congressman, that's the moral of that story—and turned out to total twenty-two thousand dollars. Feigen and Gossage turned it all over to the Anguillan Island Council. Gossage says, "There was, of course, no gratitude, though I have learned not to expect gratitude. Feigen was disgusted."

Gratitude. In the first issue of the *Beacon,* six weeks later, Atlin Harrigan described the San Francisco Group this way: "They are a group of professional and business men, inspired by high ideals, who hearing of the needs of Anguilla, have thrown in their time and resources to help Anguilla. Without their help, we would never be in the healthy position we are to-day. They have inspired us with their altruistic ideals, and have been instrumental in focussing the attention of the United States, and the whole world on the cause of Anguilla."

It came down at last to divvying the loot. Three thousand dollars' worth of checks weren't good, leaving nineteen thousand in response to the ad. All from people whose imagination had been touched, and who had sent money from their own pockets to a romantic dream in Howard Gossage's head. But when the envelopes were opened the dream wasn't there anymore; the pot was split up among people financing a rebellion on the one side and people recouping their expenses on the other; five thousand dollars to the San

Francisco Group, fourteen to Anguilla.

And the Anguilla Liberty Dollars? Newhall says, "We sent 500 coins to Anguilla, about 300 to send to the donors of the money—or were supposed to be—and the rest they could do with as they like. The other 9,500 we hope to sell, slowly, to recover as much of our tremendous expenses as we can." They figure their tremendous expenses at fifty thousand dollars.

But what *are* these tremendous expenses? Well, fifteen thousand in fun-loving one-dollar bills was money given to the Anguillans in connection with the Liberty Dollar proposition, but that still leaves thirty-five thousand dollars' worth of tremendous expenses in six weeks' time. What are they?

Why, they're a suite at the Lombardy in New York, a suite at the St. Francis in San Francisco, a corner suite at the Caravan on St. Thomas. They're Howard Gossage's butterfly net, and the boys controlling the situation. They're receptions, airline tickets, lamb chops, long-distance telephone calls. They're flags, letterhead stationery, bordelaise snails and tape recorder.

The San Francisco Group used the fact of the Anguillan rebellion to live a Technicolor movie full of mad dashes, zany ideas, wonderful guys, breathless arrivals—and the whole thing paid for by money generated by the existence of Anguilla. The San Francisco Group spent thirty-five thousand dollars in six weeks of *fun*, and paid for it with schemes that were supposed to be getting money for Anguilla.

And which did get money for Anguilla. Fifteen thousand dollars in one-dollar bills. Seven hundred and fifty Anguilla Liberty Dollars. Fourteen thousand from the ad. Something over thirty thousand, all told, and money that was very sorely needed. So the San Francisco Group, despite all, did no harm and did quite a bit of good.

It's just a pity about the bitterness at the end. Two years later, Scott Newhall did a series of three articles in the San Francisco *Chronicle* and the bitterness is teeth-rattling. He did them under a pen name, F. Scott Valencia, but at the end of the last piece ripped off his mask and revealed himself, explaining, "Newhall did not wish to use his own byline because he has preferred to keep his own name out of the paper." But he said this *in* the paper. There's a consistency of style in the San Francisco Group that becomes recognizable after a while.

The San Francisco Group does not exist in the Anguilla story as it unfolds in Newhall's *Chronicle* chronicle. In a parenthetical sentence, for instance, he refers to the Anguillan Liberty Dollars—which were his own brain storm—this way: "(Earlier, the Anguillans had arranged for the minting as coinage of 10,000 silver 'Liberty Dollars,' which already have achieved collectors' prices of up to $100 for the rare items.)"

(If I may be parenthetical myself, the San Francisco Group kept 9,250 of the coins to cover their enormous expenses. At one hundred bucks a shot, that's within spitting distance of one million dollars. Even in one-dollar bills, that would take care of a lot of enormous expenses.)

In the *Chronicle* Newhall comes as close as the libel laws allow to calling Jerry Gumbs a crook: "He became 'Mr. Anguilla' and formed an association of Anguillans who donate various sums to aid the homeland. Jeremiah Gumbs was the funnel through which these funds were poured. There has been some debate about the size of the downspout."

A little later, in parentheses again, Newhall explains another reason for his bitterness toward Gumbs: "(Gumbs even designed a new flag to replace that used by the first independent government.)" He forgets to mention it, but the first flag was the one he designed himself. (Jerry Gumbs didn't design the current Anguillan flag; it was done by an American firm that specializes in that sort of thing.)

Newhall is also bilious about Ronald Webster. Here's a typical sentence: "The spear-carriers in this pageant were a pair of Anguillans—Ronald Webster, a thin, seemingly-devout Seventh-Day Adventist, and an Americanized Anguillan from Perth Amboy, N.J., who has the delightful name of Jeremiah Gumbs." It's interesting that he still thinks the Anguillans are the spear carriers in the Anguillan rebellion.

Roger Fisher also gets gummed by Newhall. "Fisher is a gangling Harvard law professor who could play successfully the lead in *Charley's Aunt.* He has capered about in the background of this Caribbean pageant as the 'legal adviser' of the Anguillan government." And, "Fisher somehow ferreted out Gumbs a couple of years ago, and has had him in the pouch ever since."

But this sort of thing isn't entirely one-sided. Jerry Gumbs is himself one of the Anguillans who came around to the idea that the San Francisco Group, having failed to be philanthropists, must be profiteers. About the ad, he told me, "They were here again, trying to create this ad, figuring that if it went over big they would maybe make a million dollars, clean up, and just use the people of Anguilla. It was another form of exploitation."

And so it goes. Dr. Kohr, the gentle and not-entirely-practical man who was described by *Scanlan's Monthly* as "theoretician of the Anguillan revolution," is no longer connected with Anguilla, nor with the Caribbean. He left the University of Puerto Rico and went to the University of Wales, where he got involved with the Plaid Cymru, Welsh nationalists with whom the San Francisco Group would feel right at home; Dr. Kohr has described them as "beloved friends and fans of mine."

13

The isle is full of noises,
Sounds and sweet airs, that give delight, and hurt
not.
—William Shakespeare, *The Tempest*

After a summer as jam-packed with incident as *Flash Gordon Conquers the Universe*, the fall and winter of 1967 passed with placid serenity on the island of Anguilla, as free from action as a Saul Bellow novel. Colonel Bradshaw had demonstrated his inability to mount an invasion of the island, and all his potential allies had demonstrated their unwillingness to help him, so the danger of military conflict had at least temporarily receded.

All Anguilla's diplomatic overtures to Great Britain had met with the same dense response. The United Nations was or was not considering the problem, but in either case there was nothing left for Anguilla to do on that front either. Other countries—the United States, Canada, various Caribbean islands, and so on—were consistent in their refusal to get involved without an okay from the U.K. Nothing was being done to Anguilla, and there seemed to be nothing for Anguilla to do, so the island merely settled into the independence it didn't want and waited to see what would happen next.

It was obvious that *something* would have to happen sooner or later, since the island's economic problems weren't getting any better. Colonel Bradshaw was still holding back the mail and blocking bank accounts and refusing to pay Civil Servants' salaries or pensioners' pensions. (The United States was routing Anguillan mail through St. Thomas, so that some expatriates could still send their remittances home, but Great Britain was blandly accepting mail for Anguilla and then sending it to St. Kitts.)

Walter Hodge, formerly Chairman of the Peacekeeping Committee and now in charge of island finances, was keeping the island government solvent—mostly through postage-stamp sales and customs collections—but as he explained to me in the spring of 1970, they had kept in the black only by eliminating all capital expenditure—no road building, no school construction, virtually no expenditures except salaries and necessary supplies. This could be nothing but a short-term arrangement, and the Anguillans knew it but couldn't find anything to do about it.

They were getting some financial help from outside. Medical supplies came from the United States and the U.S. Virgin Islands and other places. Money came from a couple of American foundations. And there were also some real-life philanthropists involved.

One of these was Herbert B. Lutz, a New Yorker who lives most of the year at one or another of his homes in the Caribbean. (His New York operations include coproducing a 1970 off-Broadway production of *Waiting for Godot,* a play which is in many ways a perfect summation of the Anguillan rebellion). Lutz had taken an interest in Anguilla a few years before the rebellion and, seeing how skimpy medical care was on the island, had at that time tried to give the Anguillans a mobile operating unit (This was a complete operating room, fully equipped for most general operations and containing its own electric generating equipment, mounted on the frame of a Dodge truck. Incredibly expensive, and incredibly generous.) Since this was *before* the rebellion, the gift had to go through St. Kitts, and a representative of the St. Kitts Government told Lutz, "What you want to care about those bubber-johnnies for? Give it to us here on St Kitts." "Bubber-johnny" is the contemptuous Kittitian word for Anguillans; some say it is a bastardization of the Dutch word for "monkey," but whatever the source, it means "hick." The people of St. Kitts, most of whom never in their lives travel more than twenty miles from the shack of their birth and most of whom still work the same sugar fields their grandfathers worked as slaves, call the Anguillans, who build the boats and travel around the world, hicks; it seems a strange sort of insult.

Lutz had been forbidden by the Government of St. Kitts to give the mobile operating unit to Anguilla, but after the rebellion he dealt directly with the Anguillan Island Council, and gave them the unit.

He also helped with cash, paying salaries for teachers and administrators whose wages had been cut off by St. Kitts, and also helping pay for other talent brought in after the rebellion.

For instance, Roger Fisher had arranged for a young man named Frank McDonald to stay on the island and form a sort of liaison between Fisher and the Island Council, to give advice whenever any problem in Fisher's domain might arise. Lutz paid a part of McDonald's salary and an American foundation paid the rest. (In a somewhat tactless move, all of McDonald's salary was sent to him on Anguilla. Since he was being paid according to American standards, his income was twice that of the Council members; this amount of money, to a young man fresh from his graduate studies and taking his first job, eventually caused some bad feeling on the island.)

McDonald tells a story of one of Lutz's charities that gives the flavor both of the man and of Anguilla's circumstances at the time. The Island Council found they didn't have any cash to pay teachers' salaries for the month of December 1967 and sent McDonald to St Thomas to ask Lutz if he could help. McDonald told Lutz the problem, and Lutz said, "How much?"

"Ten thousand U.S."

Lutz wrote a check, then and there, and drove McDonald to the nearest branch of his bank to cash it; but the branch didn't have ten thousand dollars in cash, so they had to go to the main bank, where the manager was startled but willing. Lutz and McDonald and the manager all stood around in a back room of the bank while a teller carefully counted out ten thousand dollars—not in one-dollar bills—and then McDonald stuffed it all in a money belt and took the next plane back to Anguilla; the money paid the teachers' salaries for two months.

But McDonald did more things than go places and collect money. Shortly after his arrival on the island, the Great Esso Crisis took place, and his role in that was to get on the phone to Roger Fisher. The St. Kitts Government had ordered Esso to stop delivering gasoline and fuel oil to Anguilla; if Esso were to refuse, St. Kitts would shift its own trade to Shell or some other competitor. Esso didn't refuse.

The first the Island Council knew about any of this was a letter from Esso, saying it couldn't make deliveries anymore. The big storage tanks on Anguilla were Esso property, but they could stay on the island for the time being.

Whatever electricity there is on the island—such as in the hospital—comes from gasoline generators. In places without electricity, like most private homes, light at night comes from lamps fueled by Esso kerosene. Esso deliveries were, in a lot of different ways, very important to the life of the island.

Frank McDonald went over to St. Martin, called Roger Fisher in Boston and told him the situation. Fisher looked in his law books and found the proper legal justification for governmental expropriation of private property. He gave McDonald the references and told him to tell the Island Council to send somebody over to the Esso tanks and stencil on them "Property of the Government of Anguilla."

Next, the Esso office on Puerto Rico was told its property had just been expropriated, and Fisher's legal references were cited. The Esso people were told the Anguillans would buy their petroleum products henceforth from the pirate tankers that work the Caribbean from bases in Venezuela.

Esso management said, in effect, "Hey, wait a minute." A meeting was organized on St. Martin, with two representatives from Esso, plus Ronald Webster and McDonald. Every time the Esso people said something smooth and multisyllabic, McDonald got on the phone to Fisher up in Boston, and Fisher hit them long distance with his law books. Finally, the men from Esso surrendered. They agreed to resume deliveries; as for Colonel Bradshaw, they'd tell him the Anguillans had forced them into it. Which was, after all, simply the truth.

Not long after this, Esso had an accident while making deliveries and spilled several thousand gallons of gasoline all over the ground. The ground of Anguilla is *always* thirsty; it drank up the gasoline in nothing flat. Esso chalked it up to profit and loss, but the Anguillans looked at the ground and thought about things. They thought about the fact that their island has a thin soil over a coral base, and that the coral is full of salt water, and that gasoline is lighter than water and therefore floats on top. If we dig down, they thought, we should come pretty quick to pure undiluted gasoline. And so they did, and so it happened, and for a while after that the Anguillans were digging gasoline out of their back yards. They may not have electricity, the Anguillans, but they're bright.

McDonald, to return to McDonald, also came in handy another way. The indefatigable Jerry Gumbs had come up with an idea for a "Bank of Anguilla," to be owned by himself, of course. The big thing with this bank, anytime Gumbs talked about it, was that it would have anonymous numbered accounts; why should Central American dictators send their loot all the way to Switzerland? The Island Council wasn't entirely sure this was proper, but they were willing to listen, particularly when Gumbs told them he had a bona fide American banker to set the thing up and run it for them.

The bona fide banker was named A. Hunter Bowman, and McDonald met him with Gumbs in New York in October. Gumbs talked to McDonald about numbered accounts for a while and said that he and Bowman were on their way to Anguilla to present the idea to the Island Council. McDonald wished them well and went off to dinner with some friends, where he mentioned Bowman's name, at which someone else at the table said, "A. Hunter Bowman. Isn't he the one who was just indicted for embezzlement?"

McDonald never did finish that dinner. He quickly looked into the background of A. Hunter Bowman, and there it was; only three months before, in July, Bowman had been indicted in New York City for embezzling nearly half a million dollars from the Rockefeller Center branch of the Marine Midland Trust, a major New York bank in which he had been a vice-president. Of course, Jerry Gumbs had already come up with the doctor in trouble with the American Medical Association, so it was probably inevitable that when he went out looking for a banker he would come back with A. Hunter Bowman.

McDonald next phoned Fisher, told him about Gumbs and Bowman, and Fisher decided to take a trip to Anguilla. He and McDonald followed Gumbs and Bowman south, and the confrontation took place at the meeting with the Island Council. Bowman had brought along a lawyer and a tape recorder, and he very ostentatiously started both. What was read into the tape recorder's microphone, however, were the details of Bowman's indictment.

Bowman and Gumbs responded with a rhetorical question: Shouldn't a man who has slipped once be given a chance to prove himself, to rebuild his shattered etc.? (In January of 1971, Bowman was still slipping; he appeared in court on a charge of violating probation.) Council members also say that Bowman claimed many ties with the Kennedy family, saying that Ethel Kennedy was paying his defense and the Joseph Kennedy Foundation was repaying the embezzled money; the Council waited for the pictures of Hubert Humphrey. They were not forthcoming, however, and eventually the Council bade good-bye to A. Hunter Bowman.

Another American who showed up around the same time was a veterinarian from Chicago who was seeking a place that was quieter and warmer than his home city; most places are, but he picked Anguilla. There was then no regular channel Anguilla could go through in buying weapons, so Ronald Webster was looking for something similar to the source found a few months earlier by St. Kitts. The veterinarian managed to make arrangements in Chicago, and Webster paid for the guns out of his own pocket.

And so the year waned, a restful pause after the helter-skelter summer. On October 7, 1967, the Island Council announced that the first Anguillan election, for a new five-man Council, would take place on October 25; but on nomination day, the seventeenth, there turned out to be only five candidates, so there wasn't an election after all, just a declaration that the five had won. Ronald Webster was among them and was made Chairman again. According to the rules they'd set up ahead of time, the five then got together and appointed two more members, to bring the Council strength back up to seven.

Anguilla dozed. The economic problems were chronic and occasionally acute. The Council was forced to accept loans of several thousand dollars each from both Ronald Webster and Jerry Gumbs. They knew they couldn't count on gifts and charity from outside forever, but there seemed nothing to be done about it.

In Great Britain, some Anguillans and some of their English friends were still making local efforts to attract Whitehall's attention, but for a long time it seemed as though nothing was going to come of that, either.

And then something did. Or did it?

14

The Walrus and the Carpenter
Were walking close at hand;
They wept like anything to see
Such quantities of sand;
"If this were only cleared away,"
They said, "it would be grand!"
— Lewis Carroll, *Through the Looking-Glass*

Here come Fisher and Chapman, all things to all people.

In the beginning of December it was announced in London that two Members of Parliament, Nigel Fisher and Donald Chapman, would be leaving very soon for the Caribbean to solve the Anguilla problem. The two M.P.'s had all the necessary qualifications; one was a Conservative, the other was Labour, and both were old friends of Colonel Bradshaw's.

As Nigel Fisher said before leaving, "Our job is to try to find ways of reuniting Anguilla with St. Kitts." Of course, immediately after that remark he also said, "We have no intention of being seen to be taking sides."

The Delegation was preceded by a small administrative team, containing a radio and a radio operator and a cipher clerk, and led by a man named Anthony Lee. Lee didn't know it but he was on his way to the worst mess of his life.

But to begin with, Lee was merely running the administrative team for the Parliamentary Delegation. He was forty-four when he first landed on Anguilla. The son of an Anglican clergyman, he'd served in the Royal Navy in the Second World War, went to Cambridge, and afterward joined the Colonial Service, but always on a contract basis, never as permanent staff. After serving ten years in Africa, mostly in Tanganyika, he spent two years in private industry but apparently preferred working for the Government; he applied for a post with the Commonwealth Relations Office, got a new contract, and went off to Aden until the British had finished setting up their ghastly Southern Yemen federation. After his Aden tour he was offered the job as secretary to Fisher and Chapman's Parliamentary Delegation. It was suggested that an English administrator might be assigned to Anguilla for a period of time and that he might turn out to be the man.

Anthony Lee is a gentle, soft-spoken man who prefers a simple life in which he can follow simple orders. He is six feet four inches tall, so that he towers over just about everybody else in the Anguilla story, but despite his height—or perhaps because of it—he is not at all a forceful personality. He moves with the tide, he follows orders competently and diligently, and in a normal circumstance he is probably the ideal representative of a far-off Authority: the unabrasive vessel through which Authority's desires are made manifest.

Unfortunately, Anguilla never has been a normal circumstance.

When Fisher and Chapman arrived, the *Beacon* ran a Delegation Special supplement that pretty well covered the events of their stay.

The advance guard [said the paper] consisted of Mr. Tony Lee with radio operators and equipment to be in constant touch with London, and a team of secretaries, which shewed that they intended to do an efficient and comprehensive job. Prior to the arrival of the M.P.'s, Mr. Greatorex, the British Representative, and Mr. Lee inspected the island and were seen climbing down the Fountain, and nearly getting lost in the bush.

And also:

Along with the two parliamentarians came two others, Cecil Greatorex and Tony Lee, both astute figures in the British Foreign Service, ranking among the authorities in colonial affairs, both with colourful experiences in Africa, the Middle East and the West Indies. Mr. Greatorex we have already welcomed to our island before, and each time we have grown fonder of him. Mr. Lee we have just come to know, and find him a most charming and helpful diplomat.

And what of the Parliamentary Delegation itself? The *Beacon* says:

Our guests are Mr. Nigel Fisher and Mr. Donald Chapman, members of a parliamentary delegation sent to work out possible solutions to our political impasse with St. Kitts and the other world States represented in the United Nations. *Mr. Fisher*, 54, married and the father of two children, previously an Under-Secretary of State for the colonies, with a vast experience of West Indian affairs, is the President of the Delegation. *Mr. Chapman*, 44, unmarried, is Chairman of the Delegation, representing the present Labour Government, also with long experience in the Caribbean. These two men were specially chosen from the whole of Parliament as having the greatest understanding of our local problems.

A two-man Delegation, and one of them is President and the other one is Chairman. If it had been a three-man Delegation, what would the third man have been? Emperor?

And what did Fisher and Chapman think of the Anguillans, now that we have seen what the Anguillans thought of them? Novelist John Updike was staying at Jerry Gumbs's Rendezvous Hotel while Fisher and Chapman were there; in a piece he did later in *The New Yorker*, Updike writes, "One of the Englishmen in the Parliamentary mission referred to the Anguillans as 'the poor dears,' and another, as we lay on the beach, in answer to my question as to what St. Kitts was like, answered, with a wave that included the immaculate beach and the turquoise sea, 'Bout like this. A bloody 'ole.'"

Fisher and Chapman arrived at the bloody hole and were greeted by the poor dears. Ronald Webster made a speech: "Mr. Greatorex, Honourable Gentlemen of Parliament, Mr. Lee. On behalf of the Council and the people of Anguilla we wish to express our warm welcome to you, especially at this time. We are indeed grateful for having you here, and may your stay be an unforgettable one. I can assure you that there is law and order in our beautiful island, and I am asking you while you are here to guarantee our safety from any attacks, and I am sure that you will have a wonderful stay in Anguilla. Anguillans are peaceful, loving and law-abiding people. Our desire for freedom is still as resolute as on the eleventh day of July 1967. It is our firm desire to negotiate and achieve some amicable solution. Now you are free to go from home to home and get the views of the people, have a nice lunch, a sea bath, visit anywhere in our island, and judge for yourself. Friends, I thank you."

This was on Monday. According to the *Beacon:*

> On Tuesday the 5th the Delegation visited the Valley Schools, and were really shocked at the overcrowding there, and said it was the worst they had ever seen. They also visited the hospital and saw the improvements there effected since the secession.
>
> In the evening there was an official party at the house of the Medical Officer to meet the Anguillan notabilities informally. Unfortunately, there was no room to invite the wives....

Fisher and Chapman met with as many Anguillans as they could during the next few days, impressed the local citizens with their apparent desire to listen and understand, and wound up with a social event nicely reported by the *Beacon:*

> On the Thursday evening, our visitors were invited to attend a Cantata at St. Andrews Church East End, which had been arranged some time before it was known they were coming. In getting there they experienced most of the hazards of Anguilla—running out of petrol, the rocky roads, and the dust. Mr. Ronald Webster welcomed them to the Cantata, and gave them the opportunity to introduce themselves to the crowd there.
>
> Mr. Webster himself took part in the singing of a trio with two young ladies, and revealed that he has a very good tenor voice. The Rector announced that he would have loved to say that the next item was a duet by Mr. Fisher and Mr. Chapman, but had to pass on to the next item of the full programme.

It's a pity they didn't get to do their duet, but as the Delegation Special supplement of the *Beacon* says in its windup:

> It is obvious that we cannot expect any pronouncement from the Delegation while they are on this island. The real battle has got to be fought in St. Kitts. Anything may happen there, as the people of St. Kitts are getting very restive, and the Anguillan problem is part of a bigger problem involving St. Kitts and Nevis. We are grateful for having had two men of such great friendliness and understanding, and while we are standing firm to our legitimate demands, we realize the very difficult task that lies ahead of them when they land in St. Kitts. Perhaps they may pay us another visit

before they return to Britain.

The prayers of all Anguillans go with them, that they may find a solution acceptable not only to us, but to the other islands.

Good-bye. God be with you.

Fisher and Chapman next went to St. Kitts to see Colonel Bradshaw. There was no published account of that meeting, but apparently it didn't run very smoothly. "The distrust on both sides was very great," Nigel Fisher said later. "On a small scale, it was quite a difficult negotiation, because neither side would meet the other, and we had frequently to go to and from Anguilla and St. Kitts to get agreement."

About two weeks were spent traveling back and forth between the two islands. Almost from the beginning Fisher and Chapman realized the best they could hope for was a temporary agreement; the distrust on both sides was so great that no permanent solution was likely to be worked out in the short time they had available. So they aimed at the idea of leaving Tony Lee on Anguilla for an interim period of about a year, to give some semblance of legality to the island while a more permanent arrangement could be hammered out.

But even an interim arrangement was difficult to achieve. Neither side wanted to seem to be giving in on any of its positions. The British accepted Bradshaw's dominion over Anguilla, and therefore had to have his permission to assign Tony Lee there. They also, for more obvious and fundamental reasons, had to have the Anguillans' permission before leaving him there. In order to get it all accomplished, Fisher and Chapman apparently had to behave rather like insurance salesmen; a lot of vague promises were spoken, most of which had faded like morning mist when it came time to write things down.

For instance. Bradshaw agreed to the interim period because he thought he would get Anguilla back when the year was up. On the other hand, the Anguillans thought the idea was a step-by-step breaking of the link with St. Kitts, with the interim year to be followed by an adjustment either to Crown Colony or Associated State. As Atlin Harrigan put it in an editorial in the *Beacon* a month later:

We are like a man sitting down to a many-course dinner at a big hotel. He knows that by the time dinner is over he will have had all he can eat, but it will be served to him course by course, and the next course will come when he is ready for it. The whole dinner is not put on the table at one time. No, Mr. Bradshaw, we have got all we want for the present, and we are sure that at the end we will be quite satisfied, and not the least because everything has not been handed out on a plate, but we are going to have the satisfaction of working for it ourselves.

Meanwhile, Bradshaw was announcing, in a speech on Nevis, "The people of Nevis are saying, 'See, Anguilla has got what it wanted, and we have to get what we want, too.' But I want to go on record as saying, Anguilla has *not* got what it wanted, and Nevis will never become another Anguilla."

Also, the Anguillans had been left with the impression that Colonel Bradshaw's clutch on their savings in Kittitian banks would be loosened and that the island's Land Registers would be turned over to the Island Council by the St. Kitts Government; two things Bradshaw hadn't the slightest intention of doing. In fact, Chapman himself, a year and a half later, pointed out that the savings and the Land Registers were Bradshaw's "trump cards, and if he gave them all away he would never get Anguilla back."

A short while after the Interim Agreement had been worked out, Lord Lambton, a Conservative M.P., visited both St. Kitts and Anguilla, and wrote, "Anguilla believes that its independence has been established. St. Kitts believes that Anguilla will be returned to it by the British Government at the end of the year. A settlement based on such misunderstanding will do more harm in the long run than an unpopular decision would have done now."

Fisher and Chapman disagree. "No one was misled in any way about the interim solution," Fisher says, and Chapman says, "There were no misconceptions about the interim settlement."

This perfect understanding was attained by December 18. Nigel Fisher has since described the windup on Anguilla, saying, "The Anguillans are not at all easy people to negotiate with, because, perhaps through lack of political experience, they are not politically very sophisticated. Mr. Webster is honest but not very articulate, deeply religious but rather obstinate, an ardent patriot for Anguilla but not a very self-confident leader of his own people. He was nervous of leadership and wanted always to carry his followers and the people with him at every stage of the negotiations. He had no idea of negotiating privately, and even when agreement was reached we had to obtain all the signatures from all the leading people all over the Island of Anguilla ourselves. We also had to announce at a great public meeting the solution that had been agreed. It was rather embarrassing that we should have to do that, but we did it because Mr. Webster was unwilling to do it himself until he saw that the agreement was acceptable to the people."

Another English politician had here run into the thorny problem of Anguillan democracy. We dwellers in the metropoli have been calling our republics "democracies" for so long that we tend to be baffled and uneasy when we run across the real thing. We are more comfortable with somebody like George Thomson, Secretary of State for Commonwealth Affairs, who announced the Interim Agreement to the House of Commons at the end of January (six weeks after Fisher's embarrassment in Anguilla) with the words, "We have made some progress towards finding a solution to this difficult problem. I think in some ways the less I say about some of the details the better."

---

15

*"I'll be judge, I'll be jury," said cunning old Fury; "I'll
try the whole cause, and condemn you to death."*
—Lewis Carroll,
Alice's Adventures in Wonderland

Back in September, three months before Fisher and Chapman's Caribbean trip, Colonel Bradshaw had gone to England. He had told reporters in London, "I am going to tell the Commonwealth Office that Britain should act with military force to disarm the rebels and land a force on Anguilla. We must go back and disarm the people who have the guns there." He also said Anguilla was controlled by "a group of gunmen financed by dirty money."

Shortly after his arrival in London, a solicitor's clerk interrupted these pronouncements by serving several writs on him; one from James Milnes Gaskell and two from Diane Prior-Palmer. Milnes Gaskell wanted damages for false imprisonment and Miss Prior-Palmer wanted her diary back.

The Colonel returned to St. Kitts.

The detainees had been there all along. After popping in and out of jail all summer, life had quieted for them, too, until at last the trials started on October 16, four months and six days after the detentions began. Judge Eardley Glasgow, who was to have presided, asked to be excused for "certain reasons," which he didn't go into, and was replaced by Judge St. Bernard, from the island of Grenada.

The first defendant was an Anguillan, Collins Hodge, who was charged with "shooting with intent" while wearing a plastic Batman mask. A confession was introduced, but Hodge said he'd signed it while a pistol was being held to his head. The trial ended in an acquittal. A "spontaneous demonstration" objecting to the verdict was immediately delivered to the Blakeney Hotel, where the judge and the defense attorneys were staying. The judge immediately got in touch with the Government and said that if something wasn't done about that mob at once he'd contact England and ask them to send in a warship. The spontaneous demonstration spontaneously went away.

The *Beacon* had some interesting things to say about the trial of Collins Hodge. From the issue of October 21:

On the Monday afternoon of October 16th we were all tuned in to the radio station of St. Kitts, feeling sure we would hear some news of the trial. All we heard were some trivialities and advertisements, but of the trial—nothing. But thanks to Radio Antilles we heard the truth; that the Government of St. Kitts had been reprimanded for keeping the accused in prison; for not letting their counsel see them; and that they were all released on bail. We have heard eyewitness accounts of the ovation they received as they joined the crowd outside the court; the kisses from the women; the handshakes from the men.

A week later:

With great joy we welcomed back to Anguilla Mr. Collins Hodge, the *first* of the accused in the St. Kitts trials to be found not guilty. Dr. Herbert's father took him to the LIAT plane at St. Kitts, bound for St. Martin. He then came on a chartered plane to Anguilla on Wednesday, the 25th. He was taken on a motorcade through the island, visiting the homes of the other accused. Asked what his plans were, he said that he would take a few days' holiday and have some sea bathing, and then go back to work at Expan Company here in Anguilla.

And in an editorial the week after that:

With the return home of Collins Hodge, freed, every true Anguillan rejoices, and feels a change in the heavy atmosphere which has hung over our little island during the last few months. Earnest lawyers from St. Kitts and other Caribbean countries are diligently employing legal procedure, well-learned from British jurisprudence. Before this onslaught, false implications and lies are withering away.

The falsity apparently included bribery and coercion of prosecution witnesses. One police officer testified he'd been ordered to lie in court. An Anguillan, Clarence Rogers, told of being bribed to give false statements about Billy Herbert. According to an affidavit signed by Rogers, the bribe was paid in a hotel room on St. Thomas, and the bribers were two men connected with the St. Kitts Government, plus an American couple, John and Vera Randall.

Enter the Randalls. Not long before the rebellion, the Randalls had bought a piece of land on Anguilla from the St. Kitts Government. Apparently they'd used most of their savings to do it and were planning to build guesthouses as well as a home for themselves. They got their own house built, the rebellion broke out, and they put their money on the wrong horse. They backed St. Kitts, and apparently even took an active role once or twice on St. Kitts's behalf. The fact that four years later they were still alive and intact and living in the same house on Anguilla—particularly after the Clarence Rogers story and some other rumors that traveled around the island—is a fair indication of the savagery of the Anguillans.

But back to the trials. In addition to the spontaneous demonstration, the judge also got a telephone call and a letter threatening him with death if there were any more acquittals. So there were more acquittals.

The second trial, with five defendants, was simply a choral repeat of the Collins Hodge solo, and all five were found not guilty. Three of those acquitted were Anguillans; as they left the court on November 13 after the acquittal, these three were immediately rearrested and charged with taking policemen's rifles back on May 30. The crowd outside the courthouse was pro-defendant, but the police held it at bay with cattle prods.

The next day, Colonel Bradshaw did an odd thing, considering there were more trials coming up. He called his House of Assembly, led a debate on the trials, broadcast live on ZIZ, in which matters that hadn't been decided yet by any court were presented as facts, and rammed through a resolution that said that the House of Assembly of St. Kitts felt a "lack of confidence in the administration of justice in this State." Colonel Bradshaw also caused to be created a document called "Complaint Against the Judge," accusing Judge St. Bernard of "bias," "maladministration," "perversion of justice" and corruption. The document was sent to the Chief Justice of the Associated States Supreme Court, who replied six days later by slamming the St. Kitts Government up, down and sideways, accusing St. Kitts of contempt of court, attempting to prejudice a fair trial, using the Government-controlled radio and newspaper as clubs against the court, and general lack of decent behavior. The Chief Justice also said he was making his response public with the full knowledge and approval of all the other judges on the High Court.

At the third trial there were seven defendants, including Billy Herbert. But the prosecution announced it didn't have any evidence to offer beyond what had been presented in the first two trials, so they might just as well find the defendants not guilty right at the beginning. Which they did.

Thus ended the trials—or almost. There were still the three Anguillans who'd been rearrested behind cattle prods and charged with taking policemen's guns away from them. They were out on bail, and so was a fourth Anguillan, Lemuel Phillips, who had been detained from the beginning but had never been tried for anything. The bail money had been raised from friendly Kittitians and legally the Anguillans were required to stay on St. Kitts until the Government could figure out some way to try them, but one dark night they stepped aboard a northbound schooner and went away from there. (After a short rest in Anguilla, they headed farther north, to St. Thomas, to earn enough money to pay back to their Kittitian friends the bail money that had been forfeited.)

Just after the final trial, the six-month period of the Emergency Regulations was up. As expected, Colonel Bradshaw got his House of Assembly to renew them for another six months. He also announced that all Kittitians who had been defendants would have their passports withdrawn. This was reasonable and justifiable, he explained, because the defendants had been charged with plotting against the state. That they'd been found not guilty didn't matter.

He also expressed again his irritation with the way the trials had gone and increased his reputation as a statesman by saying, "Next time, evidence will be picked up in blood in the street."

But nobody was entirely happy about the conduct of the trials. The Bar Associations of ten Caribbean islands had a meeting to discuss the trials, at the end of which they published a paper condemning the St. Kitts Government's actions "as being contrary to the principles of the Rule of Law and being inimical to the due administration of Justice and as constituting an affront to basic human rights and dignity.' They documented their charges with six specific points and sent the paper around to lawyers and judges and government leaders all over the world.

But the legal profession wasn't through with Colonel Bradshaw. The next thumping was delivered by the International Commission of Jurists in a report on the St. Kitts trials; it said, among other things, "The indictment against the St. Kitts Government is a long one: it has repeatedly shown contempt for the courts, has refused to accept their decision and has flagrantly attempted—by threats and the misuse of the mass media—to use the courts as an instrument of its policy. When the courts proved to be instruments of the Rule of Law, it resorted to government by emergency regulation and trial by 'Commission of Inquiry.'"

But let's give the last word on the St. Kitts trials to Atlin Harrigan, in the *Beacon:*

> There lingers in the minds of thinking Anguillans a feeling of shame, shame that we have ever been associated with St. Kitts' Government as it stands today; a system so deteriorated that a police state has resulted ... That Government is one of hate which uses its laws as weapons to castigate, muzzle and punish any hapless individual brave enough to stand up against the system ... Did we really rebel? Or did the St. Kitts Government, weakened by ailing politican conditions, lose its wavering grip on us and slip back into its quagmire of corruption (with just a little local help)?

16

The most dramatic event of 1968 took place on January 1; that's the kind of year it was. The event itself was dramatic enough: a mysterious murder. A nineteen-year-old girl, Robena Diego, was shot by a bullet from a .38-caliber gun and died on the way to the hospital. She had been walking along the road with her boy friend, a twenty-year-old former Kittitian. His story was that they had been strolling together, he pushing his bicycle with the hand that wasn't holding hers, and suddenly she fell down. However, as there didn't seem to have been anyone else in the general vicinity, the boy was arrested by the Anguillan police and charged with murder.

The gun was quickly found; a revolver in a brown paper bag behind a low wall thirty feet from where the girl was shot. Roger Fisher's young assistant, Frank McDonald, spent a few days flying around the Caribbean with this gun, trying to get some island's police force to check it for fingerprints, but nobody wanted to cross Colonel Bradshaw, so he finally had to give up. Also, since a murder charge was far above Peter Adams' even theoretical jurisdiction, and since the Anguilla Police Department had no experience or training or equipment for investigating a case like this, there was little anybody could do. The boy friend stayed in jail, the gun was locked away in the police safe, and Robena Diego was buried.

Meanwhile Tony Lee was on the island, waiting for Lord Shepherd in England to finish the formalities of setting up the Interim Agreement. This finally happened on January 16. Now everybody had a year in which Anguilla would be run more or less directly from Great Britain, with Tony Lee as our man in Anguilla under the title Senior British Official.

Nothing had been changed legally—the murder charge, for instance, still couldn't be tried anywhere but in St. Kitts—but there was a temporary period in which everybody had agreed not to raise a fuss, the idea being that the Interim would be spent trying to find a solution with some permanence in it.

Very very slowly passed 1968. On March 8, the anniversary of the burning of the Warden's house, Dr. Hyde's house was burned. Dr. Hyde understandably took his wife and mother and children and went home to England. Anguilla was at loose ends for a doctor until an American, Dr. Felix Spector, arrived to take over. Dr. Spector was a Philadelphian with twenty-five years' medical experience, but he had run into some trouble with the law concerning an operation that is legal in some parts of the world but not in the particular place where Dr. Spector performed it. He was tried and convicted, and the judge sentenced him to two years' practice in an undeveloped part of the world in lieu of jail.

Also in 1968 Burrowes Park underwent a name change. This was the place where Ronald Webster made all his public announcements, and several of his followers decided the park should bear his name. And so it was done, and Burrowes Park became Ronald Webster's Park.

It was also the year that British journalist Colin Rickards asked Colonel Bradshaw why, since Anguilla was a financial drain on him and he didn't like Anguillans anyway, he didn't let them go ahead and secede, to which the Colonel replied, "That would not be statesmanlike. There would be fragmentation throughout the West Indies. Barbuda would secede from Antigua, Tobago from Trinidad, possibly Carriacou from Grenada and even Bequia from St. Vincent. It is up to me as a Caribbean statesman to prevent this from happening. I must shoulder my responsibilities. Anguilla is the cross that I must bear."

It soon became obvious that what the British intended with the Interim Agreement Year was to play a game of Masterly Inactivity, waiting for the Anguillans to calm themselves and march obediently back to St. Kitts, as though this were simply a case of hysterics. Tony Lee soon came to understand that there was no way to make the scenario run like that and kept telling his superiors so, but there must be something peculiar in the air of Anguilla—Great Britain can't hear anybody from there.

Possibly because a connection with Great Britain now seemed so much more hopeful, or possibly because of tensions aggravated by the passage of time, various relationships on the island began to undergo a change; practically none of them for the better. The Island Council decided it didn't want Frank McDonald around any more and also told Roger Fisher they'd let him know if they ever needed *him* again. Relations between Ronald Webster and Atlin Harrigan became increasingly strained as they moved more and more into new roles, Webster becoming the solitary leader, shrugging off the restrictions of working with the Island Council and eventually packing the Council with yes men, and Harrigan becoming the island's—and Webster's—Jiminy Cricket, sniping away at local errors and peccadilloes via the *Beacon*. On March 2, for instance, he wrote, "What is happening to our Council Members? How many more pieces of bad legislation will be passed? Cannot any of them think before they make a move?"

But Harrigan didn't confine himself to watchdogging Webster and the Island Council. Very early in 1968 he saw what a foot-dragging operation the Interim Agreement really was and began complaining about it. On February 24 he published an "open letter to Lord Shepherd," which said in part:

> Two months have passed since Anguilla accepted the interim agreement, and with the presence of Mr. Tony Lee on the island we realize that there is no longer a danger of overt hostile action being taken against us ... In other respects there has been no alleviation of our difficulties. The savings of many hundreds of Anguillans are still frozen in the Treasury of St. Kitts ... the share of the U. K. grant which should have come to Anguilla last year never reached us ... Mr. Tony Lee is here in Anguilla (in the words of your letter of January 16th, 1968) "to assist with the administration of Anguilla, with the object of working towards an agreed long-term solution for the island." Both these objectives are being hindered by the delay in settling these eight-month-old grievances.

The bank had also been a problem, but that was in the process of being resolved—not through any activity on the part of the British,

131

however, whose Inactivity was at that time at its most Masterly.

There had originally been two banks on Anguilla, one a local branch of Great Britain's Barclays Bank and the other the Mid-Atlantic Bank with its home office in Basseterre. Barclays had shut its doors very early in the proceedings, while the Mid-Atlantic was still open and trying to do business without any money.

But the Mid-Atlantic Bank was a strange little outfit, straight out of an Eric Ambler novel. It was started in the sixties by a man named Sidney Alleyne, who has the kind of past history that makes frequent use of the word "alleged." He is from Barbados and was involved with a racist-*cum*-Communist political party on Jamaica in 1962, none of whose candidates got enough votes to save their deposits; you put up a deposit and if you don't get an eighth of the vote you lose the money. They lost the money.

It is alleged that in Trinidad he passed counterfeit money. It is also alleged that he did some gunrunning to various African nations in the sixties; for this or some other reason, he was named an Honorary Colonel in the Algerian Army. He also got involved in politics in his home island of Barbados in 1964, but it is alleged he passed some queer money on a high official and had to go somewhere else.

From somewhere in this forest of allegations, Alleyne picked up nearly half a million dollars. With this money and some personal contacts in the St. Kitts Government, he set up the Mid-Atlantic Bank and became its major shareholder. The original idea was that it would be an investment bank with numbered accounts (shades of Jerry Gumbs!), but since there wasn't at that time any other bank on Anguilla the Mid-Atlantic became a general-purpose bank.

Enter, in dramatic lighting, a Swiss citizen named Walter Germann, who lived in New York and had started the Bank of Panama. (If only Sydney Greenstreet were alive to play the role.) The Bank of Panama had been put together with Nazi money from Argentina, Teamsters Union money, Nevada and Puerto Rico gambling money and (here comes an "alleged") alleged Mafia money.

But the finest asset of the Bank of Panama was a piece of paper. It was letterhead stationery from a reputable American geological survey and assaying company, and it said that rich gold-ore deposits had been found in Ecuador on a piece of land owned by the Bank of Panama. This letter was signed by a well-known member of the firm who had recently died, so nobody could ask him if that was really his signature.

I'm not suggesting that anybody was out to sell gold-mine stock, not in this sophisticated day and age. You don't need a gold mine, and no gold has been mined on that bit of land in Ecuador; all you need is the piece of letterhead stationery. You borrow all the money you want and put up the land as security.

These two bankers, Alleyne and Germann, allegedly met when both were wearing their gunrunning hats. Germann had a Swiss corporation called Interhandle, and it is alleged that Interhandle handled the gun sales to Boumédienne in Algeria, Tshombe in the (Belgian) Congo and Colonel Ojukwu in Biafra.

Back in the Caribbean, Germann saw what a nice little bank Alleyne had on St. Kitts, and one way or another he hustled Alleyne out and took over the operation himself. It is alleged Alleyne lost a lot of money and was very bitter about it. Germann sent down two assistants, improbably named Labe and Schwarm, to run the Mid-Atlantic Bank for him.

Unfortunately, a little difficulty had come into Walter Germann's life. A Federal Grand Jury in New York decided that much of what he was doing, particularly with the Bank of Panama, required their attention. This was in March of 1965. Germann said he really couldn't give comprehensive answers to their questions unless he looked in his account books, which were in Switzerland; could he go get them? The Grand Jury said Yes. Walter Germann went to Switzerland and refused to come back, putting him in contempt of court in New York. He didn't seem to mind.

The end of the Walter Germann story—or maybe it isn't the end—is also imitation Eric Ambler. Germann committed suicide by shooting himself in the face so that he was no longer recognizable. The final allegation is that the body in Walter Germann's grave over there in Switzerland is somebody other than Walter Germann.

So that's the bank. The miracle is that the Kittitians didn't wake up one morning and find the whole building gone.

Early in 1968, the Bank of America stepped in and bought the Mid-Atlantic Bank, from whoever was left to sell it. The Bank of America agreed with the Anguillans that their branch would not be administered from St. Kitts, but from St. Croix, one of the U.S. Virgin Islands, a shift in responsibility that made banking possible once again on Anguilla.

It also made it possible at last for Anguillans to withdraw their savings, which just about all of them did. The result was a run on the bank, ending with the only instance in the history of the Bank of America that one of its branches had to shut its doors. The closing was only temporary. More money was brought in from another branch, and when the Anguillans saw that this bank was businesslike in its behavior most of them deposited their cash right back in again.

A murder, a bank opening; the story of Anguilla had shifted from international politics to small-town commonplaces. At the end of August, with more than half the year of grace already gone, Tony Lee went back to London and met with officials there. Sluggishly the bureaucratic machinery began to respond to reality. In October, Mr. Willian Whitlock, Parliamentary Under-Secretary of State for Foreign and Commonwealth Affairs—and a Labour M.P.—invited Ronald Webster and Robert Bradshaw to London to talk things over.

The talks started on October 14. But nobody was sure what would happen if Webster and Bradshaw met face to face so the first week was spent with everybody simply talking to Whitlock. The Kittitians chatted with him in the morning, and the Anguillans chatted with him in the afternoon. Finally Whitlock offered both sides three possible plans for ending the stalemate; Webster liked only plan one, Bradshaw liked only plan three.

The *Trinidad Guardian* summed up the meetings: "Interim report on the current interim Conference on the 'Interim Agreement' on Anguilla:—No progress, no confrontation, no compromise, no cash, no comment."

These meetings marked the low point in Jerry Gumbs's relationship with his home island. While in London, Ronald Webster said in public that Jerry Gumbs was "an evil man who would not be allowed to have any part in Anguilla's affairs." But when the London meetings were over, and the British—who had been talking so strongly against Gumbs—had managed once more to accomplish nothing, Webster's opinion of Gumbs very quickly rose again, until eventually it was higher than before.

By the time Webster got back to Anguilla the Interim Agreement was a shambles and the future was a mess. Webster was talking about *really* going independent on January 9, the day after the Interim Agreement would drop dead. Anguillans were choosing up sides as to whether he was right or wrong.

Among those who opposed the idea was Atlin Harrigan, who flailed away with his *Beacon* at everything that moved: "For some time an element existed in Anguilla that attempts to destroy anything that does not coincide with their own cabalistic views. These persons are only looking for personal financial gain and don't give two hoots about the individuals and will use dirty methods to achieve their aims, if and when Anguilla declares her independence from Britain."

But Jerry Gumbs, who'd been back talking about the Bank of Anguilla again—still with numbered accounts as the main feature—was all in favor of independence. So was Wallace Rey, a member of the Island Council. Wallace Rey, an excitable man at a public meeting, owner of a prosperous hardware store, had run the island's Department of Public Works until there was some question as to whether or not he was hiring out bulldozers and other equipment belonging to the Government and forgetting to give the rentals to the Treasury. (Of all the people I talked to in preparing this book, Wallace Rey was the only one who offered to sell me information.)

And three Americans who had become friendly with Webster also counseled independence. They were an odd assortment, unrelated except by their citizenship. One was a Baptist minister from Kentucky named Freeman Goodge, a fire-breathing believer in dramatic solutions to all problems. One was a man named Lewis Haskins, who, with his two teen-age sons, owned and operated a small mica-sorting and plastic-jewelry-making factory on the island; back in January of 1968, the Anguilla Alphabet in the *Beacon* had included, "*H* is for Haskins, the Father and Sons; Dad runs the business, the Boys hold the guns." The father had been a moderate for some time before coming to the conclusion that Anguilla would never get anywhere with Britain, but the sons had been hanging around with the rougher young people from the beginning, and of course that group inevitably favored whatever decision was likeliest to start a fight.

Goodge and Haskins had both been living on the island since

long before the trouble had started, but the third man was a recent arrival. His name was Jack Holcomb, and his life was somewhat less alleged than, say, Sidney Alleyne's. He was forty-one, he said he was a businessman, and his intention on the island was to start a "basic-materials industry," meaning stone and brick and concrete and other elements used in construction. But his background wasn't in construction. Most recently he had run something called Solar Research Enterprises in Florida, an outfit that made surveillance devices for private detectives—"bugs," they're called in the trade. He had gone out of business when his plant had mysteriously burned down.

He had been involved in "surveillance" work before in his life; in Los Angeles in 1955, while running a predecessor of Solar Research Enterprises, he was tried for illegal wire-tapping but was not found guilty. Much more recently, in 1967, he had become police commissioner in a small suburb of Fort Lauderdale, Florida, called Sea Ranch Lakes, but was fired when it was discovered there had been a narcotics charge in his youth; he'd been arrested in Long Beach, California, for possession of barbiturates and a hypodermic needle (and a blackjack), but the charges had been dropped.

More prosaically, Holcomb was involved in real estate in Florida. Less prosaically, he made business trips to the Caribbean, though the business matters were vague. (When I wrote to him in December of 1969, he wrote back, "Purposefully I have omitted writing on a letterhead until such time as I determine you are not one of the British agents still trying to acquire certain information about Anguilla ... I could give the story with documentation far greater than anyone since I was privy to the most guarded secrets both of government as well as individuals involved. However ... I would doubt that my inclination would be to release the information at this time." In my response, I said, "You say British agents are still trying to acquire certain information about Anguilla; of course, I won't try to get you to tell me the answers they're looking for, but would you feel it possible to tell me the questions they're asking?" He never replied.)

In the fall of 1968, Holcomb presented the Island Council with a spiral binder containing "A Proposal to the Government of Anguilla for Basic Building Materials by Jack N. Holcomb, P.O. Box 23130,

Oakland Park, Florida." Complete with maps and illustrations, the binder started with a suggestion about the manufacture of concrete blocks, but soon began to spiral upward.

First, Holcomb wanted a guarantee that he would be the sole supplier of all building materials on the island for twenty-five years. Second, he wanted it tax-free. Third, he had some other ideas in addition to building materials. "Fantastic growth and development possibilities exist," the proposal said. "In the investment capital market of the world, nothing appears as attractive as complete and total tax exemptions." Anguilla could set herself up as a flag of convenience for shippers (the pseudo-Onassis offer again); she could offer incorporation for international holding companies and give them "exemption from special taxes, corporation taxes, personal income tax, customs duties and tariffs." Land deals could be worked, money deals (numbered accounts?), all sorts of deals.

There could be Anguillan "participation" in all this, but the "stockholders in all companies would principally consist of United States citizens interested in this type of operation." And Holcomb himself would be in charge and exert "direct control."

For all of which the Anguillan Government would be paid a total of five hundred dollars a year.

The Island Council decided not to accept Holcomb's proposal, but he did have several supporters on the island. Jerry Gumbs was unhappy at the turndown: "He was gonna invest plenty. He wasn't gonna make money for four years. *Then* you'll let someone *else* in? These people don't understand economics. If Webster could worry he'd be worried. He was gonna build that road, open up that whole area. Put value on people's property. Houses going up alongside the road. But these people don't understand."

Jerry Gumbs understood. So did Wallace Rey, and so did a few others.

So the Interim Agreement Year wound down, with nothing accomplished. Things must grow or rot; that's a fact of life, in everything from flowers to love affairs, from brains to nations. In 1968, in the political life of Anguilla, nothing grew.

17

We've a war, an' a debt, an' a flag; an' ef this
Ain't to be inderpendunt, why, wut on airth is?
—James Russell Lowell, *The Biglow Papers*

On January 8, the Interim Agreement on Anguilla came to an end. With it, British aid—technical and economic—also ended. On January 16, Tony Lee left the island.

The next two months got a little rough on Anguilla. Anguillans have always fought among themselves as boisterously as any people on earth—it took someone like Colonel Bradshaw to make them all stand together, even briefly—and now that they were alone, with neither a goal nor a way to get to it, the factions began to split like the ground over an awakening volcano.

There was no longer any question about whether or not to separate from St. Kitts; they'd done that, they'd made it stick for almost two years, and they'd amply demonstrated that neither Bradshaw nor anybody else could get them back with St. Kitts again. Now the question was what to do next, and it boiled down to two choices. Either *really* declare independence and try to survive alone, or go on struggling to make the connection with Mother Britain.

The Island Council was split down the middle on the issue. Wallace Rey and two others favored independence, while Atlin Harrigan and another two wanted to stay in the Commonwealth and go on trying to attract Great Britain's attention.

The tie-splitting vote was held by the Chairman, Ronald Webster, and Webster was spending most of his time with four men: three Americans and an Americanized Anguillan. They were Lewis Haskins, the Reverend Freeman Goodge, Jack Holcomb and Jerry Gumbs. All four preached independence, and that was the way Ronald Webster went.

So there was another independence referendum. This one was

tied in with a new Constitution that had been written to replace the one Roger Fisher had tapped out on his portable typewriter in July of 1967. Most of the new document was a rehash of the American Constitution, but a couple of parts rang echoes from Jack Holcomb's "Proposal" of the preceding fall.

The anti-independence faction on the island was also anti this Constitution and was by this time very anti Jack Holcomb. However, the phrasing of the referendum stacked the deck in such a way that the pro-British group had no way to announce itself. The voter was given a choice between an A statement and a B statement as follows:

A: Affirm declaration and approve Constitution Government of the people of Anguilla;

B: Reject declaration Constitution return to St. Kitts.

The vote was 1,739 A's and 4 B's; I don't know which member of the Lloyd family didn't vote that time. The referendum was held on February 6, and the next day Ronald Webster went into Ronald Webster's Park and read out a new Declaration of Independence.

But this one didn't fool around; when this one said independence, it meant *independence.* "When the political ties of one people have deteriorated with another," it started, "and the common bonds of their future no longer exist, it becomes necessary to separate and assume their own destiny among the nations of the world."

Meanwhile, there was another Conference going on, only peripherally involved with Anguilla. This was the Fifth Conference of Heads of Government of Commonwealth Caribbean Countries, and it was held in Port-of-Spain, Trinidad, from February 3 to 6, 1969. While Ronald Webster was publishing his Declaration of Independence, this Conference was publishing a statement that included the following: "The Conference called upon the Government of the United Kingdom to take all necessary steps in collaboration with the Government of the State to confirm the territorial integrity of St. Kitts-Nevis-Anguilla."

Which was a lot tougher than they'd been a year and a half earlier, when Lord Shepherd had asked for just this kind of statement to support a landing of British troops on the island. What made the big change?

Primarily, it was the simple fact that a year and a half had gone by without a solution. Anguilla was a continuing aggravation and worry in everybody else's back yard, and the anticipated British handling of the problem hadn't worked out. Also, there was the usual terror of fragmentation. Colonel Bradshaw had been sending telegrams all over the Caribbean for a year and a half warning everybody about fragmentation, claiming that a successfully independent Anguilla would cause other subcolonies to act the same way, and it was actually beginning to happen. Though whether the discontent was caused by the example of Anguilla or more personal problems at home is another question.

Still, at the very time the Heads of Government Conference was going on, there were stirrings and trouble in three places besides Anguilla. First there was Nevis, which was also starting to give Colonel Bradshaw a bad time; when Nevis had gotten its Local Council at long last, PAM had run candidates for five of the six seats and all five PAM men had won, a result that was sure to cause friction between the Nevis Local Council and the St. Kitts Government just about any time they'd meet.

Then there was Barbuda. A smaller island than Anguilla, with a population of around two thousand, it was governed from Antigua, thirty miles away, and had much the same stepsister complaint about Antigua that Anguilla had about St. Kitts. Rumblings of discontent had become louder from Barbuda since Anguilla's successful secession.

On the South American mainland, there was Guyana's trouble with the people of its own hinterland. While the Heads of Government Conference was going on, Guyanese troops were operating in the interior, breaking up a "Republic of Rupununi" that had been set up by some dissident ranchers there.

At the moment, Trinidad wasn't having trouble with Tobago, nor was Grenada having trouble with Carriacou, but who knew when it might start? No, the best thing was to ignore the details of the Anguilla situation, look upon it not as six thousand people struggling against petty repression but as a "disturbance" having an "effect," and give the British the okay to go on in there and clean it up.

Which the British didn't do. Instead, they announced in the middle of February that William Whitlock—whom Webster and Bradshaw had talked to separately in London last October—would be making a tour of the Caribbean at the end of the month and would hope to be able to produce some new proposals for both sides. As an editorial in the *Beacon* of February 15 said:

It is a pity that this announcement came after Anguillans had gone to the polls and voted to be independent of the Crown and Commonwealth. Any talks that Mr. Whitlock can venture upon, would only serve a purpose, if he is prepared to start at a level where Anguilla's secession from St. Kitts is acknowledged. Although it is said that Mr. Whitlock will be visiting St. Kitts, no question is raised as to a possible visit to Anguilla. In 1967 when Mr. Lord Shepherd came to Barbados to try a settlement to the dispute, he was invited to Anguilla, to see the island first hand for himself, and he refused. This is no doubt why H. M. G. has continually misunderstood the whole situation.

In the same issue of the *Beacon,* the further deterioration of Anguilla's domestic scene was shown in an angry reply by Atlin Harrigan to an attack against him by Ronald Webster, which had appeared both in the *Windward Islands Observer* over in St. Martin and in the *Anguilla Observer,* a short-lived newspaper competing with the *Beacon* and supported by the anti-British faction.

This is a willful attempt [Harrigan wrote] to whip up anti-feelings against the *Beacon* and its Editor, in the eyes of the public ... Will Mr. Webster level his reputation to that of Mr. Wallace Rey? After saying all this, it is expected that people will size the Editor (Atlin Harrigan) and Mr. Webster, as the two persons who started the revolution, now pulling apart. We may not share each other's ideas, but that does not give anyone the right to say one hand is working for the enemy ... Our aim we felt would have taken us to the same destiny (Independence) but envisaged it taking longer, but on a sound basis. Mr. Webster's course was the short way, Independence immediately. The people accepted it, and we all must now make the best of it.

They were also making the worst of it. The following week's

Beacon contained this notice, without editorial comment:

> This is to certify that Mr. Jack N. Holcomb has been duly licensed as an Attorney to engage in the practice of Law, in the Republic of Anguilla, having been approved by the Government on 18th February, 1969. All privileges of Legal Practice are conferred hereby. This is to further attest that the Republic of Anguilla has certified Mr. Holcomb with the Courts to enjoy all Rights of Representation and confidence as an Officer thereof. 19th. February 1969
>
> > *Ronald Webster*
> > Chief Executive Gov't. Republic of Anguilla

Holcomb's relationship with Anguilla had altered quite a bit since the Island Council had turned down his spiral binder the preceding fall. Holcomb was now claiming that he represented five big-money investors in Florida, two of them "in heavy equipment and the construction industry with Government contracts for air bases and things," two in electronic manufacturing, and one "widely represented in insurance." He also said, according to Emile Gumbs, that he "had inside information from the White House that the United States would recognize Anguilla within ten days after the island's Declaration of Independence."

As to the second, it didn't happen. As to the first, those five investors that Holcomb never stopped talking about but never named, there's this exchange between London *Daily Express* reporter Henry Lowrie and Holeomb's wife, Dorothy Jean, at the Holcomb home near Fort Lauderdale:

> What about her husband's link with Webster? "Oh, no. My husband is strictly on his own."
>
> Was he acting for a group of investors? "Well, if he did find something worth developing, I suppose he could bring in some investors who would back him."

Mrs. Holcomb was asked by another reporter if she had a profession: "'No,' she said wistfully. 'Unless you could call tidying up after Jack a profession. I'm his sort of secretary.'"

Asked to respond to a British official's charge that her husband was an "evil genius," she said, "He may be a genius, but he is certainly not evil." And as to his having been declared the first lawyer in the Republic of Anguilla, she explained that he had "an extensive law library."

Having a lawyer of its own, regardless of the extent of his law library, didn't solve much for Anguilla. Trouble was starting on the island again. The guns were coming back out, and this time the enemy wasn't a callous but unreachable Government seventy miles away on another island; this time it was the neighbor next door. The sides were moving steadily farther apart, and the threat of Colonel Bradshaw was no longer real enough to keep the factions united.

Anguillan individualism has one unfortunate side effect; Anguillans make lousy team members. "The common good" is a phrase that doesn't make any real sense to Anguillans. Once the immediate problem of Bradshaw was solved—political settlement or no political settlement, they were no longer being governed from Sc. Kitts—they were free to return to their natural state, and the natural state of Anguillans is to be independent *from one another.* If a public official wants to take the opportunity to work some private hustles, the majority of Anguillans couldn't care less; they have their own lives to think about. If their leaders want to make odd business deals with passing Americans, why not? If Webster and Harrigan, whose agitation had started the secession in the first place, want to squabble in public, the majority of Anguillans won't bother to take sides, they'll just enjoy the spectacle.

The trouble with this kind of attitude is that things can be allowed to get completely out of hand before anybody starts to worry. In the days when a Bradshaw invasion had seemed a possibility, Webster had imported some guns and had assembled the boys and young men of the island into a Defence Force. Elements of this Defence Force had now become a kind of teen-age gang, roaming the island and looking for action. The most justifiable action they could think of was to roust the opponents of Ronald Webster, and that's what they started to do. It's unlikely that Webster gave them any orders, or that anything he could have told them would have made any difference. They were dumb kids looking for adventure and finding it right at home.

So independence was turning out to be even more of a mess

than the pro-British faction had suggested. On the one side, a pro-moter like Jack Holcomb was being made the new nation's first lawyer, and on the other side, some bored boys were practicing to be vest-pocket terrorists. While Ronald Webster, with undiminished conviction in his own infallibility, was going around quoting from the Bible, lashing out at anybody who disagreed with him, and building a sixty-five-room hotel.

Where you see a jester a tool is not far off.
—Thomas Fuller, *Gnomologia*

"The time spent has not been wasted, and Mr. Whitlock will have gained a deep knowledge of the personalities and problems involved, which will stand him in good stead on the final day of reckoning." That's what the *Beacon* said in summing up the deadlocked talks in London between Webster and Bradshaw in October of 1968. The final day of reckoning for William Whitlock came on the eleventh of March, 1969, and it turned out the *Beacon* was wrong; the time had been completely wasted insofar as giving Mr. Whitlock a deep knowledge of the personalities and problems was concerned. Particularly the personalities.

William Whitlock made two trips to the Caribbean in the early part of 1969. The first had been spent in talking with various Caribbean Governments, trying to find out what solution would please all of Anguilla's neighbors. Also on that trip, Whitlock talked with Colonel Bradshaw and one way or another managed to get from the Colonel concessions he'd never been willing to make before. There were a number of development schemes for St. Kitts, involving British money, being considered in London at the time—updating Golden Rock Airport to take jumbo jets, turning Frigate Bay into a tourist area—and one doubts that Whitlock failed to make reference to these things while chatting with Bradshaw. Whitlock himself later explained that Colonel Bradshaw had shown a "statesmanlike recognition of the strength of feeling in Anguilla," and that "because of this statesmanlike recognition by the Government of St. Kitts, Nevis and Anguilla that there was this terrific feeling in Anguilla, my proposals were agreed to by the State Government."

The Colonel agreed to let another Interim Agreement be set

up, except that this time the interim would be open-ended, and instead of the Senior British Official advising the Island Council, the British official would be in charge and the Island Council would advise *him.* (This was the transfer of authority from St. Kitts to Great Britain that the Anguillans had been requesting for 147 years.) He also agreed to let the British arrange for an Associated States' magistrate on the island, which would permit the Anguillans to have the court they'd been wanting without forcing them to accept Bradshaw's authority through Bradshaw's selection of the magistrate. And he further agreed to let Great Britain handle the Land Registry, which was one of what Donald Chapman had called his "trump cards."

Technically, Anguilla would remain part of the Associated State of St. Kitts-Nevis-Anguilla, but for the indefinite future the administration would be handled totally by the English.

Which was a good 90 per cent of what Anguilla had been asking for.

So all that remained was for Whitlock to go back home to London, have the new proposals put down on paper in careful proper form, take the paper to Anguilla, and show it to the people. That's all that had to be done, and it doesn't seem as though anything could possibly go wrong.

19

That fellow seems to me to possess but one idea,
and that is a wrong one.

—Samuel Johnson

ANGUILLA REBELS FIRE
AT BRITISH MINISTER
By Ian Ball

ST. JOHN'S, ANTIGUA—Warning shots were fired at Mr. William Whitlock, 50, Parliamentary Under-Secretary, Foreign and Commonwealth Office, in a tense confrontation with rebel leaders on Tuesday on the breakaway Caribbean island of Anguilla in the Leeward Islands

London *Daily Telegraph,* March 13, 1969

Now what went wrong?

On March 9, Tony Lee arrived on Anguilla with his radio and
radio operator, just as he had done in advance of Fisher and Chapman. This time, he was in advance of Whitlock, and when he told
Webster and the Island Council that Whitlock was coming with
new proposals, almost everybody was delighted, including Webster.
Independence had been a very bad strain on Webster, whose increasing uncertainty had shown both in his inability to control his
followers and his growing dependence on Jack Holcomb and Wallace Rey and a few others. He would be grateful for some reliable
help if he could take it without seeming to surrender.

Webster went so far as to have a luncheon prepared for the
Whitlock party. He had the best cars on the island cleaned and polished and made ready for a motorcade that would take Whitlock
from the airport to Jerry Gumbs's Rendezvous Hotel, where the luncheon would be held.

Whitlock was due at noon on the eleventh. The motorcade was

there at the airport, and so were Webster and the rest of the Island Council (which was now calling itself "the Provisional Government"), all dressed up in morning coats and white gloves; they were, after all, about to meet a representative of the Queen.

Also present were the usual crowd of demonstrators, carrying posters reading "We Want Britain" and "Welcome Mr. Whitlock" and "Britain not Bradshaw." And there was a bunch of school children, let out for the occasion and just waiting to rip into a rendition of "God Save the Queen."

It still looks as though nothing can go wrong.

The plane carrying Whitlock and his five assistants was nearly an hour late, but that didn't much matter; planes are almost always late in the Caribbean, and so are people. As Whitlock stepped from the plane, everybody sang "God Save the Queen" and there were smiles on all faces, on the faces of Whitlock and his party and on the faces of the Anguillans there to greet him.

Everything is still okay.

Now Webster stepped forward and shook hands with Whitlock. The two had gotten along well together the previous fall in London, and in fact Webster had subsequently written to Whitlock, thanking him for everything he had tried to do on Anguilla's behalf. Meeting again, they exchanged brief hellos, and Webster offered Whitlock the terminal steps from which to address the crowd if he liked. Whitlock made a short speech, thanking everybody and saying he'd brought along proposals that he thought they would all like. The response was more cheers and another round of "God Save the Queen."

Things are about to go to hell now.

Whitlock had brought with him some leaflets explaining the new proposals, and he decided to distribute them at the airport, *before* talking to the Provisional Government. "They were distributed by members of my party," he said later, "and the crowd scrambled eagerly for them."

They had to, considering the way the leaflets were "distributed." Anthony Rushford, the Legal Counsellor with the Whitlock group, described it this way: "It was like handing out oranges at a children's party. Mr. Whitlock's private secretary stood up and tried to scatter them over the crowd in a perfectly good-humored way. They came down like great snowflakes. There was something quite comic about it. Nothing derogatory."

Nothing derogatory. Handing out oranges at a children's party; nothing derogatory. Something quite comic, but nothing derogatory.

The *Anguilla Observer* described it this way: "Whitlock literally threw his pamphlets at the crowd as a farmer might throw corn to fowl."

Ronald Webster later said of the leaflets that Whitlock "threw them at the people."

There was also nothing derogatory about Whitlock's refusal to ride in the cars Ronald Webster had had polished and spruced up, nor in his refusal to have lunch with Webster.

The Whitlock party hung around the airport for forty-five minutes while Tony Lee made some last-minute arrangements to get them fed without forcing them to see Anguillans at table. Lee set up an alternate lunch in the home of the manager of the Bank of America (called the Howard House) and rounded up different cars, and the Whitlock group, having finished its first lesson of the day in the arts of diplomacy, went off to lunch.

Various British Government officials later explained that this is always the way a British minister enters other people's countries. "Protocol," they call it. The minister arrives, shakes hands with whoever among the 'locals" has come to greet him, and then goes off for lunch with the Senior British Official (in this case Tony Lee) to get an "appreciation" from him before talking with local leaders. But *is* that protocol? On his earlier trip through the Caribbean did Whitlock really leave one Government official after another standing around at one island airport after another, with nothing to show for his day but a handshake and a leaflet and egg on his face? If that's protocol, give me rudeness.

Whitlock was later to say he hadn't known about the Webster lunch, but surely *somebody* at the airport in those embarrassing forty-five minutes must have mentioned the luncheon and pointed to the very shiny cars out there in the sunlight.

Did Whitlock think Webster and the other Council members always wore white gloves? In the Caribbean?

It is now approaching two o'clock, and the Whitlock party—including Tony Lee—has gone off to the bank manager's house for lunch. Whitlock intended to meet the Provisional Government at the Administrative Building at four o'clock, but there's some question as to whether anybody told the Provisional Government or not.

Which raises the question of Tony Lee's part in all this. He knew the island and its leaders by now better than any other Englishman, and his role in this day's activities was essentially liaison between the British and the Anguillans, but the depth of ignorance that each side showed about the other's plans and attitudes makes one wonder. Maybe Tony Lee actually did fail to give Whitlock an accurate picture of the circumstances on the island. Or maybe Whitlock thought so little of Lee—a "diplomatic mercenary," as Sir John Rodgers later called him—that he didn't bother to listen. Or maybe it was both, with Lee soft-pedaling anything that would conflict with Whitlock's preconceptions and Whitlock busily giving him less than half an ear. One recalls that Lee's reports about Anguilla had been ignored in London for something over a year.

The house of the Whitlock lunch is on the side of Sandy Hill, the place from which the Anguillans drove the French back into the sea in 1796.

While relaxed good cheer was the order of the day inside the house, growing irritation and confusion were rampant outside it. So far as the Anguillans could see, Ronald Webster had been snubbed. No one was happy about it, but the most actively unhappy were the young hooligans of the Defence Force. They went home and got out their rifles and tried to decide how to even the score for Mr. Webster.

The first thing they did was kidnap a turkey.

Tony Lee had arranged for a turkey to be cooked and delivered to the Howard house for the ministerial lunch. As it was being delivered, the car containing it was stopped by a bunch of young men with rifles. They took the bird and sent the driver away.

At the house, they finally gave up waiting for the turkey. The bank manager had some cold chicken, so they made do with that.

Ronald Webster had been looking forward to Whitlock's arrival. He'd had to overrule the more strident supporters of complete independence in laying on such a lavish welcome, and all he'd gotten for his pains was humiliation in front of his people. He used the lunch hour to prepare a leaflet of his own, insisting on independence. "The hell with the British" was the basic attitude of the leaflet.

At twenty after three the Whitlock party started organizing itself for a return to the center of the island and the four o'clock meeting with the Government that the Government hadn't been told about. Then somebody looked out front and saw that a chain had been put across the driveway and that a group of men had gathered on the high ground overlooking the house. One of them seemed to be an American in steel helmet and battle dress and carrying a carbine. (Probably one of the Haskins boys, dressed up to play War.)

Anthony Rushford again: "Some very tough-looking fellows were putting stones in the road, and there were other people with firearms … I saw some people who looked like Americans wearing steel helmets and carrying arms." If "some" means two, they were the Haskins boys; if more than two, I can't think who it might have been. Wheeler-dealer Jack Holcomb? The Reverend Freeman Goodge? The veterinarian from Chicago?

Rushford again: "I couldn't swear to the number in court, you understand, but I think there were ten to fifteen guns in the drive, and at least two rifles at a house on the skyline."

One of the tough-looking fellows in the driveway went up to the house and told the people there, "Mr. Webster says he's coming to see you. You will not leave the house."

Rushford says that after the tough-looking fellow had gone back down with the other tough-looking fellows, Whitlock suggested the English get into their cars and try to drive on through the blockade. But Rushford told him, "Sir, be careful, there are armed men around. You are a Minister of the Crown as well as a male human being."

So they waited for Ronald Webster, who, says Rushford, "came down in a somewhat autocratic manner." He behaved, in other words, like a proud man who'd been humiliated in front of his followers and was determined to make up for it. He entered the house and said to Whitlock, "Sit down, I have something to say to you."

Whitlock said, "Don't tell me to sit down. *I* have something to say to *you*. Listen to me. I am, after all, a Minister of the British Crown and you have threatened me with armed men. I wish to give you an extremely solemn warning that this will have extremely se-

151

rious consequences for you."

While the leaders bickered, the Englishmen in the house maintained a low profile and the armed men on the ridge of the hill maintained an ostentatious profile. Webster handed over his leaflet, and there was more sharp talk on both sides. Webster told them they should leave the island within thirty minutes because "I can no longer guarantee your safety."

Rushford says he took that "as a threat. I am not quite a greenhorn after twenty-five years in the legal profession." But the statement was at least as much warning as threat. Although Webster denies it now, this group of armed boys and young men was out of his control by the time Whitlock arrived on the island, and remained out of his or anybody else's control until the British took over. The British had created a power vacuum in February of 1967, and it had taken two years for the island to be reduced to mob rule. All things considered, that's a very long time.

As one of those whose ignorance and indifference had contributed to the mess on Anguilla, it's fitting that Parliamentary Under-Secretary of State for Foreign and Commonwealth Affairs William Whitlock was present on the island when its social structure hit bottom.

Webster, having delivered his threat—or his warning—left the house. The Whitlock party tried to decide what to do next. The suggestion of blasting through the blockade had already been made and rejected; now another idea came up. The bank manager, their inadvertent host through all this, was an American and not a part of the fracas, and would therefore not be bothered by the tough-looking fellows outside; at least that was the theory. He could carry a message through the enemy lines to Snowi!

Of course, Webster had told them they could *all* go. In fact he had suggested it was a good idea. But this is what they did instead. They drafted a message to Snowi and the bank manager carried it out in his shoe.

The message is full of a kind of pedantic hysteria, even to the point of giving the latitude and longitude of the house—the latitude twice—and mentioning the next day's date in a parenthetical aside. It reads:

To SNOWI repeated FCO

(Flag)

Minister and party, 9 persons in all, now surrounded at SANDY HILL BAY (Howard's house) on southeast shore of island (latitude eighteen degrees thirteen minutes forty-five seconds north, longitude 63° 00' 30" West Lat 18° 13 mins 45 secs N. by armed Webster supporters. Communications base at THE ROAD (3 men) also behind similarly cut off. Minister has seen Webster who called at Howard House and he warned him of consequences of his action. We may be forced off the island, although we shall try to avoid this.

Please reconnoitre SANDY BAY and THE ROAD areas first light tomorrow (12 March)

"Snowi?" Senior Naval Officer, West Indies. "(Flag)" means flagship. "FCO" is the Foreign and Commonwealth Office, to whom Whitlock wanted a copy of the message sent.

Two words from the original were crossed out and replaced, both of them in the first line. The phrase "9 persons" had originally read "seven," meaning that somebody had been a little too shaky to count heads right on the first try. And the word "surrounded," with all its implications of melodrama and derring-do, had been put in place of a much odder and perhaps more accurate word—"isolated." Whitlock, and his misconceptions, and his assistants handing out oranges at a children's party, had been isolated. Which happens to rude people the world over.

Not long after the bank manager had slipped through the enemy lines by the clever stratagem of getting into his car and driving to the bank, Sergeant Thomas Ryan of the Anguilla police went to the Howard house and told Whitlock that Webster would like to see him.

A word about Sergeant Ryan and the Anguilla police generally. The people of the island had had their fill of hard-nosed Kittitian cops. The Peacekeeping Committee, forming its own police force, had gone out of its way to find peaceable friendly men who could be relied on to calm disturbances rather than start them. When I was on the island in the spring of 1970, the police motor pool consisted of one green Volkswagen beetle, which would start only with a push. Twice in three days I saw that beetle rolling slowly down the road, one blue-uniformed policeman seriously at the wheel and another earnestly pushing from behind. On both occasions I was in my rented jeep and was able to give them a push. I have never been as fond of any police force as I was of those two cheerful indefatigable officers, and I was happy on my visit in 1971 to see that they now had a black Volkswagen capable of starting with no outside assistance at all.

So we have Sergeant Ryan, a slow-moving and soft-bodied man with a round face and cherubic smile, a man who likes peace and dislikes trouble. Sergeant Ryan is not your typical terrorist agitator.

Webster had gone to Howard's house and talked to Whitlock, and Whitlock had done most of the talking. Now Sergeant Ryan was there to say that Webster wanted Whitlock to come up to the house on top of the hill. Whitlock said he definitely was *not* going up there to talk to Webster in the middle of an armed mob. Ryan stepped out front and bellowed this news up the hill.

Rushford tells us what happened next. "Someone blew a whistle and there was a fusillade of shots fired from the house on the height. They may have been fired into the air. I don't think they were aimed at the house. You can hardly miss a house, can you? There were at least four distinct shots. Someone said to us: 'The General wishes you to leave.'"

So they left. They got into their cars and drove to the airport and flew away.

Or, as Whitlock himself was later to describe it, "After several threats and the bringing of more and more nasty armed men and the firing of shots I was hustled off the island."

20

*Man is made for error; it enters his mind naturally,
and he discovers a few truths only with the greatest
effort.*

—Frederick the Great

"Force is the only solution to the problem," said Colonel Bradshaw. "Minister Whitlock's expulsion from Anguilla, part of my country, is tantamount to an expulsion of Britain herself. The dastardly act fully substantiates what I have been saying for two years, namely that the Anguilla rebels are the front men of a sinister external gangster element and that only the use of force can properly bring Anguilla back to constitutional rule within the State."

For two years, Colonel Bradshaw had been practically alone in talking about gangsters and Anguilla in the same breath. But now watch the Mafia come leaping center stage, in its black shirts and white ties and snap-brim hats.

The first claim in the British press that Anguilla was run by mobsters came in the magazine *Private Eye*, a satirical muckraker that is a kind of cross between the American magazines *Ramparts* and *Mad*. In its issue for January 17, 1969, two months before the Whitlock visit, *Private Eye* offered this little item:

The controversy between plucky little Anguilla and the tyrant Brandshaw, Premier of the St. Kitts Federation, has its roots in the American underworld, notably in the so-called Mafia, led by Meyer Lansky in Florida. Lansky has recently been making a bid to break British monopoly control over gambling casinos in the Bahamas, and has already taken some of the casinos over. It was Lansky's "mechanic," Dino Cellini, who visited Anguilla the year before last with an offer to build a casino there in opposition to the Bradshaw plan to build a casino on St. Kitts. The "independence movement" is, in the main, financed by Lansky and is believed to be not entirely a question of freedom.

That came from a young man named Paul Foot, who is the son of Hugh Foot, whom we have already met under his more official name, Lord Caradon. The question arises: Does Paul Foot talk too much to his father or too little?

In a full-page piece called "Last Year's Bradshaw" in *Private Eye* for March 28, 1969, Foot offered the following:

> Hardly anyone reported a meeting on 2nd August 1967 between Bradshaw and Peter Adams the elected MP for St. Kitts, in which Bradshaw undertook to establish an Anguillan local council. Adams, delighted with the agreement, sailed for Anguilla to promise his people everything they had been asking for. He was thrown out of the island by armed thugs. He has not been able to return since.

I don't know which Peter Adams he has in mind. The one I've met was never thrown off the island, never delighted with anything about Bradshaw, and never able to sail to Anguilla from anywhere with a promise that his people were going to get everything they had been asking for.

In the same article, Foot had this to say about the trials on St. Kitts: "The other prisoners came to trial after six months in jail (only marginally more than the average 'wait-for-trial' period in Britain). Their trial evoked a quarrel between Bradshaw's Government and the judges, as a result of which the trial was suspended, and the prisoners released."

Suspended?

Here's Foot on Ronald Webster. First he mentions the Dino Cellini visit to the island, and then: "Several months after the visit, Ronald Webster, the self-styled leader of Anguilla, told Lord Lambton, Tory MP, that the island's monthly deficit was £3,000 and that this had been bridged 'by sale of property.' (Evening Standard: 19.2.68) He did not say to whom the property was being sold."

I guess we're all supposed to leap to the assumption that the land was sold to Dino Cellini. However, since the land was on St. Martin, Foot's concern seems a little curious. Even if it *was* Dino Cellini who bought that land on St. Martin—it wasn't—what good would that do Meyer Lansky in his evil plan to take over Anguilla?

One final bit of Footwork. In *Private Eye* for April 11, 1969, appeared the following item:

> More light on the "arms for Anguilla" rumours. In the July of 1967, a BBC producer, working on a film in Havana, made the casual acquaintance of a rich entrepreneur with a large loud pseudo-American accent and three passports (Canadian, Israeli, Dutch) called Van Gurp. Van Gurp entertained the producer on his 85-ft. luxury yacht, and showed him round the inside of the hold. Proudly, he uncovered cases of M1 carbines and repeater rifles.
>
> "This was God-Damn full to the brim," boasted Van Gurp. "Full to the brim. But I've just got rid of almost all my stock doing a roaring trade in a little island not far from here … somewhere I'd never heard of before … called Anguilla."

What a lovely picture that makes: an itinerant arms seller traveling back and forth in the Caribbean in a yacht loaded with rifles, shooting off his mouth to passing strangers and making deals with people he'd never heard of before. Does Paul Foot really think that's the way illegal arms are moved from seller to buyer in this world? And if the mob was running things on Anguilla, don't they have weapons sources of their own? Is the Mafia really dependent upon some passing nut with a shipful of carbines? Van Gurp says he'd never heard of Anguilla before; does Foot contend that if Van Gurp hadn't stumbled on Anguilla in July of 1967 the whole Anguillan rebellion wouldn't have happened?

Nearly two-thirds of "Last Year's Bradshaw" is devoted to PAM. Foot suggests PAM is dominated by evil landowners trying to bring down an upright trade unionist (Colonel Bradshaw) and that PAM created the Anguillan rebellion itself as a roundabout way to defeat Bradshaw. *Private Eye*'s Foot behaved here like what has been called a "knee-jerk liberal"; he leaped to his liberal political stance before being sure of his facts. On the one side he saw a black (check) who was a union leader (check) and head of something called the Labour Party (check). On the other side he saw white exploiters of black men (check) with upper-class English friends (check) and supporters in the British Conservative Party (check).

That's all Paul Foot needed to know, and I think it's obvious it's all he ever found out.

In the course of preparing this book I spoke with or wrote to several journalists, needing clarification on things they'd reported or attempting to unravel contradiction between different reports on the same event. Of them all, only Paul Foot showed any reluctance to talk to me. I phoned him and I visited the offices of *Private Eye* on Greek Street, and I got nowhere. It had all been a long time ago, he didn't remember the articles well enough to talk about them, and he wasn't really that interested.

So the Mafia, which had first been talked about by Colonel Bradshaw and then very briefly mentioned by Lord Shepherd, entered British print in January of 1969 via Paul Foot and *Private Eye*. The next mention was by William Whitlock in an interview on the BBC: "I think there is a danger that in certain islands at any rate, undesirable elements can take over. Remember that there are so many small islands in the Caribbean scattered around which might be occupied or taken over by almost Mafia-type elements who would form a threat to the security of the Caribbean."

Whitlock made that remark in February, before the *first* of his Caribbean trips and almost a month before he landed on Anguilla. It suggests attitudes that might already have been in his head when he did land there.

We know what was in his head after he left. "I will say, unhappily," he told the first reporter he met, "that a small number of people dominate the affairs of Anguilla, and that they are armed." He was asked about the Mafia, and said, "I have no doubt at all that this type of organization is on the island."

When he got back to London he called a press conference at the Foreign and Commonwealth Office and said, "The Anguillan people are completely dominated by gangster-type elements." He also said they were "gangster-like characters who are holding the Anguillans in complete subjection." When he was asked about the Mafia he was only slightly more restrained: "This I don't know. I think the phrase which has been used is 'Mafia-type elements.' We have no proof that in fact they are members of the Mafia. The general feeling throughout the Caribbean—I don't know if anyone has proof—is that they are somehow like Mafia characters. We know their names. But we have no knowledge that they are part of the Mafia at all. All that we do know is that Webster is accompanied and advised much of his time by an American."

That was Jack Holcomb, of course.

But saying "Mafia-type" and "gangster-like" is a little too subtly seedy; it's like calling a non-sports car "sporty" or a dog food full of cereal "meaty." The British press simply dropped the shabby qualifiers and had a field day.

From an editorial in the London *Daily Telegraph* for March 14: "Anguilla finds itself in the grip of a bunch of about 50 gangsters of American origins who want to set up gambling and other rackets."

From the London *Sun* for March 13: "American gangsters linked with the Mafia have made approaches to Mr. Webster, hoping to set up gambling casinos on Anguilla."

A headline in the *Sun* on March 14: "GANGSTERS 'CONTROL BREAKAWAY ISLANDERS.'"

A headline in the London *Evening Standard* for March 14: "GUNPOINT ISLAND PUTS MR. WILSON ON THE SPOT."

From the *Daily Telegraph* of March 14: "Officials are now inclined to believe reports that have been circulating in the Caribbean for several months that the American Mafia or associated crime interests are interested in Anguilla."

From the London *Times*, a headline on March 13: "ANGUILLANS 'RULED BY FEAR.'"

My personal favorite is from the *Evening Standard* on March 14: "There are about 6000 people on the island. Most of them are believed to have guns." If we remember that thirty-five hundred of the six thousand are children and two thousand of the remainder are women—if, in fact, we remember that British and Kittitian neglect have resulted in an island run by remittance, in which most able-bodied men must spend years in exile to send money home for their families to live on—that particular line becomes first funny and then merely stupid.

21

Desperate deeds of derring do.
—W. S. Gilbert, *Ruddigore*

On Anguilla the tough boys had been only nominally under Webster's control until the Whitlock incident. Once they'd managed to throw a British diplomat off the island there was no stopping them. They were in charge to whatever extent they wanted to be in charge.

Fortunately they had no program, no goals and no plans. They weren't Mafia or even Mafia-like; they were simply thirty overgrown brats with guns in their hands. Which meant that for the most part life on the island continued as before. The Provisional Government continued provisionally to govern, and the juvenile delinquents did much less damage than might have been expected.

Their worst act was reported in the *Beacon*, which under the circumstances deserves the right to describe it:

On Wednesday, March 12th, the day after Mr. William Whitlock was expelled from the island, eight men, some armed, walked into the premises of the *Beacon* and took away the *Beacon* press. Spokesman for the men said that they were sent for a press which belonged to the people of Anguilla. My wife and her mother, who were home at the time, did not argue with the intruders, who took the press away. On hearing this, I approached Mr. Webster, who said that he had no knowledge of what had happened. Mr. Webster returned the press the following day, with an excuse for the men. It said, "The press was taken by citizens who believed that the *Beacon* printed news that was treasonable." The press was out of order when it was returned. Thanks to two persons a new roller was brought in from Boston on Saturday, 29th March. The *Beacon* holds no ill feelings against these men. We feel that the press was taken as a result of a meeting held at Sandy Hill's Government Building the night before, by some Government officials. Mr. Jack Holcomb and Mr. Jeremiah Gumps were also present at the meeting.

22

When the foeman bares his steel,
Tarantara, tarantara!
We uncomfortable feel,
Tarantara.
—W. S. Gilbert, The Pirates of Penzance

In the outside world, the Mafia story had begun to spring some leaks. Jerry Gumbs carried to the United Nations a letter from Ronald Webster asking for a fact-finding mission from the U.N. to come see for itself if there were any gamblers on Anguilla. When the Committee on Colonialism agreed to give Gumbs another hearing, the British delegation walked out. But the walkout failed to keep Jerry Gumbs from being news again. *The New York Times* quoted him as saying, "The Anguillans are a Christian, churchgoing people who do not want gambling casinos." And the London *Daily Telegraph* also quoted him: "A United Nations mission can see for themselves that there is no Mafia there. The people of Anguilla are not going to have gambling on the island. Nobody that I know of is attempting to introduce gambling there."

Reporters had descended on Anguilla the instant the Whitlock story broke, and their reports were significantly free of news about the Mafia. The vagueness of the Whitlock remarks on the subject began to be more noticeable as the first excitement faded, and within four days a certain skepticism had entered the news reports. No one in the press had as yet come out with the flat statement that Whitlock was wrong. But when another member of the Whitlock party announced that the island's leaders had met Whitlock in "a Black Power type of dress," and it turned out he meant morning coats and white gloves, the absurdity was out in the open.

Now the reporters began to get more specific. The *Telegraph*'s Ian Ball wrote, "The oblique reference to the Mafia, first made by

Mr. Whitlock ... may turn out to be a particularly embarrassing one for the Government. Those of us who have tried to find substantiation for the charge are still looking." And Andrew McEwen of the *Daily Mail* reported, "The nearest thing to A1 Capone and Miami thuggery is a bunch of schoolboy hoodlums who play soldiers and carry guns." And in *The Guardian,* Adam Raphael calmly said, "The Americans in Anguilla may not for the most part be very likeable, but they are hardly sinister characters and the extent of their influence seems to have been to encourage the islanders to break away both from St. Kitts and Britain."

But that was all in the newspapers, not in the halls of Government.

The British Government made its first official response to the Whitlock ouster three days after it happened. In Barbados the Permanent Secretary of the Ministry of Overseas Development announced that Great Britain was scrapping all financial aid to Anguilla. What the *Trinidad Guardian* had in 1967 called "the most empty diplomatic threat in history" had now become a reality. Two months after British economic aid to Anguilla had stopped because of the end of the Interim Agreement, the British decided to stop all economic aid.

Unfortunately, the British Government was also making other decisions, less empty in their threatening aspect. As the weekend of March 15-16 approached, it became increasingly obvious from newspaper reports that the British were planning a military invasion of Anguilla. On Friday the fourteenth, Ronald Webster told his people the British were probably going to invade and said it would surely lead to bloodshed. "If they take our land they must take our life first," he told them, and said they should "be calm and do not despair, as God is with us through these troubled times."

Webster tried the same bluffing tactics against the British that had worked so well against Bradshaw. In an interview with *Daily Telegraph* reporter Ian Ball, he started talking again about his military preparedness. Ball writes:

> I questioned Mr. Webster at length about the weapons his "Anguillan defence force," a Home Guard type of army, had at its disposal. When I asked him exactly what firepower his regime could muster he threw his

arms wide in a gesture of mock surprise.

"Oh, please! ... How do you expect me to answer that? All I can say is that they are up-to-date weapons, very destructive."

Were they obtained legally? "They came in legally to me, yes. I can say they did not come from the States, but I cannot tell you the source."

I asked him what he would do if the British Government dispatched the frigate *Minerva*, 2,860 tons, now in Antigua a few hours' steaming distance away, to deal with his revolt.

He boasted that his Defence Force could handle "one British frigate. Two boats, I might have to resort to something else. But one frigate I can handle."

This fairy tale was believed by the British Government just as thoroughly as its predecessors had been believed by Bradshaw. The difference was that it didn't make the British change their minds about invading; it simply made them increase the size of their invasion force.

On Sunday the sixteenth, Webster tried another tactic to forestall the invasion. There were four Britons on the island—two nurses, a teacher and Canon Carleton, cofounder of the *Beacon*—and Webster informed them they would have to leave, temporarily. They would be welcome back, "as soon as the threat of an invasion is past," he said, and explained he was afraid the British Government would claim it had to invade Anguilla to protect its citizens there. To rob London of the excuse, he was asking the British citizens to go somewhere else until calm returned. Jack Holcomb typed the deportation orders.

That same Sunday, Jerry Gumbs went back to the United Nations, claimed that two British frigates were on their way to Anguilla, and asked the U.N. to intervene and help avoid bloodshed. A British "spokesman" denied that frigates were heading toward Anguilla, which was technically true. They weren't; not yet.

By Monday the seventeenth, the Anguillans were getting very nervous. Their tough-talking bluff had worked, but not the way they'd wanted it to; instead of scaring the British off, it had made them decide to get tougher.

It was St. Patrick's Day, but the Irish in the Anguillan blood wasn't being stirred at the thought of a donnybrook with the British.

Webster grew less talkative with reporters. He traveled everywhere with Jack Holcomb at his side and more often than not deferred to Holcomb to answer the questions put to him. Ian Ball once again defined Webster's mood: "I asked Webster whether his defence force would fight British paratroops and police and perhaps a naval and marine force. 'I am prepared,' he said somberly."

His preparations included moving a motorboat he owned, which had always been docked around on the north side of the island, over to Sandy Hill Bay, near his home, and hiding it there under some brush, so that if the British actually did invade, he and his family could escape to St. Martin. Unfortunately some Defence Force boys who lived in the area stumbled across the hidden motorboat, which they didn't recognize as belonging to this bay. Thinking it might have been left there by an assassin from St. Kitts, they took their rifle butts and smashed it to kindling. As it turned out, Webster didn't try to leave the island when the British landed, so it was several days before he discovered what had happened to his boat.

On Monday Jerry Gumbs showed up at the U.N. once more, and by now the bluff was almost completely out of him. He wanted the U.N. to stop the British from invading; he wanted it very badly. "It would be a mass murder—a bunch of gorillas rushing into an orphanage," he said. "Don't they know that if you use force you get murder, rape and kidnaping? They are going to go to this island of ours, which has no murder, no rapes, no crime at all, and murder our people." And, "Mr. Webster and I could sit down with Lord Caradon and sort out the whole situation with very little difficulty, if we were just given the chance."

But on the island itself there were those who wanted the British to invade. The guns had come out and they hadn't liked it; no matter how troubled they might be at the thought of invasion, uncontrolled juvenile delinquents troubled them even more. Cabdriver John Rogers told the *Daily Mail*, "I hope Britain will send in a force as soon as possible. And it must be a massive force, otherwise the defence force will resist." And Canon Carleton, before leaving the island, told Ivor Key of the *Sun*, "The only solution is for Britain to invade. Somewhere along the way, Webster has gone wrong, and, with American influence, he now wants complete independence. The whole trouble stems from when Holcomb came in July last year and now it seems the island is under his influence."

Ian Ball talks of meeting Wallace Rey and being shouted at, and adds, "The encounter with Mr. Rey in which pro and anti-rebel Anguillans standing nearby almost came to blows, was indicative of the brittle tensions on the island."

The situation on Anguilla was becoming more complex by the hour. Here was fragmentation with a vengeance. The range of opinion on the island now from David Lloyd through to Wallace Rey included someone who defended just about every possible shade. Men who had been rebel leaders for two years were now asking the British to invade. Ronald Webster was talking about "blood on the beaches" while the man who was supposedly representing him in New York, Jeremiah Gumbs, was claiming the whole mess could be resolved by a simple discussion with Lord Caradon. The brats on the Defence Force had stopped intimidating other people now that they had been intimidated themselves; reports were getting out that the Defence Force was losing membership.

On Tuesday the eighteenth, Webster made an about-face; the bluff wasn't doing what it was supposed to so he switched tactics. He called a news conference and said his people weren't going to fight after all. "There is no sense in making ourselves martyrs on the battlefield," he said. "We are not a bloodthirsty or trigger-happy lot. We are just defending our island for independence."

Perfectly reasonable. "I am willing to negotiate now," he said. "We could not withstand a heavy bombardment from warships. We could not expect to fight against trained men from Britain and I think the world would look down on Britain as a big baby if it tried to bully Anguilla back to St. Kitts."

Sweet reason now lights all the dark corners. The Webster change of mind didn't untangle the whole mess, but it did simplify things to the point where forward motion could be made again.

However, the British—the big baby—had already determined on a move that simplifies all situations, no matter how complicated. Nothing in this world strips away the complexities like a good rousing war.

23

Something may come of this. I hope it mayn't be human gore.
          —Charles Dickens, *Barnaby Rudge*

The frigate *Minerva*, 2,860 tons, steamed northward through the sultry night, approaching her rendezvous with destiny. At her side moved her sister ship in Great Britain's Royal Navy, the anti-submarine frigate *Rothesay*, 2,600 tons.

The date was March 19, 1969. Belowdecks within the two ships waited the sleepless troops, checking their weapons, their buttons, their cigarettes, covering their insignia with black tape. In addition to the twenty Royal Marines normally carried by each frigate there were now 315 Red Devils aboard, men of the Second Parachute Battalion of the Sixteenth Parachute Brigade of the Parachute Regiment. They would enter battle today not by parachute but by rubber boats.

All British paratroops are called Red Devils because they wear red berets. Or perhaps they wear red berets because they're called Red Devils.

These particular Red Devils were normally stationed in barracks at Aldershot, near London, but a group of them had been moved, day before yesterday, to transit barracks at Devizes. From Devizes yesterday morning, before dawn, they had been loaded onto four Army trucks on which all markings had been masked over with black tape. They still looked like Army trucks, but no one could be sure *which* Army trucks. They had been driven via roundabout country lanes to the troop-ferrying center at the airfield at Lyneham. Tight military security was maintained by floodlighting the airport and chasing reporters away with guard dogs and jeeps; taking a page from the St. Kitts Secrecy Manual, apparently. The troops boarded two transport planes of the Royal Air Force Support Command, one Britannia and one Hercules.

Meanwhile, their places back at Aldershot had been partially taken by some forty-odd London policemen from Scotland Yard's Special Patrol Group, commanded by Assistant Commissioner Andrew Way. Way had originally been an officer in the mounted police, but as his weight had risen above three hundred pounds it was thought best he not ride horses anymore. He and his forty constables, three sergeants, two inspectors and one superintendent had arrived at Aldershot the night before to be given kit bags and military clothing suitable for the tropics. Unfortunately they didn't have anything in Commissioner Way's size, so he had to go along in blue serge.

Now these policemen, plus the rest of the Red Devil invasion force, were also on the move. Riding in two private fifty-seat buses marked "Wilts & Dorset," they were driven at ostentatiously high speed to the RAF airfield at Brize Norton and on through the ostentatiously heavily guarded Gate Number 2. What later that day the London *Evening News* was to call "Britain's worst-kept security secret," what the military authorities had designated "Operation Sheepskin," had begun to unroll. (The tightness of the security can be judged by a headline in the London *Daily Express* a day and a half before the actual landing on the island: "*Invasion Plan:* FRIGATES TO LAND PARATROOPS AND LONDON BOBBIES ON ISLAND.")

Unfortunately, a slight hitch now developed; it was too foggy at both airfields for the planes to take off. The two at Lyneham and the five at Brize Norton, filled with Red Devils, London bobbies, guns, jeeps, leaflets, trucks, radios, bullets, medical supplies, clothing, forms to be filled out, parachutes, gasoline, loud-hailers and all, sat on the taxiways and waited for the fog to lift. When at last it did, so did they.

Ten hours later, the whole farrago landed again in Antigua. The Premier of Antigua was a man named Vere Bird, whose background was similar to Robert Bradshaw's—labor organizer, union leader, and now Premier with working-class backing. The British, stumbling around in the Caribbean like a—well, it *was* like a bull in a china shop—merely stopped off in Antigua on their way to "help" Robert Bradshaw but in so doing bumped into Vere Bird and helped knock him off his shelf. Most ordinary Antiguan citizens had taken the Anguillan side in the dispute and were annoyed with Bird for helping the British. Bird had been in political trouble anyway, but every little bit helps; in his next bid for re-election, he was defeated.

Having helped bump Bird, the troops and policemen and equipment traveled by truck from the airport to the deepwater harbor at St. John's, the Antiguan capital city. Along the way they passed unfriendly natives who shouted "Shame!" and political slogans, none of which made too much sense to the men in the trucks, who really didn't know what was going on. All they knew was what they read in the papers.

"There are about 6000 people on the island. Most of them are believed to have guns."

Minerva and *Rothesay* were waiting in the harbor, and the men and equipment boarded at once.

Now the two-frigate fleet, under the command of Commodore Martin N. Lucey, the Senior British Naval Officer for the West Indies (the same SNOWI to whom William Whitlock had written the week before), steamed north to do battle with an enemy so clever and shifty that nobody even knew exactly who he was. The enemy might be the Mafia, formerly Sicilian but more recently American, armed with machine guns, possibly in violin cases. Or the enemy might be the Black Panthers, also American in origin, armed with God alone knew what—possibly blackjacks. Or the enemy might simply be bloodthirsty Wogs indigenous to the Caribbean. Or all three, combined together.

The firepower of the rebels—who may have been joined by American gangsters and Black Panthers, the trigger-happy wing of the Black Power movement—is unknown.

London *Daily Mail* March 18, 1969.

But the firepower of the Red Devils was definitely known. They were armed with automatic rifles—Sterlings and Belgian-made SLR's—and machine guns. The frigates were armed with their naval guns and had a pair of Wessex helicopters. They also carried leaflets that they would drop on the island and that said, in part, "Our purpose is to end intimidation ..."

And they had, finally, their leader, Lieutenant Colonel Richard Dawnay, who had flown out to Antigua four days earlier, on the fifteenth, for a "reconnaissance and appreciation." After reconnoitering and appreciating from Antigua, 112 miles south of Anguilla, and after discussions with a few Englishmen, Lieutenant Colonel Dawnay worked up a tactical plan for the military operation and cabled it to London. The plan was modest at that stage, but somebody in London decided this was a good opportunity to give the boys of the Parachute Brigade some practice at military maneuvers. So the plan was blown up to make it possible for more of the troops to play.

The engorged plan had as its first objectives the cross-roads in the center of the island, the jetty area at Road Bay, the airport, and the road from Crocus Bay to Forest Point. Following the securing of these objectives, the plan called for the troops to disarm the local inhabitants of all ages, to detain known ringleaders, and to search the island for caches of arms.

At one point the plan had also included the presence of William Whitlock, by his own request. He canceled his appointments and got ready to leave, but when the word filtered upward about his intentions he was told to forget it. Stay home, stay home.

Now the plan was going into operation. *Minerva* and *Rothesay*, sailing north-northwest through the sultry night, steamed past the tiny sleeping Leeward Islands—Nevis and St. Kitts off to the left, Barbuda off to the right; then St. Eustatius and Saba to the left and St. Barthélémy to the right; then the U.S. Virgin Islands far away to the left and St. Martin close by on the right; and finally the Gunpoint Island itself, off the starboard bow.

The frigates steamed past the western tip of the island, turned right, and at last dropped anchor off the northwest coast, between Road Bay and Crocus Bay. Ahead, in the predawn darkness, stretched from left to right the low profile of Anguilla.

It was 5:16 A.M. when the troops landed. Paratroops and Marines from *Rothesay* touched ground at Crocus Bay, where the Anguillans had routed the first French invasion of their island in 1745. More paratroopers from *Minerva* landed at Road Bay, near the salt pond. The troops, ducking and weaving, dashed from the open boats across bare stretches of white beach, their automatic rifles held at the ready. They ducked behind bushes and upturned fishing boats before moving again, cautiously, into the interior. Meanwhile, Royal Navy helicopter R424 was landing four Red Devils inland at the all-important crossroads by the famous mahogany tree.

Aboard *Minerva* and *Rothesay*, gunnery control officers tensed as they saw sudden white lights streaming across the island in the darkness—automobile headlights moving toward the beachheads and the landing parties. The automobiles stopped. The gunners waited, hands gripping their gun mounts. Up on the bridge, Lieutenant Colonel Dawnay watched through binoculars. Suddenly on the beaches there was a barrage of flashes.

"I fear the worst," said Colonel Dawnay.

It was photographers' flashbulbs.

24

*'Twas brillig, and the slithy toves
Did gyre and gimble in the wabe;
All mimsy were the borogoves,
And the mome raths outgrabe.*
                    —Lewis Carroll, *Through the Looking-Glass*

"'Shotgun' Said The Sergeant ... [London *Evening Standard*, March 19, 1969]."

Ronald Webster was taking a bath when the troops landed. He didn't know about the invasion until a reporter went to his house to ask his reaction.

Most other Anguillans were still asleep. With all the security leaks in the British and American press about the oncoming invasion, the islanders had had plenty of time to reconsider the notion of having a war with Great Britain. So they had carried all their guns over to St. Martin and buried them. They're still there.

The troops were very nervous and jumpy. Later on it was going to be a joke, but right now they kept waiting for the war to start. As sleepy Anguillans emerged from their houses, troops carrying machine guns shoved them against walls, searched them, questioned them. Troops mounted machine guns on building roofs, made tense little comments back and forth on their walkie-talkies, and kept waiting for the goddamn war to start. They were here for a war, they were dressed for a war, they were primed for a war, they'd stayed up all night thinking about war. Where the hell was the war?

The boy, not more than 15, spun around a corner and his motor-cycle backfired.
    "Right—a shotgun: Get him," a sergeant shouted.
                    London *Daily Mail,* March 20, 1969

The British reporters were heartily disliked by both sides, though only yesterday everybody had thought they were nice fellows. But today here they were strolling around in shirts open at the neck, taking pictures, interviewing soldiers who were trying to keep their minds on the war, and generally making the troops self-conscious, which the troops didn't much care for. As to the Anguillans, they'd just been invaded by Great Britain; for the moment they didn't like *any* Englishmen.

The Randalls did. Vera Randall told a reporter, "I grabbed a flag and it was an American one, ran out with it and waved like mad and cheered the helicopters."

The Anguillan flag had been flying over the Administrative Building, but when the Red Devils captured the building—it was one of the high points in their tactical plan—they took it down. They were assisted in this by a cheerful young local citizen, very helpful; but when it turned out he was the prisoner still waiting to be tried for murder in the death of his girl friend, the troops shooed him back to his cell.

Lieutenant Colonel Dawnay and his troops commandeered some cars; that is, they took people's cars away from them. With these they were able to spread out more quickly and capture the entire island. They set up roadblocks and searched every car that came along without troops in it. When they asked one Anguillan, "Whose car is this?" he said, "Well, it's not the Queen's, that's for damn sure."

Cars containing reporters were also searched. The *Daily Mail's* Andrew McEwen wrote, "Troops stopped my car at cross-roads. 'Get out and sit down over there,' a sergeant ordered. Twenty minutes later, after having it searched, he let me return. 'We had to make sure there was not a bomb in it,' he said."

This seriousness was occasionally matched by the Anguillans. A woman came out of her house and watched a group of paratroopers walk by in the dawn light. Very indignant, she called, "Does the Queen know you're here?"

One loud BANG sent some of the paras leaping into defensive positions. It was only a backfire from the motor-cycle ridden by a smartly dressed schoolboy on his way to morning lessons.

There were no lessons at The Valley School that day. The paratroopers had taken it over as their supply dump and command post.

The helicopters had awakened most of the population by now, but there was nothing to do but stand around and admire the precision of the soldiers. Or not admire it; as one helicopter landed in a cloud of dust and a rush of wind and a roar of noise, a farmer said, "Look at all that filthy mess. It is going to upset my cow."

Evening Standard reporter Jean Campbell was in Ronald Webster's Park when a helicopter landed there and four Red Devils leaped out. She described what happened next.

Old William Harley from the Agricultural Station, with his yellow crash helmet on, stood gaping by his bicycle. "Miss, Miss, what manner, what class of people are these?"

I could not answer "Red Devils." So I grinned and said, "Friendly English soldiers, they are just practising."

"Uncle William," screamed a 16-year-old. "Why are they running toward us?" Uncle William shook his head. "I just cannot tell what class of people these are, son."

Four fresh-faced Red Devils from Beckenham, Nottingham and the North came rushing toward us. Silence.

"Good morning," I said hopefully as the young lieutenant arranged his machine gun. We looked a motley bunch, Old William with his bike and a little group of Anguillan teenagers.

Still there was silence.

"Are you from London?" I asked politely.

"Beckenham," came the answer with a broad grin. "But you can't have my name, not on your life."

And Ian Ball of the *Telegraph* reported a Scotland Yard inspector in blue wool uniform sweltering amid the troops, but he wouldn't give his name either.

Also sweltering in blue serge was Commissioner Way, another early arrival with the troops. Apparently he'd found some tropical wear to fit after all, because he explained his discomfort by saying, "I blame the Navy for this. They dropped my case with my light clothes in it out of one of their helicopters."

One sharp report sent the parachute troops leaping into defensive positions—until they found that it came from a backfiring motor cycle being
ridden by a young islander.

London *Times,* March 20, 1969

One American lady on the island told Jean Campbell, "Imagine
… I slept in my brassiere to be ready for this invasion. Never did
that before in my life."

Reporter Bill Bruns wrote, in *Life* magazine, "At a strategic
bend in the road one soldier had dug a foxhole, but the only creature
to challenge him was a cow grazing 20 feet away. His buddy sat
nearby cradling his rifle. I didn't see any ammunition clips, so I
asked him if his rifle was loaded. 'No, but don't tell anybody.'"

Thousands of leaflets were being dropped from helicopters
shushle-shushling back and forth. They were headed "Message to
the people of Anguilla from the British government," and they
started by telling the Anguillans they hadn't been very nice to Mr.
Whitlock. They then went on, in boldfaced lettering, "It is not our
purpose to force you to return to an Administration you do not
want."

But if the troops weren't there to force the Anguillans to do
something they didn't want to do, why were they there?

The leaflets attempted an explanation: "Our purpose is to end
intimidation so that you can live in peace and express your opinions
without fear." A purpose attained with machine guns.

The leaflets next said that Tony Lee was coming in with the
troops to be the Commissioner in charge of the island: "He comes as
your friend." But very few friends come visiting in quite that fashion.

Finally the leaflets requested cooperation, and ended with a
platitude: "The quicker law and order is restored, the sooner you can
resume a normal and peaceful life."

Before the invasion had started, it had been announced that
Colonel Dawnay had been given by the Foreign and Commonwealth Office a list of forty "baddies," to use the newspaper word,
who would be "rounded up" once the war had been won and the

island secured. The war was won and the island secured so fast that by six-thirty, an hour after the landings, SNOWI could cable London, "OPERATION SHEEPSKIN HAS BEEN A SUCCESS." (Actually it had been a failure, since it had given Anguilla everything it wanted.)

And the roundup began. The London *Times* reported, "Many of the people caught in the first roundup by troops were reporters and press photographers, already ashore to cover the landings." So they let the reporters and photographers go and started again.

By now, the official word was that there were only twenty names on the list of baddies, but of these only five names were ever made public, and they were all Americans: Jack Holcomb, Lewis Haskins, Raymond Haskins, Sherman Haskins, and the Reverend Freeman Goodge.

Reverend Goodge started his day in an irreverend manner, screaming at Andrew McEwen of the *Daily Mail*, "You British bastards. You are no reporter—you're a Scotland Yard man sent here to spy on us." He was shortly introduced to real Scotland Yard men, for comparison. Ten Red Devils went to his house and rounded up the Reverend Freeman Goodge and his wife and his three children. They searched the house, and Goodge later described it this way: "They went through the chicken coop, even searched my wife's underwear and went through a new Bible leaf by leaf." He was then taken away to be questioned by Scotland Yard men, but when it turned out he wasn't a Mafia chaplain they let him go.

One down out of the forty; or the twenty; or the five.

Lewis Haskins was arrested and questioned and his premises searched, but he too failed to live up to the advance billing and was released. His sons Raymond (20) and Sherman (22) had fled to St. Martin the night before.

Four down, leaving thirty-six; or sixteen; or one.

Jack Holcomb.

Holcomb had been staying at Jerry Gumbs's Rendezvous Hotel. That's where two Red Devils carrying automatic rifles picked him up. He was taken to the schoolhouse, now being used as invasion headquarters, where Detective Inspector Harry Nicholls of Scotland Yard greeted him with "Good morning, Mr. Holcomb. I am a police officer."

Holcomb was then taken out to the *Minerva* and questioned for two hours. The British had spent something over a million dollars to save the Anguillans from Mafia terrorism, and Jack Holcomb was their last possible hope to prove that the money hadn't been a total waste. Holcomb *looked* good. He was, in the first place, from Florida, and everybody knows that everybody from Florida is in the Mafia. He talked a lot about mysterious big-money backers, and everybody knows that mysterious big-money backers are always Mafia men with *dirty money* to invest. He had turned Ronald Webster against Britain—so unfairly, so unfairly—and why would he have done a thing like that unless he was in the Mafia?

After two hours Holcomb was returned to the island and deported. Nobody said anything about the Mafia. In fact, the British pretended they never had said anything about the Mafia. The deportation order gave no particulars, outlined no charges against Holcomb, made no specific points of any kind. No reasons were suggested other than that the British didn't like him, that they had to show *something* for their morning's work, and that he was unwelcome.

Holcomb asked permission to get his things from the hotel. He was told he could go, with military escort, but not in a military vehicle. He had to take a cab. They drove out to Rendezvous, Holcomb packed, and then he paid his bill. The last act of this conspirator in the great plot to take over Anguilla and run it by mobster fear was to write a check for his hotel bill and hand it to Jerry Gumbs's sister, Aunt B.

"Right—a shotgun: Get him," a sergeant shouted. Three Sterling sub-machineguns were pointed at the boy ...

London *Daily Mail*, March 20, 1969

Back home in London, a BBC announcer reported the invasion of Anguilla in a somewhat awed voice: "British troops have landed," he said. "It is a phrase we thought we would never hear again."

Only one shot was fired in the course of the invasion; appropriately enough, it was fired at reporters. A charter plane was bringing in a group of British correspondents, and when it came inadvertently close to a Hercules transport air-dropping equipment, a warning shot was fired in its direction. Other than that, it was a very peaceful war.

> British paratroops leaped to defensive positions as a sharp report rang out after they had landed on Anguilla. "Shotgun," shouted a sergeant. His men swung their guns round—to cover a sheepish young Anguillan riding up on a backfiring motorcycle.
>
> London *Evening Standard*, March 19, 1969

What if they had killed that boy?

25

*He had merely considered him a humbug in a Pick-
wickian point of view.*
        —Charles Dickens, *The Pickwick Papers*

The world's press was not kind. "WHAT A LAUGHING STOCK" was the headline on the London *Daily Mail*'s story announcing that the invasion was about to start. And on the very day of the land-ings, *The New York Times* was running an editorial titled "No Case for Invasion," which began, "Developments on Anguilla have been bizarre and baffling but they do not justify a British military seizure of the tiny eastern Caribbean island. Frigates loaded with paratroop-ers are en route to the island, but an outright order to invade would reflect no credit on British arms or judgment."

The London *Times,* under the heading "A CARIBBEAN TRAGI-COMEDY," wrote, "In the near future, perhaps today, we shall possi-bly be treated to the rather absurd spectacle of British paratroopers descending on the 'rebel' island of Anguilla, like a re-run of a jerky-film of colonial times." And continued, "What has happened so far has drifted from inattention to muddle and to farce; it should be pulled back from the brink of tragedy."

The next day *The New York Times* remarked, "The British lion has subdued the Anguillan mouse that roared, without spilling any blood. That is one of the few credit marks earned by any of the parties ..." And, "Skeptical outsiders will expect early evidence to support the notion that the real enemy here is some mafioso descen-dant of Captain Kidd."

Nabil Zaki, a columnist in Cairo's *Al-Akhbar,* called the inva-sion "a bloody comedy reminiscent of the age of gunboat diplo-macy," and the Nairobi *Daily Nation* said, "The prospect of British might deployed against the tiny Caribbean island of Anguilla is more than faintly ridiculous. The situation is a cartoonist's dream."

African newspapers generally compared the British reaction in Anguilla to the British reaction in Rhodesia, and were not amused. In Lagos, Nigeria, which has problems of its own, the *Daily Sketch* said, "Britain could be rightly accused of using double standards as long as it suits her interests to do so. Is the world now to understand that Britain is not opposed to the use of force so far as Anguilla is concerned, while it still insists that force cannot be used in the case of the Rhodesians?" And in Kampala, Uganda, *The People*, the ruling party's official newspaper, said, "When a handful of white racists in Rhodesia defied Britain and set up a racist regime to rule the black millions, Britain stepped aside like the toothless bulldog she was said to be."

Great Britain had after all been faced with just the two UDI's (shorthand for Unilateral Declaration of Independence, which in turn is longhand for revolt) in the nineteen-sixties, and they were Anguilla and Rhodesia. Comparisons were inevitable.

Other comparisons were more vicious. The Chicago *Tribune* observed, "British valor has, at one stroke, wiped out the stain of Dunkirk, Singapore and other debacles of British arms of recent memory."

"BRUTE FARCE AND IGNORANCE" was a headline in the London *Sunday Times*, and the London *Evening News* headlined its invasion story "THIS WAG THE FLAG AND FLOG THE WOG' FARCE." (In this story, by Stephen Claypole, reference was made to Whitlock's Mafia: "From the way Mr. Whitlock spoke I expected to find the island crawling with dark-jowled mobsters prowling the island with violin cases under their arms.")

Time magazine's headline on its invasion piece was "BRITAIN'S BAY OF PIGLETS," and *Newsweek*'s was 'THE LION THAT MEOWED."

New Statesman: "HIGH WIND IN ANGUILLA." *Spectator:* "WAR OF WHITLOCK'S EAR."

But this wasn't the only reaction. Like a man adjusting his tie in an avalanche, there were reporters prepared to behave as though Anguilla were simply another sensible action in a calm and rational world. Two days after the invasion, Charles Douglas-Home, Defence Correspondent for the London *Times*, wrote a piece on Anguilla from the standpoint of military medicine, titled "ACTIONS

THAT SAVE LIVES." In it he wrote, "Our natural relief at the blood-lessness of Operation Sheepskin might lead us to forget one of the most important officers in the Anguilla expedition—the medical officer. The fact that he has not had to tend battle wounds may be welcome both to him and to us, but there are many other most important aspects of his role in the operation which seldom receive recognition." The article then went blithely on to count the angels on the head of the pin.

The next day the London *Times* ran another editorial that counted angels in a different fashion. In closely packed and utterly impenetrable reasoning, it dealt with the legal justifications for the invasion, worrying them like *The People's* toothless bulldog gumming a bone. It began, "The Anguilla (Temporary Provision) Order 1969 is likely to be discussed in the House of Commons on Monday. There are indeed a number of points about its propriety and even its legality on which the Foreign Secretary will no doubt wish to offer elucidation."

The *Times* editorial also said such crystalline things as:

In law the Government are covered by the later clause 18 (1) which empowers the Secretary of State to issue a certificate saying that in the Government's opinion ... Yet when one looks at clause 3 ... though the question whether an Order in Council goes beyond the power of the original Act is one the Courts can consider ... Parliament must examine whether the order is not illegal, because ultra vires, as well as unjust, and should ask whether the original action of the Government was not also illegal as well as absurd.

But deadpan reportage reached its apex in the following item from the *Daily Telegraph* for March 20, the day after the invasion: "It seems most unlikely that any campaign medal will be issued for the operation in Anguilla."

26

The House of Peers, throughout the war,
Did nothing in particular,
And did it very well.

> —W. S. Gilbert, *Iolanthe*

And what of Parliament, through all this? What was going on in the House of Commons before, during and after the invasion?

Before. On March 18, Michael Stewart, the Secretary of State for Foreign and Commonwealth Affairs, was asked by various Conservative M.P.'s to tell the House what was going on, and explain these invasion rumors in the newspapers, and he said, "I shall be making a statement on Anguilla later this week." Since this was less than thirty-six hours before the invasion—a fact he didn't mention—it was a pretty safe bet he would be making a statement later that week, but a statement made *after* an invasion wasn't what his questioners had in mind.

M.P. Stanley Henig pointed this out the next day, the nineteenth, very few hours before the invasion: "It would be most unfortunate if Britain were involved in a military intervention overseas and the House of Commons would only be presented after the event with a *fait accompli.*"

Other M.P.'s, both Conservative and Labour, chimed in. Edward Heath said, "The House of Commons seems to be the last place to be informed about this." George Brown, a onetime Foreign Secretary himself, said, "I do not press the Foreign Secretary for a statement; he should be the judge of when he should make it. But will he take into account that both he and I over a period of some years have refused to resort to what we scornfully called 'gunboat diplomacy' in issues which had much more interest for Britain than this."

During. Stewart at last made his statement, in which he talked about what had happened to Whitlock. "After this reception, an armed minority decided that the proposals must not be further discussed with the people of the island."

Since nobody had been killed, and since nobody knew yet whether Stewart was telling the truth or not, the discussion mostly centered on the legality of the invasion. If St. Kitts-Nevis-Anguilla was an independent nation, hadn't the United Kingdom just invaded a friendly nation and muscled into that nation's civil war?

The Mafia was mentioned, and Stewart began to back-pedal from that one. "As to the use of the word 'Mafia,' I think this is an exaggerated term. I draw attention to the phrase which I used, 'disreputable characters.' They were disreputable characters, and had arms."

Conservative M.P. Nigel Birch asked Stewart, "Will you convey to the Prime Minister the congratulations of the House on at last taking on somebody of his own size?"

Stewart said a remark like that "illustrates the contrast between the greatness of the issues involved and the littleness of the right honorable Gentleman."

Another M.P. suggested that Prime Minister Harold Wilson was "a sheep in sheep's clothing."

It was left to George Brown to mention Rhodesia, indirectly, as he'd done the day before. Today he said, "How are we, on the basis of the arguments you seem to use today, going at the United Nations to answer those who demand that we should do exactly the same on exactly the same grounds elsewhere?"

To which Stewart replied, "Whenever you consider the use of armed force, you consider what the results of it would be. An attempt to try to solve the Rhodesia question by force would have resulted in such a destruction of life and wealth, and such bitterness throughout Africa, that the end we all want in Rhodesia of a just regime for men of all colors would have been indefinitely postponed."

To which Brown replied, "Are we going to say we can do it where there is only a rusty gun?"

After. The tone the House would take, once its surprise and relief were over and the Members had time to think about things, was pretty well established by Mr. Goodhart, Conservative for Beckenham, who said on the twenty-first, as reported in the London *Times,* that "all M.P.'s were anxious that British forces on Anguilla should draw every penny to which they were entitled. There was, for instance, two shillings six pence a day payable for other ranks for Arctic or tropical experiments. Clearly the Anguilla expedition was a tropical one and in the nature of an experiment. He suspected the lesson to be drawn from it was that it was far less expensive in blood and treasure to invade one's friends than to get into serious conflict with one's enemies. Would the troops on Anguilla be entitled to an entertainment allowance?"

On the twenty-fourth, nearly a week after the invasion, Anguilla was shoehorned into a debate on the general subject of British foreign policy. The M.P.'s began by questioning Whitlock about his experiences, and not showing much sympathy for him. Mr. Martin: "What evidence has the honorable Gentleman actually adduced which has been corroborated by other sources of these undesirable elements before sending over two hundred parachutists to deal with them?" Mr. Rose: "Will my honorable Friend in due course give an undertaking to let the House have full details of these Mafia-like elements in Anguilla ...?"

Whitlock: "There will be a debate on foreign affairs at a later stage today, and no doubt all those points will come out during the debate."

Edward Heath, Opposition Leader, said, "So far, however much we may have disagreed with some aspects of policy or the implementation of policy, they can be fitted into a pattern, but I think the imagination boggles at the task of doing that with the recent operation in Anguilla." He then proceeded to raise six questions about the handling of the Anguilla affair, covering the past, the present and the future. Stewart replied with a quick gloss on the past, a spirited defense of the present, and a promise of joy and contentment and universal understanding in the future.

Several M.P.'s felt there were more questions to ask. They included Sir Dingle Foot, the brother of Lord Caradon (Hugh Foot) and uncle of *Private Eye*'s Paul Foot. Sir Dingle Foot spent most of his time arguing against federations—no two Foots seem to have the same attitude about things—and concluded with a suggestion that a Commission of Inquiry be put to work to sort the whole mess out.

Mr. John Hynd spoke mostly about the imperfections of associated statehood, and said, among other things, "This problem is one of the many Imperial chickens coming home to roost."

Sir Cyril Osborne followed Hynd and said, "In the earlier part of the rather long speech of the hon. Member for Sheffield, Attercliffe (Mr. John Hynd)—"

"It was no longer than any of the others," Hynd said.

Sir Cyril Osborne: "It lasted twenty-five minutes."

Sir Cyril wanted to talk about Rhodesia and other matters. The debate ranged around the world for a while, to be brought back to Anguilla by Viscount Lambton, who said, "I think it is worth digressing for a moment upon the personality of Mr. Bradshaw. This, again, is something which has been ignored. When I saw this Prime Minister he struck me as being a man who was in very bad health indeed, to put it mildly. He had the strangest delusions: he always supposed he was about to be poisoned. He dressed up in fancy dress clothes; he parades around the island; and he is served by men who really are not fit to be in any Government in any country in the world."

The House of Commons would get the range better a little later, but in this first long debate little was accomplished. In fact, the whole day was best summed up early on, in the middle of Mr. Heath's opening statement:

MR. HEATH: There was no sign of the Government's endeavoring to tackle what they must have realized to be very fundamental difficulties in the relationships between Anguilla and St. Kitts.

MR. ROY ROEBUCK (Harrow, East): On a point of order. Is it in order for the hon. Member for Walsall, South (Sir H. d'Avigdor-Goldsmid) to be asleep during the speech by the right hon. Gentleman his leader?

MR. DEPUTY-SPEAKER: That is a frivolous point of order.

27

Every hero becomes a bore at last.
— Ralph Waldo Emerson,
Representative Men

The war is over. Anguilla won, in the first second of play, but it took the British two years to fall down. They had more mistakes to make first.

Beginning with Tony Lee. He knew from early in the Interim Agreement Year that nothing would ever reattach Anguilla to St. Kitts, yet he failed to communicate this awareness to his superiors. Perhaps nobody could have broken through their complacence and their obtuse determination to live theoretically, but the point is that Tony Lee didn't.

When the Interim Agreement Year ended, Ronald Webster desperately wanted the connection with Great Britain to be kept alive somehow, as long as it could be done without it seeming to his people that he'd sold out. Tony Lee knew that and must have told his superiors so, but not in any way that made them listen or understand.

When Whitlock arrived on the island in March, Tony Lee had been there for two days. He knew about the motorcade-and-lunch arrangements Ronald Webster had made. There is no question of that, because *Lee* had made no other arrangements for either transport or lunch.

A great muffled silence seems to hang around Tony Lee, through which messages have a great deal of trouble traveling. It begins to seem he is simply a man who doesn't want to disturb his bosses. He will tell them what he knows, but quietly, without a great deal of emphasis, and if they fail to act on what he has told them, he seems to let it go at that.

But the largest blunder involving Tony Lee is yet to come.

The troops had invaded before five-thirty in the morning; by eight o'clock, Tony Lee was on the island. Had he come in two or three days later, he would have been the islanders' old friend, come to rescue them from the paratroops. But coming in *with* the paratroops, and with his name on the leaflets fluttering down from the helicopters, he became—permanently and forever—the Anguillans' enemy.

Ronald Webster told reporters, "I don't trust Mr. Lee. I no longer trust the British." As usual, what he said reflected the feelings of the people of the island.

Ronald Webster is not really a leader. In a way, he is the ultimate follower. He senses which way the majority of the people are going and then gets out front and shouts, "Follow me!" He may be the world's first hesitant fanatic.

Webster had liked and admired Tony Lee for a year and a half, but the British bungled with Lee, and the people of Anguilla turned against him. So Webster turned against him.

Jean Campbell of the London *Evening Standard* reported this remark by an Anguillan named Charlie Gumbs, referring to the Whitlock visit: "Of course, we blame Tony Lee for all this, for he knew the island and was supposed to understand our feelings. Whitlock was a stranger."

In the spring of 1971 I talked with Ronald Webster. I mentioned the number of people whose careers or reputations had been damaged in the four years of the rebellion. Neither of us named any names, but Webster said, "Oh, yes," and explained to me that there had always been a plan, every step through this maze had been part of the same master plan, and that some people had been useful in the plan only up to a point. When they began to steer a course away from the plan, he explained, "We had to put them to one side." Seated in a chair, he gestured down and back with both hands, as though pushing a bag of laundry around behind him. "To one side, you see," he said.

Of course the British had the same thing in mind for Webster. He would be treated as a "prominent citizen," no more. As Foreign Secretary Michael Stewart told the House of Commons, "We cannot, of course, treat him as the president of an independent Republic of Anguilla ... we can treat him as one would any other Anguillan."

As Whitlock, for instance, had treated him.

When Tony Lee arrived on the island two and a half hours after the troops had landed, the job he had been given by his superiors was to supplant Webster. Apparently, at the time, he thought it was possible.

While Lee was setting up a temporary headquarters in the schoolhouse, Webster was holding a press conference, telling reporters, "I had ordered the Defence Force not to resist. But we will not surrender. We will not accept Mr. Lee unless the people decide they will have him." Very few leaders with no army behind them and with their entire nation occupied by foreign troops would have the brass to announce, "We will not surrender."

Ronald Webster has no previous political experience and very little experience of the outside world. His own speaking manner is stiff and awkward, and he tends to listen with perhaps too much naïve confidence to people who speak more fluently than he. He contradicted himself dozens of times in those four years, partly because of the contradictory shifts of mass opinion and partly because of his tendency to move on the basis of whomever he has talked to last. Senior British diplomats were complaining after a while that they had never had to deal with so erratic a personality in their lives.

Webster himself sees no contradictions in his performance. He started out with certain objectives in view, he never doubted he would win them, and eventually he won them. In the spring of 1971, with no consciousness of the extravagance of the statement, Ronald Webster seriously told me that he had never been wrong.

Most Anguillans agree with him. In the symbolic family surrounding the Anguilla affair, in which Bradshaw is the stern father (Papa Bradshaw, run you run) and Great Britain the neglectful mother (Seeking the choice of Mother's care), Ronald Webster is not exactly a member of the family; he's the family priest. He moves always with the assurance that God has judged his plans and found them good. And when Tony Lee landed at Wall Blake Airport on Anguilla in the wake of the paratroops, one of the signs being held by the inevitable crowd of demonstrators read, "God first, R Webster after."

Lee, naturally, now assumes the inadvertent role of Pontius Pilate. Originally, he had been Senior British Official and his role was to advise the Island Council led by Webster. Now, he was to be Commissioner and the Island Council was to advise *him*. In fact, it would be called the Advisory Council.

Since Lee isn't the sort of man to throw his weight around, this technical shift in power wouldn't have changed much, but British officialdom decided to go farther. Apparently they had the idea that Webster should be punished for what had been done to Whitlock. So Lee, in addition to being Commissioner, would be Chairman of the Advisory Council. In other words, he was to take Webster's job as well as his own.

Webster, unsurprisingly, told him to go to hell. He announced to his people that he had been deposed and they rallied round him at once.

Way back in 1967, on Statehood Day, there had been an anti-independence demonstration in which a small coffin draped in black had been carried around the island bearing a sign saying "Anguilla Is Dead." Now that same coffin was brought out by the same demonstrators, but with a new sign: "If Lee Don't Go Anguilla Dead."

The invasion had come on Wednesday. On that same day Webster and Lee had a couple of cool meetings. Pro-Webster demonstrators accompanied Lee wherever he went. By Thursday, Webster knew he still had a majority with him so he announced it was impossible to negotiate with Lee. In fact, he said, it was impossible to negotiate with *any* Englishman until the troops left. Then, on Friday, Webster fled the island.

The flight had clear Biblical and symbolic overtones. It was also good public relations; it's impossible to have a triumphal return unless it's preceded by a flight. In addition, at the time, Webster thought there were also more practical reasons for escape, since he believed he was about to be arrested.

Two things had led him to this impression. The first was a London *Times* report that "Britain was determined not to negotiate with Mr. Webster." It went on: "What is more, sources close to both Mr. Kerr and Mr. Cecil Greatorex, another senior British official in the area, said that every effort will be made to discredit Mr. Webster in the eyes of his people."

Just after reading that, Webster was told Commissioner Way

was looking for him. He didn't wait to find out what Way wanted. In fact nobody seems to know what Way wanted.

Webster spent six days in the wilderness of Manhattan. During that time the Anguillans never ceased to bedevil Tony Lee. When he tried to enter his office on the day after Webster's flight, a crowd of demonstrators blocked his path. *The New York Times* reported:

> Several hundred angry Anguillans prevented the British Commissioner, Anthony Lee, from entering his office here today ... The tall phlegmatic representative of the British Crown beat a quick retreat after receiving several blows. But he refused to force the issue ... This morning, about 400 persons gathered in front of the building with signs demanding that Mr. Lee leave the island ... Although warned of the crowd, Mr. Lee appeared an hour later in a green Volkswagen. The only security forces present were unarmed London policemen who could not prevent the crowd from surrounding the car.
>
> Mr. Lee received some roughing up, but was uninjured. His car, however, was dented on the hood and roof. Two policemen received slight injuries. One was hurt in the hand when he attempted to wrest a bicycle pump from a woman who was beating him with it.
>
> Mr. Lee went back to his little white house overlooking the sea ... He acknowledged that the situation had deteriorated. Asked what he would do if the situation did not calm down, Mr. Lee answered, "That of course is the obvious question."

Another obvious question, considering Lee's background with the island and the events of the preceding three days, was how he could go on to what he said next: "Mr. Lee insisted that the demonstrators did not represent majority opinion on the island and that they had been goaded into action by a small group with extreme views."

By Monday, Lee was getting snappish. Ronald Webster and Jerry Gumbs had been getting a great deal of publicity and sympathy at the United Nations, and on Monday Ronald Webster became the second Anguillan in history to be "Man in the News" in *The New York Times.* The same paper also reported that back on Anguilla, "Mr. Lee said he had seen 'with my own eyes' young men going around exhorting people to demonstrate against him. He described them as hoodlums."

And the same paper quoted a "vehement" young Anguillan woman as saying, of Tony Lee, "He just has to go. We won't eat him or shoot him. We have nothing to shoot him with."

In New York, Ronald Webster was saying, "We are depending on the United Nations as a young child on its mother."

The next day, Tuesday, Lee took a page from Ronald Webster's book and reversed his field. "I consider Mr. Webster has done a great service for Anguilla," he announced. "He has put the island on the map. He has given Anguillans dignity. If people make enough noise something will happen."

Much will happen. Suddenly Lord Caradon announced that he would go to Anguilla at once to "make an assessment of the situation."

"I'm sure he will help us," Ronald Webster said.

Lord Caradon later described his involvement with Anguilla to me this way: "I'm the only Permanent Representative of the United Nations who is not an ambassador. I am a Minister of my Government, so I can go in that capacity. So I went down there, and we had a couple of noisy days, and wrote out an agreement together after a long discussion. And it was a perfectly sound agreement, the terms of it are well known, and it's been an agreement which has in fact been worked since then. What's the answer? That we should—the British and the Anguillans should—work together; why not? And we want a period of constructive cooperation. Oh, yeah? Okay. Well, then it went bad a bit after that, because very shortly after that Mr. Ronald Webster denounced the agreement. I had to go down a third time and we had these discussions with him and his remarkable gathering of his committee, all of them men of outstanding—character. And we had worked out together over these three meetings, as far as I'm concerned, an understanding. That's all."

Actually, it was a bit more complicated than that. But Lord Caradon's skill is to smooth complications, which is why he was the one going down there in the first place. He told me, "The great quality of the West Indians whom I know—I'm more of a West Indian than an Englishman really, I spent about ten years of my life in Jamaica, I was there as what they call Colonial Secretary, acted as Governor, then went back for seven years as Governor of Jamaica—the great quality of the West Indians is their individuality. You sit down with those fifteen or twenty members of that committee, every one of them is a highly developed personality. Each different. There's no uniformity amongst these chaps. They've got a fascinating capacity to express themselves. I fell in love with the people of Anguilla. I do it naturally, because I fell in love with any West Indians."

It *still* wasn't quite that simple. "Well, they had one bad time when I was there," he told me, "when they were rioting, when I was there. But it was accident as much as anything else."

The day before Lord Caradon arrived on the island, on Thursday the twenty-seventh, Tony Lee came up even with Ronald Webster again; he too was "Man in the News." The report began, "Perhaps the most nonchalant man on the island of Anguilla these days is the man most under attack." The story called him "calm, matter of fact and good-humored," "convivial and informal," and "extremely moderate." However, the flavor of his anti-dynamism showed clearly in this passage:

Mr. Lee admits to feeling uncomfortable about the military display Britain put on for his latest return. When asked why it was done, he answered laconically, "To install me, I suppose."

His nonchalant, muddling-through, almost flippant air comes through in other answers to newsmen's questions. Asked about a letter from Mr. Webster ... demanding an immediate referendum, he answered, "I really haven't read it carefully." Asked to explain parts of the stringent local regulations, just issued, that give him sweeping powers, he had difficulty making precise references to them. "I really naven't done my homework," he explained.

The "stringent regulations" were defined more stringently by the London *Times*. A paper not given to overstatement, it ran this headine: "DICTATOR ROLE FOR LEE."

But if anybody is miscast in the role of dictator, it is Tony Lee. The regulations did put him in about the same position in Anguilla that Douglas MacArthur had in Japan in the late forties, but Tony Lee is not a man to throw his weight around. And anyhow he hadn't done his homework and didn't know what his powers were.

Nevertheless, the London *Times* pointed out that the Order in Council that had installed Tony Lee as Commissioner "goes a very long way to putting the Commissioner outside the law altogether. What has he in fact done so far? He has introduced several hundred soldiers to the island, together with two score policemen. He has instructed or permitted security officers to arrest, hold and interrogate, apparently without warrant, citizens of the Federation and citizens of the United States. He has used powers of expulsion. He has instructed or permitted a general search for arms, with all the patting of buttocks and covering with guns which such searches involve."

But of course Tony Lee hadn't done any of that, had he? *Tony Lee* didn't mount an invasion involving three hundred fifteen paratroops, forty Marines, four helicopters, two warships, seven transport planes and forty-nine London policemen; but Tony Lee was responsible. And *Tony Lee* certainly didn't pat any buttocks; but Tony Lee was responsible.

Lee very early had tried to limit his responsibility to things he had some control over. When a reporter asked him where all the Mafiosi were, Lee replied, "Are you asking me to substantiate something someone else said?"

But it was too late to protect himself. Lee had been shoved into the pit with the alligators, and it was only a question of time till they noticed him. Being very quiet might help delay things, but it wouldn't alter them.

For instance. During one of the scuffles that marked Lee's first week on the island, an Anguillan woman complained to reporters that she'd stuck her arm in Lee's car and Lee had bitten her. Among those who heard that story on the radio was Lee's wife, Thelma, waiting on the nearby island of Antigua for Anguilla to quiet down enough to permit her to join her husband. "How silly," she thought. "Now they're saying Tony's biting people." That evening at dinner with friends, the subject of Tony's biting people came up. The hostess said, "You know, I've been thinking about that, and what I think must have happened was, Tony was probably saying something to somebody and this woman stuck her arm in the car, and her hand just went in his mouth." Thelma Lee told me about this much later, and even then her laugh was still uneasy. "Until that moment," she said, "it never occurred to me anybody would *believe* Tony was biting people. But she *knew* Tony, and she was an educated intelligent woman, and she was trying to find explanations for how it had happened."

It was coming at Lee from every side by now. The London *Times* was calling him a dictator, *The New York Times* was calling him laconic, Anguillans were parading around with a coffin with his name on it, the London *Times* was saying he was responsible for people's buttocks being patted, an Anguillan woman was saying he bit her on the arm, and Jack Holcomb claimed Lee had asked him for a job.

"Tony Lee asked me for a job last year," Holcomb was quoted in the *Evening Standard* of March 22. "He said he felt his work would be done by this January and as he would like to stay on in Anguilla after they became independent, he would have liked the chance to manage my proposed basic-materials industry."

Tony Lee had argued against Holcomb and his basic materials on Holcomb's first visit in 1968. He had enough experience in the Foreign Service to know how much of a mess would be created if he asked for a job in private industry while still in Government employ and while his Government job was having an effect on that particular private industry. He and Jack Holcomb had disliked each other from the minute they'd first met. Holcomb was enraged by the very thought of Lee when he arrived in the States, having been deported in an order signed by Lee. (It was Holcomb, remember, who had typed the orders deporting the four British citizens the week before.)

What I think must have happened was, Lee was probably saying something to somebody and Jack Holcomb stuck his arm in the car . . .

Webster arrived home on Anguilla on Thursday, the twenty-seventh of March, 1969. The invasion was a week old and the protests were beginning to wane. Like most people, Anguillans prefer to live their own lives. They had done all they could about the British, so now they returned to their own concerns. Only two hundred of them showed up to greet Webster at the airport. Nothing terrible had been done to the Anguillans by the British in the week since the invasion, so passions had cooled.

Webster announced to the little crowd that Lord Caradon was

coming to the island the next day, as "my guest," and that negotiations would start then, but no real negotiating could be done until the British soldiers left. "We cannot negotiate looking down the barrels of guns."

When Lord Caradon did arrive, the political split in Anguilla was reflected for the first time in a demonstration. The usual five hundred demonstrators with their signs greeted Lord Caradon at the airport, but this time they formed two opposing factions, one pro-British and one anti. Four hundred fifty anti and fifty pro. The antis almost all carried posters declaring their support of Ronald Webster. The pros, who included Peter Adams, supported Great Britain rather than Tony Lee.

Lord Caradon began by buttering his hosts. "I should be sitting in the Security Council on the Middle East, but I'd much rather be here," he said. He also promised "talk, talk and more talk until we get this thing sorted out."

The talks took three days, during which Lord Caradon showed himself as agile at recognizing public opinion as Ronald Webster. He tacitly accepted Webster as the island's leader and for most of the talks Tony Lee wasn't invited to attend.

In the end, Lord Caradon and Ronald Webster published a joint declaration, which described how the island would be governed for the next period of time, though it later turned out Webster hadn't understood it: "The administration of the island shall be conducted by Her Majesty's representative in full consultation and cooperation with representatives of the people of Anguilla. The members of the 1968 Council will be recognised as elected representatives of the people and will serve as members of a Council to be set up for the above purposes."

Her Majesty's representative would be boss. That was the part Ronald Webster didn't understand.

Webster told his people, "Today is a happy day for Anguilla. Anguilla and Britain are working side by side. Now that Britain is willing to work with us, let us forget quarrels and work together for the target."

The London *Times* said, "Anguilla's national revolution appeared to have petered out today in a web of peaceable vagueness spun by Lord Caradon."

Seeing Lord Caradon off at the airport, Ronald Webster gave him an Anguillan flag.

The next day, the *Beacon* reappeared. This first post-invasion issue said, "At this point we feel that all the past differences that caused a split among the people of Anguilla should be forgotten," though editor Harrigan apparently hadn't forgotten them, since his paper also said, "The intervention of the British at this stage is well welcomed, though a bit late, and we hate to comment on the way in which they became involved as we cannot totally agree that all was well in Anguilla at the time."

The *Beacon* also included a letter to Lord Caradon from Ronald Webster that said, "We would like to confirm some things we told you but which you asked to be excluded from the Declaration we signed yesterday." It made it clear that Webster still thought he was running things.

This was going to cause trouble, but not yet. The immediate trouble would be caused by something else in the *Beacon* of the same date.

This was twelve days after the invasion. The situation had altered heavily in those twelve days, but the "dictator" regulations were still in force and this was the *Beacon*'s first opportunity to announce them. Which, of course, it had to do.

> Mr. Tony Lee, Her Majesty's Commissioner in Anguilla, has put into effect as from 19th March 1969, two regulations for the island. Regulation No. 1 gives any member of the Police, or of Her Majesty's Naval, Military or Air Force, the power to enter and search premises and make arrests without warrants. It also allows them to search and control persons, control arms, weapons and explosives. Appropriating and requisitioning of property, to deport undesirable aliens, restriction of planes and boats from calling at any unrecognized port. And it also imposes penalties for violators. Regulation No. 2 sets out the powers of the Anguilla Police Unit, and makes provision for a Chief Immigration Officer.

The timing of this announcement was, well, Anguillan. The island had been living under the regulations for nearly two weeks, but since the day of the invasion itself there had been none of the searching and appropriating and deporting and restricting they allowed. When the Anguillans saw the notice in the same issue of the *Beacon* as the agreement signed with Lord Caradon, they thought these regulations were about to start *now*. There was trouble.

But not immediately. It took a few days for the impact to be felt. In the meantime, Ronald Webster found out what had actually been on Lord Caradon's mind when they'd signed that Declaration in perfect mutual understanding. He found out at the first meeting between Tony Lee and the Island Council.

What happened that day was best described by the *Spectator:* "It now appears that Mr. Ronald Webster has been upset because the British commissioner, Mr. Tony Lee, insisted upon taking the chair at the first council meeting of the new regime. Mr. Webster thought that he ought to be the chairman ... It is embarrassing to think that the British Empire has dwindled to this—a nursery struggle with a thin-skinned island politician for the best chair."

Webster now made another dash from the island. It wasn't musical chairs he complained about though, but the regulations announced in the *Beacon.* He went to Puerto Rico and claimed that Tony Lee had declared martial law *after* the Lord Caradon visit. He also charged that Lee had dissolved the Council and had increased the number of British troops on the island.

The dissolving of the Council, when the dust settled, turned out to be the game of musical chairs. (The "Island Council," of which Webster had been Chairman, had been turned into an "Advisory Council" with the exact same membership, but without a chairman.) As to the increase in British troops, the Red Devils were in the process of being withdrawn, a few at a time, while Army engineers were coming in to start some development work.

"I don't care if they do call themselves engineers," Webster said. "The British are taking out ten men and returning fifteen armed men."

In London, Sir Con O'Neill, former Deputy Under-Secretary of State in the Foreign Office, was saying on the BBC, "Anguilla? Well, I don't know much about it. It has hardly involved diplomacy."

From Puerto Rico, Webster went on to New York to confront Lord Caradon, who agreed to go back to Anguilla later that week. But before he got there, things on the island took—incredible though it may seem—a turn for the worse.

The British suddenly decided to deport Dr. Spector, since he was an osteopath and osteopathy is not an adequate medical credential under British law. Why the British decided to throw a burning stick on that particular sheet of gunpowder at that particular moment defies, like everything else in British behavior toward Anguilla, rational analysis.

It was also defied by the Anguillans. They met Dr. Spector and his deporters at the airport, took the doctor away with them, and hid him elsewhere on the island. This was not done without scuffling, and during the scuffle Commissioner Way knocked a microphone out of the hand of BBC correspondent Barry Sayles and ordered *him* to leave the island. Sayles declined and lodged a formal complaint against Commissioner Way. So now everybody was fighting with everybody.

Webster returned to the island on April 10 and arrived in the middle of yet another blowup. The British had brought in a magistrate to get the courts moving again, and the magistrate they brought in was—inevitably, I suppose—a Kittitian. His connection was with the judiciary of the Associated States and not with the St. Kitts Government, but it was another of those subtleties hard for the Anguillan eye to see.

When the magistrate showed up at court, there was more scuffling. Detective Inspector Harry Nicholls, he who had greeted Jack Holcomb, was hit in the head with a brick. The five defendants in the minor cases that were supposed to be tried that day were hustled away by the crowd, which also nailed the courthouse door shut. There were no legal proceedings that day.

Later the same day, Dr. Spector quietly left the island of his own accord.

The anti-Lee tone of the demonstrations was building up again. Lee had been put in charge of the island, he and Webster had clashed head on, and everything that happened was seen to be Lee's responsibility. The clamor to be rid of him was building and building. Lee told a reporter, "It's personal. They are after me for personal reasons."

They were also, like the British, fighting among themselves. One of the strongest pro-British Anguillans was Walter Hodge, first Chairman of the Peacekeeping Committee and still the island's Treasurer; twice crowds tried to beat him up and Webster had to step in and protect him. But Webster's control was slipping again; even a messiah can't keep the Anguillans in check forever.

Which everybody discovered the next day, when Lord Caradon arrived and the crowd wouldn't let Webster talk to him. The people had come to the conclusion it was impossible for an Anguillan leader to talk to the British without being either conned or sold out. So they took upon themselves the simple solution of keeping their leader from talking to the British. Lord Caradon went to the Administrative Building on the island, but when Webster tried to go in and meet him the crowd wouldn't let him do it. Instead, they surrounded the building and chanted, "Lee must go. Lee must go." Finally police and troops managed to get Webster through the crowd, and he met briefly with Lord Caradon. Webster told Lord Caradon that Lee really did have to go. Lord Caradon said, "It's impossible to have talks in a situation like this."

The snarl in the situation was not the crowd, though, or even Tony Lee. It was Ronald Webster's lack of understanding of the diplomatic meaning of the word "understanding." Once again, as in Barbados, as with Fisher and Chapman, as with every British diplomat who'd ever tried to deal with Anguilla, diplomacy looked very much like the practice that when done in conjunction with selling a used car is called fraud. The British hand had once again been quicker than Ronald Webster's eye, but Webster doesn't take it like a good sport when he finds he's just been razzle-dazzled. He gets angry, he digs his heels in, he refuses to go along. As he said at one point, in what must be the most deeply felt remark of the whole affair, "You can't fathom British diplomacy. They use it to hit you."

Webster, like the crowd, deals in simpler things. Such as that Lee must go.

The crowd was very strongly out to make this point to Lord Caradon. Having so far prevented Webster from meeting with him, the crowd then got into cars and trucks and headed east out the road to Tony Lee's house at Sandy Ground. Lee was home, guarded by one policeman. More than two hundred people showed up to chant "Lee must go" and shake their fists. A few of them grappled with the policeman, knocked him down, cut his forehead by hitting him with a stick, and bit him. Possibly that was done in retaliation by the woman bitten by Tony Lee.

The policeman broke free and ran up the stairs to the front door of the house, where he pulled out a revolver; up till this point, the publicity had been full of "unarmed" London policemen taking the places of the armed paratroopers, but this particular policeman, Constable Jack Gooday of Essex, had a gun on him It's probably just as well he did.

Constable Gooday and his pistol held off the crowd until Marines were landed twenty minutes later from H.M.S. *Rhyl*, another frigate.

The people had spoken; so did Webster. "The British representative must go, the troops must go, the regulations must go, the police must go and Lee must go."

Lord Caradon at last responded. On the thirteenth, before departing once more, he announced that Lee would shortly be going on "leave"—"well-deserved leave," as he inevitably put it—and his place would be taken temporarily by John Cumber, a career Foreign Office administrator.

Nobody believed it was temporary. Even Lord Caradon didn't work very hard to make anybody believe it. But in London, Michael Stewart muddied the waters again by saying, "Mr. Lee has not been fired. He will shortly be going on leave, during which time his place will be taken by a deputy. But after his leave he will be returning to Anguilla."

Lee's response to this, when reporters asked him what he thought about the idea that he'd be coming back after his leave, was typical: "It's news to me." So was Webster's: "It won't work."

But Webster wasn't pleased about John Cumber either: "There's no difference between them." But in the end he said he'd try to cooperate with him. "I don't want to embarrass Her Majesty's Government too much because we may have to depend on these same troops one day," he said.

He also said the demonstrations on the island were getting too violent and he thought it time to calm everybody down and try to make peace between the different factions of Anguillans. It was the kind of sudden switch the British had come to expect from Webster, except that it was rare for the switch to be in a direction they could be pleased about.

On the fourteenth of April, Adam Raphael made this report in the *Guardian*:

> Low comedy made a welcome return to Anguilla today when the British authorities tried for the fourth time to hold a magistrate's court. Most of the world's press was in attendance, filling the rock-hard benches of the island's tiny courtroom, but as none of the defendants bothered to turn up once again the proceedings were short.
>
> After Sergeant Ryan ... boomed out the names of the defendants ... the magistrate, Mr. Roderick Donaldson, on loan from St. Vincent, strode into court dressed in a small black ceremonial vest ... The press stood, the magistrate nodded his appreciation, and he then strode out again.
>
> There begins to be something almost uncanny about the manner in which nothing goes right with our Caribbean adventure. The lesson that good intentions are not enough in these matters has never been more plainly made. It is hard even to laugh at this week's mess-up over the future of the wretched Mr. Tony Lee: it is farcical, yes, but shaming too. It's bad enough being confused about the identity of the supposed Mafia agents and about whether our intervention was meant to bring down Mr. Webster or support him; but to slither into public disagreement over the future of our own man is really a bit too much.

And on Anguilla, Webster was actually making efforts to lead his people—not with total success. After he'd made a strong plea for people to calm down and stop demonstrating—explaining to them that the troops surely wouldn't leave until the threat of violence had ended—a group of youngsters surrounded a nearby police car and tried to overturn it.

Still, the shouting at Tony Lee died down, and Webster even had friendly meetings with Cumber and Lee both present. The Anguillans had what they wanted and were just beginning to realize it. They had wanted to be a colony, and that's what they were, though the word wasn't being used. Army engineers were working on the roads, specialists in development were coming from England to talk about water and electricity and schooling and all the rest of it, and Anguilla's relationship to Great Britain was precisely that of a self-governing colony to its mother country.

On April 20, 1969, Tony Lee was given a farewell dinner by his remaining friends on the island. There aren't that many restaurants to choose from on Anguilla; the dinner was held at Jerry Gumbs's Rendezvous Hotel.

Jerry Gumbs was there, though not as a guest; he had been one of the most loudly anti-Lee people on the island. His role at Tony Lee's farewell dinner was that of host. He fussed around the twenty-four guests until they got settled and then went outside to talk with a London *Times* reporter. He told the reporter that Great Britain should be prepared to deal as equals with Ronald Webster and not try to boss him. "That is the way I work with Mr. Webster," Jerry Gumbs said. "Humility has been my lifelong companion."

28

People must not do things for fun. We are not here for fun. There is no reference to fun in any Act of Parliament.
—Sir Alan Patrick Herbert, *Uncommon Law*

Defending himself in Parliament, Michael Stewart tried among other things to pass the buck to the other Caribbean Commonwealth countries: "We were bound to take on board the views of our friends in the Caribbean and bound to take action in the way they wished."

But Mr. Stewart's friends in the Caribbean were not unanimous in their applause. Prime Minister Hugh Shearer of Jamaica said he was absolutely opposed to what had happened: "The Anguillan situation involved the right of every state to self-determination. We will not support the Government in any course that is contrary to basic rights in keeping with the charter of the United Nations. We call for prompt withdrawal of British forces from Anguilla."

Prime Minister Eric Williams of Trinidad-Tobago said, "What I want to know now is, what is Britain going to do about Rhodesia?"

Even Mr. Stewart's true friends in the Caribbean couldn't speak with very loud voices. Antigua's Premier Vere Bird was on his way out of office, and who else was left?

As to the next-door island of St. Martin, both the Dutch and the French halves sided with Anguilla. When a boatload of British policemen followed Ronald Webster over to Marigot, the French capital, local citizens wouldn't let them land, but threw bottles and garbage at them instead, while gendarmes stood around and laughed.

But facts don't seem to discommode Mr. Stewart. On April 23, he told the House of Commons that there were "undoubted cases of arson and—somewhat earlier—of murder on the island ..." There *was* suspected arson in three cases on Anguilla, two of them houses and one an airplane, but since no criminal prosecutions ever followed, the word "undoubted" is, if nothing else, premature. There were all together three *alleged* cases of arson, but there were no *undoubted* cases of arson. And the most recent had happened one year and eleven days before the invasion. What other country could claim as good a firebug record in a three-year span?

About the undoubted cases of murder. The only even alleged case of murder in the entire Anguillan rebellion was the death of Kittitian attorney Robert Crawford at the alleged hands of an alleged pro-Bradshaw surgeon, and not many people have alleged that one. But that happened on St. Kitts, not on Anguilla, and Michael Stewart has never expressed any interest in murder and arson—or disreputable characters—on St. Kitts.

It took a week for Parliament to ask about those undoubted cases of murder, and then it was William Whitlock who replied, saying there were no cases of murder after all, but there was one pending case of manslaughter. Interested M.P.'s then rooted that one out and discovered the amiable young man who perhaps had or had not shot his girl friend—not an entirely political activity. After that, Stewart finally changed his statement about murders.

But in October of 1970 I interviewed Mr. Stewart, and he started talking about murders on the island, in the plural. When I asked him if there had really been more than one, he backtracked and said, oh, well, perhaps there was only one, but even one Me was sacred, et cetera. So I asked him if that one death wasn't actually a girl and the accused killer wasn't her boy friend, and did that really have anything to do with the rebellion, and he said he wasn't sure of the details but the killing had happened in the course of the rebellion.

But other odd things were being said in the days after the invasion. Minister Without Portfolio George Thomson said, "Some critics at home and abroad are treating this as a matter of laughter and farce. What would they have preferred—tragedy and tears? ... That it has worked out this way is a tribute to the prudence with which the policy was planned and executed ... The peaceful use of military power is a rare international skill in our dangerous world."

Now the Government was giving itself tributes for having rare international skills. Thomson was also saying, whether he meant to or not, that the British Government's brand of prudence had worked things out to laughter and farce.

The laughter and farce continued. In a debate on March 25, M.P. Eldon Griffiths told Parliament, "The Government have been quick to say that they have had support from some of our allies, but they should understand that the private sentiments of important Americans on this matter are of bewilderment and derision. I shall not go into that at length. I simply make one short quotation from the words of a distinguished person in Washington. When discussing this matter, he said that, as far as he could see, the Prime Minister had 'lost his marbles.'"

On the same day, M.P. Neil Marten asked, "Did we need so many policemen? I suggest that perhaps twelve or fifteen could have gone out on a BOAC aeroplane to Antigua, disguised, insofar as police can disguise themselves, as civilians."

The Secretary of State for Defence, Mr. Denis Healey, answered a question in Commons as to why the troops on Anguilla had been equipped with CS gas, a strong kind of tear gas, saying, "The reason why we were able to deal with extremely violent civil disturbances in Hong Kong and Cyprus in the past with so little loss of life was the ability to use this type of weapon rather than guns and machine guns, as were used in similar situations in the past." To which M.P. Edward Taylor responded, "Would not supplies of laughing gas have been more appropriate for this particular episode?"

A month later, Sir John Rodgers told the House of Commons, "If we were to send to a stranger a complete record of all that has happened since the creation of the Associated State, he would think that he had been given a hitherto undiscovered manuscript of a Gilbert and Sullivan opera."

The Conservative Party published a pamphlet on Anguilla by M.P. Neil Marten, titled *Their's Not to Reason Why*, in which he said, "On 28th April, over five weeks after the Forces had arrived, Mr. Whitlock informed the Commons that 8 rifles, 22 shotguns and 4 pistols had been handed in, while 2 rifles, 2 carbines and an old anti-tank rifle had been discovered by the searching Forces. A total of 39 weapons between 6,000 West Indians!" He called it a "derisory quantity" of arms.

In *Spectator* for March 28, Auberon Waugh speculated on the real reasons for the invasion:

One is almost tempted to imagine that the whole invasion was mounted in order to save Mr. Whitlock's face. Of course, Mr. Healey's face received a much worse affront on Monday night, when it was pelted with flour and tomatoes at the East Walthamstow by-election meeting; and Mr. Healey is a more important Minister of the Crown even than Mr. William Whitlock. But Mr. Healey's assailants were Englishmen, while Mr. Whitlock's were nig-nogs. It may seem unjust to impute such a distinction to an upright, pink-faced schoolteacher like Mr. Stewart ...

But enough. The invasion was an embarrassment, and no matter how much talking Government spokesmen did it just went on being an embarrassment. Something had to be done about it, and William Whitlock was just the man to do it. On April 3, fifteen days after the landings, he told the House of Commons: "There was no invasion of Anguilla."

29

*The quarrel is a very pretty quarrel as it stands; we
should only spoil it by trying to explain it.*
—Richard Brinsley Sheridan, *The Rivals*

The normal state of Anguilla is apoplectic. Very soon after the departure of Tony Lee, Anguilla returned to normal.

One of the first things the British gave Anguilla after the invasion was a radio station, and very soon Ronald Webster delivered a speech over it. His talk rambled a bit but said in part, "We are not thinking of complete independence anymore, but to work in association directly with the Commonwealth ... I am with you and will remain with you until I am no longer required ... Friends and fellow Anguillans, have confidence in me. I have nothing to hide from you, so do not sell your leader's birthright for a dish of porridge. Remember what Judas did to Christ. So be wise, be fair-minded, be determined, be honest, be brave, be true, be sincere, be calm and beware of false prophets and wolves in sheeps' clothing." He also said, "Humility has been my lifetime companion."

The split between Ronald Webster and Atlin Harrigan was by now complete. Barely an issue of the *Beacon* appeared without some criticism of Webster. For his own part Webster was trying to unload Harrigan from the Council. That didn't work so he did the next best thing; he doubled the Council size to fourteen members, with the additional seven being mostly Webster supporters.

Things were getting rougher for Harrigan, as his July 12 editorial shows:

I have purposely refrained from printing many things that would make some of us look like idiots ... For this I am in the damnedest position; being an editor, it is my duty to comment on anything I see fit. I do not claim to be an expert, but rather far from it. But certainly I can see a pitfall ...

Every time I attempt to recommend something that conflicts with Webster's ideas, it is used as if I am the enemy and not Bradshaw ... Someone other than I would probably pack up the whole thing and leave the problem to the Hot Heads. No consistency whatsoever.

Some days Webster felt like getting along with the new Commissioner, John Cumber, and some days he didn't. Cumber knew that Webster could chop his head off just as he'd chopped Lee's head off—the Commissioner had the *responsibility* for keeping things quiet, but only Webster had the choice whether quiet would reign or not—and it was no real surprise when Cumber, on the twenty-fifth of July, resigned as Commissioner. "At his own request for personal reasons," the official announcement read.

Who would Great Britain find to take Cumber's place? Who would *want* a job like that?

The new man turned out to be Willoughby H. Thompson, known as Tommy Thompson, who had been at one time Administrator of the Falkland Islands and most recently Acting Administrator of the British Virgin Islands. A trim, tight, neat, controlled man of fifty, Tommy Thompson became the third Commissioner of Anguilla in three months, and he lasted nearly two years. When he left, in March of 1971, it was not as a result of pressure from any direction at all; he'd finished his job there and that was that.

Tommy Thompson's job was to oversee the belated development of the island, guide and guard the Anguillans as they moved at last into the twentieth century, and keep things quiet on the island. The way he did it—and the only way it could have been done—was by legitimizing the actual leadership, which meant primarily Ronald Webster and Wallace Rey.

The effect of this was that the pro-British faction on the island was undercut and betrayed by the British. There was peace on the island, there was development, Ronald Webster didn't chop Tommy Thompson's head off, and the whole crisis was, as the diplomats say, defused. But in the process Great Britain broke faith with the only group on the island that had never broken faith with her.

The last paratroops were removed from the island on September 14, barely a month after Thompson's arrival. "At least the cowboys-and-Indians stage is out," he told reporters. And so it was; Ian Ball reported in the *Daily Telegraph,* "The farewells will be handled with proper British official decorum, not the turbulent scenes that usually take place whenever anything of a political nature occurs at Anguilla's airport. The Royal Engineers have put up a wire-enclosed area beside the terminal's hutment and hung on it a large sign reading: 'Waving base.'"

Thompson was obviously the right man for Anguilla if he could get the islanders into a Waving Base to wave bye-bye to the paratroops.

The defusing had worked in both directions. In a flag-waving piece in the British Sunday newspaper *The People* on August 31, there were these quotes: A policeman: "These people are basically nice—really beautiful people. They are honest to a fault." Colonel Norrie Giles, commander of Force Anguilla: "We're making the best of our time by doing what we can for the island. We're delighted that our arms are kept in the armoury and not on men's shoulders." Ronald Webster: "I realise that the troops and police are protecting us rather than occupying us." Tommy Thompson: "My job here is made somewhat easier than it might have been by tremendous cooperation from the islanders." And the author of the piece, Trevor Aspinall, describes this encounter with Ronald Webster: "As I left Mr. Webster, he dashed back inside his bungalow for a cloth and returned to clean the windscreen of my car. 'My pleasure,' he said. 'I think you will find that all our people would do the same.'"

Ronald Webster knows a great secret of public relations: no matter what attitude you're going to show, it's impossible to lay it on too thick.

Wallace Rey was Chairman of the Public Works Committee again, and the day after Tommy Thompson was sworn in as Commissioner there was a road-opening ceremony for a mile-long stretch of paved road just completed by the Royal Engineers, with local help. Wallace Rey cut the white ribbon and made the first speech; he'd never been so respectable in his life. Thompson made the second speech, in which he called Rey a "distinguished guest," and said, "It is his day—he is our Public Works man." He also said, "As I stand here with Mr. Webster this afternoon, we represent Her Majesty and Anguilla and we at this very moment are rather at the heart of things." He spoke of the value of teamwork and finished, "I know, Mr. Webster, you agree with that, don't you?" Mr. Webster did.

With the British having allied themselves with the opposition, Atlin Harrigan and his *Beacon* were finding the pressure increasingly stiff. A Webster supporter, Clive Smith, had presented a petition from Harrigan's constituency requesting Harrigan's removal from the Council, but when it was charged that Smith had signed a lot of the names himself—including Harrigan's brother's name—that attack subsided.

Lord Shepherd visited Anguilla in November, and the *Beacon's* comment on the visit was in the form of an imaginary dialogue between two Webster supporters:

Ted: What do you think of L. S. visit?

Fred: I can hardly say. Remember he did not think very much of R. W. in Barbados in 1967? And still they were all good friends on L. S. visit?

Ted: Yes, I agree, even brought out their wives, too.

Fred: One thing got me kind of worried—

Ted: What is it?

Fred: You know L. S. saw our leader privately and after all L. S. has now sent in the Magistrate who was. held up in Antigua for some three weeks.

Ted: What's wrong with that?

Fred: Remember that R. W. did not want the Magistrate that would be appointed under the West Indies Act of 1967?

Ted: Yes, I see your point now. They kept the Magistrate in Antigua while L. S. got our R. W. to agree, then sent him here.

Fred: Now, you are thinking, old boy. But how will R. W. now explain this to the people?

Ted: He don't have to explain it.

Fred: Ah! But if he doesn't the people will start grumbling, and with the Beacon taking up every little thing it is bound to get out.

Ted: A pity they carried back the Beacon's press when they took it last March.

Fred: I hear they are making moves to close it down again but can't get no support on it.

Ted: They should be very careful about who they tell these

things to …

Fred: The other thing is that R. W. should be very careful; some of his keen supporters are now grumbling, too … Then again, he is buying up all this land from the poor people all over the island instead of giving them good advice not to sell, because someday their children will have to buy it back at exuberant prices.

Ted: Come to think of it, I agree with you …

Fred: Have you noticed this commissioner is very nice to our R. W.? He keeps him informed about everything and our R. W. is very happy.

Ted: He will have to keep his eye open, though. These British boys are smart …

Fred: What do you think about the Civil Servants planning to strike?

Ted: That is something that has to be watched very carefully … It is good our R. W. tried pushing them around, but he has to be careful and not overdo it …

Fred: Good thing about it is, how they supported the British when they came in, and now we and the British are hands and gloves with each other.

In January of 1971, when the announcement was made that Thompson would be replaced, the *Beacon's* editorial comment was: "Mr. Thompson as Commissioner has done the job he was instructed to do and should be credited for so doing; that is to say, he has been able to keep the island quiet, he has been able to work with the more militant of the Council Merbers without many problems, though many times to the dissatisfaction of others and good government … We are not criticizing the Commissioner for the lack of proper administration, for we firmly believe that he is capable of administering if given the opportunity. The stumbling block in his way was due to the gross misunderstanding of some Anguillan leaders and the need to win their loyalty."

I talked with Tommy Thompson on Anguilla in March of 1971, just before his departure, and he gave it as his opinion that Ronald Webster would soon be starting a newspaper of his own and that then the *Beacon* would wither and die. He smiled when he said it.

30

Advice: the *smallest current coin.*

—Ambrose Bierce

A month after the invasion, the Conservative leadership in the House of Commons attempted to censure the Government for its recent actions in Anguilla. On April 23, 1969, Sir Alec Douglas-Home made the motion: "That this House deplored the inept handling by Her Majesty's Government of the situation in Anguilla."

The Opposition had by now marshaled its facts and was ready to follow Government spokesmen through entire groves of inaccuracy and vagueness. The debate didn't precisely rage, but feathers were ruffled, and at the end the motion was only narrowly defeated: 286 to 239. Not a comfortable margin for a Government in power.

Sir Dingle Foot had suggested a Commission of Inquiry and one was formed at the end of May. Michael Stewart announced its formation to Parliament and gave the terms of reference the Commission would be starting with. It may be hard to believe, but the terms of reference *began* by saying, "Recognizing the fact that the island of Anguilla is part of the unitary State of St. Kitts-Nevis-Anguilla ..."

Is it necessary to know any more about the terms of reference? One can already guess, sixteen words in, the only recommendation the Commission can possibly come up with at the end of its inquiry. But just to drive the point home, the second of the three terms of reference read, "Having regard to the resolution concerning Anguilla adopted unanimously at the meeting of Commonwealth Caribbean Heads of Government ..." Which was the resolution calling on Great Britain "to confirm the territorial integrity of St. Kitts-Nevis-Anguilla."

The third term of reference? "Bearing in mind the problems and consequences that might arise from further fragmentation in the

Caribbean ..."

Given those terms of reference, the truculence of Colonel Bradshaw, and the explosiveness of the Anguillans, it's no surprise that it took six months to find somebody to head the Commission. At last a man with the right credentials agreed to take on the job. His name was Sir Hugh Wooding and he was a former Chief Justice of Trinidad-Tobago.

Having a Chairman, the Commission now quickly assembled the rest of its panel, none of them British, and they prepared to begin their inquiry.

The Commission's terms of reference caused immediate trouble on Anguilla. Webster announced that the agreement with Lord Caradon had been breached and that he would refuse to cooperate with either the Wooding Commission or Tommy Thompson. Thompson soon soothed him, assuring him that the British had no intention of reneging on any of their most recent promises, and after the Island Council had hired a lawyer from Barbados to advise them, Webster sulkily settled down again.

Atlin Harrigan was also troubled by the Commission. In an editorial in the *Beacon* of January 31, 1970, he wrote, "If the hands of the Commission are tied within the terms of reference as agreed between H. M. G. and Bradshaw, then we do not see how these 'wise men' will come up with a solution."

They didn't. The Commission spent the spring of 1970 taking testimony on Anguilla, on St. Kitts, in the United States, in Great Britain, and anywhere else that anybody wanted to tell them anything, and then retired to consider what they'd been told. The Report was at first scheduled to be released in August but there was a delay, and it gradually became apparent that the Commission had conscientiously done what the terms of reference had required, which was to recommend that Anguilla go back with St. Kitts. The British held off the storm as long as possible but finally released the Report on November 6, 1970.

The Wooding Report is in two parts. The first part describes the situation in Anguilla and the history of the rebellion, and while it tends to smooth over the rough spots it's basically a sound and sensible recital of the facts. The second part considers the potential solutions and opts for the return of Anguilla to St. Kitts, sugar-coated by thick icings of British aid and an extensive Local Council.

The Anguillan response was obvious and swift. The *Beacon*'s editorial, titled "Wooding Report—A Waste," began, "It is with a feeling of utter disbelief and a sense of having been badly let down that Anguillans at long last receive the news of the Commission report."

Ronald Webster issued a statement to his people that said, in part, "My only comment is—these proposals are nothing to worry about! We've been assured that the British Government are not going to force us to accept any administration we do not want ... In the meantime, I call on everyone to continue to cooperate with H. M. Commissioner, and the British Personnel. They are our friends ... Please be calm, do not get excited ... May God bless your dear hearts and keep your spirit primed and matured." And the Anguilla Council formally rejected the proposals.

As Atlin Harrigan wrote in the *Beacon*, "Any recommendation that means a return of Anguilla to the State of St. Kitts-Nevis would only go into effect with the vast majority of Anguillans wiped off the face of this earth."

Great Britain never formally rejected the Wooding Report. But she never tried to do anything with it either. By the time the Report was published, there had been an election in Great Britain, Government had changed from Labour to Conservative, and the entire British cast had changed.

Luckily, the new people weren't going to start the mess all over from the beginning. Immediately after publication of the Report, M.P. Neil Marten (author of *Their's Not to Reason Why*) asked for reassurance "that any settlement of this problem must be acceptable to the Anguillans." Mr. Joseph Godber, Minister of State for the Foreign and Commonwealth Office, replied: "Yes. I am happy to give that assurance. It is our intention to seek to get agreement for the solution of this problem ... we would not seek to impose a solution in any way, but would seek to get one by agreement."

Which meant Colonel Bradshaw. He was invited to London in November of 1970 to talk things over, but of course he was the one party involved who *liked* the Wooding Report.

The talks between the British Government and the Colonel eventually broke down, as they had to. At the finish the Colonel put in one more request for arms, but once again the British turned him down, even though he'd explained he needed the rocket launchers and armored trucks for "internal defence."

Before leaving London, Bradshaw spoke to reporters and assured them it was untrue that he had threatened to make the Anguillans accept the Wooding Report by starving them out until they surrendered. All he had to offer the Anguillans, he said, was "love and amity."

But what about the rocket launchers? What about the armored trucks? Well, he really needed them. As he told the reporters, "All sorts of funny things are happening in the Caribbean."

31

Reason and judgment are the qualities of a leader.
—Tacitus

By the spring of 1971, Anguilla had been a British colony under direct British administration for two years. The status hadn't been formalized and the word "colony" was never used, but that's what it was. The British still acted on the assumption that their own ground rules prohibited them from formalizing the change, since in theory they had freed Anguilla back in 1967 and no longer had the legal power to alter the island's status, and Bradshaw had made it abundantly clear that he wouldn't willingly help legalize the new situation himself, but in fact Anguilla had stopped being a part of St. Kitts-Nevis-Anguilla on May 30, 1967, and all the Queen's horses and all the Queen's men would never be able to put that particular Humpty Dumpty together again.

This was all very uncomfortable for the British Government, which has traditionally preferred to coat its actions with the varnish of legality. And the sharpest thorn in the British side in the whole mess, other than the Anguillans themselves, had been their own principal ally, Colonel Bradshaw. His unwillingness to compromise, his tough line of talk, and his eccentric behavior had contributed greatly to the British rout, and Her Majesty's Government seemed prepared to do what it could to repay him in kind.

The St. Kitts Constitution called for general elections no later than September 1971. Colonel Bradshaw had originally planned the election for the spring, to coincide with the opening of his new Government-owned television station. He intended not only to campaign on the station, but also to present himself as the man who had brought television to St. Kitts.

But there were problems. A British company was doing the work and unfortunate delays arose. Bradshaw postponed the election, but the unfortunate delays postponed the television station even longer.

Bradshaw also made a rather serious public-relations error. Just as he'd always been there with the timely *faux pas* to help the Anguillans in their hours of need, he now seemed determined to assist the British in their unstated attempt to replace him with Billy Herbert.

Here's the situation: As unemployment has skyrocketed on the islands (reaching 40 to 50 per cent on St. Kitts, for instance), more and more men from British islands have become illegal immigrants in the United States Virgin Islands, holding jobs without work permits. American authorities, with that humanitarianism and subtlety that have become the American trademark in the last decade, took to rounding up these illegal workers and booting them off the island without giving them a chance to pack, collect their wages, make a phone call or say good-bye to anybody. Public outcry resulted in a visit to the American island of St. Thomas by the Prime Ministers of half a dozen other islands. Bradshaw was among them, and started badly. He'd chosen to travel in his field-combat uniform, including a .45 automatic in a holster at his waist; American authorities disarmed him at the airport.

But it was his departure that got the attention of the Caribbean press. The other Prime Ministers released a group statement deploring American callousness, and Bradshaw released a dissenting statement saying every nation had the right to throw out foreign undesirables and he thought the Americans were doing just fine. Since many of the ex-undesirables were adult Kittitians who were now back on St. Kitts in plenty of time for the election, this was perhaps not the cleverest statement of Bradshaw's political career.

Still, Bradshaw is a politician, in a very rugged political arena, and hasn't survived all these years through nothing but luck and braggadocio. A rumor current in the islands that spring had it that the British intended to take Anguilla away from St. Kitts just before the election, as a further swipe at Bradshaw's prestige; Bradshaw certainly heard it. He could see the television station not being finished, and he knew his popularity among the voters was waning.

Suddenly, on May 1, 1971, Bradshaw announced the election would take place on May 10. And if that wasn't enough time for anybody else, too bad; it was enough time for the Colonel.

The brief campaign was hardly ever in doubt; Bradshaw was rough and ready and PAM was neither. Bradshaw threatened to fire Civil Servants who campaigned or voted for PAM, and he weeded known PAM supporters out of the voters' lists by every pretext he could find, including disqualification for misspelling of names on the list. As to the disgruntled unemployed back from the U.S. Virgin Islands, they discovered that their temporary residence off St. Kitts had made them ineligible to vote. The Labour Party romped to a victory.

Now Colonel Bradshaw came forth in yet another uniform. The man who once listed his hobby in the Caribbean Who's Who as "sartorial elegance" made his victory speech in faded bush jacket and worn fatigue cap. He obviously knows which way the winds are blowing in Caribbean politics, and though he didn't manage to grow a beard, he did call his followers "comrades," and told them, "The mandate is your call for revolutionary change in this country." The old Bradshaw resurfaced briefly when he shouted "*Vox populi, vox Dei!*" but when that got nothing but baffled looks he followed up with a quick translation: "Power to the people!"

The new Bradshaw is a complete remodeling. The Rolls-Royce is gone now, replaced by an open Land Rover. The cutaways and spats have been banished in favor of dirty khakis. He even talks differently; he used to sound like an Englishman and now he sounds like a cane cutter.

As William M. Tweed, nineteenth-century political boss of New York City's "Tweed Ring" once said, "As long as I count the votes, what are you going to do about it?"

32

Colonies do not cease to be colonies because they are independent.

—Benjamin Disraeli

The Wooding Report had been delivered, and had solved nothing, and had sunk without a trace. The election on St. Kitts had come and gone, and Robert Bradshaw was still in power. It began to seem that nothing would get the British off the hook.

So they did it themselves, and to hell with dignity. At the beginning of June, less than a month after Bradshaw's re-election, Joseph Godber, Minister of State for the Foreign and Commonwealth Office, showed up in St. Kitts with new proposals that in effect altered the legal status of Anguilla to a Crown Colony of Great Britain without ever quite using that terminology. Bradshaw turned the proposals down, as usual, and Godber carried them on to Anguilla, where the Anguilla Council talked things over with its attorney and said Yes.

And so, on July 7, a bill concerning Anguilla received its First Reading in the British House of Commons. Called the Anguilla Act of 1971, it said that "Her Majesty may by Order in Council make such provision as Her Majesty thinks fit for securing Peace, Order and Good Government in Anguilla" and went on to permit Her Majesty to "appoint for Anguilla a Commissioner" and to "provide a constitution for Anguilla." It further said that "this act shall have effect notwithstanding anything in the West Indies Act 1967," which was the Act that had made St. Kitts-Nevis-Anguilla an Associated State, independent (as Lord Caradon used to assure the U.N. Committee on Colonialism) from the United Kingdom forever.

For justification, or something that could look like justification in the dark with the light behind it, the Anguilla Act 1971 announced that "in accordance with section 3 (2) of the West Indies

Act 1967 which provides for an Act of the Parliament of the United Kingdom to extend in certain circumstances to an Associated State it is hereby declared that this Act (A) extends to the Associated State of St. Christopher, Nevis and Anguilla, and (B) is required so to extend in the interests of the responsibilities of Her Majesty's Government in the United Kingdom relating to defence and external affairs."

Whether accepting Anguilla as a colony was a defense affair or an external affair the Act didn't spell out.

But what about Bradshaw's potential, as head of an Associated State, to declare his entire nation *totally* independent of Great Britain? Wouldn't that whisk Anguilla out from under the Anguilla Act 1971? No, it wouldn't; the Act was ready for that: "If at any time ... there is introduced into the Legislature for the Associated State of St. Christopher, Nevis and Anguilla a bill or a law terminating the state of association of that State with the United Kingdom, Her Majesty may ... direct that Anguilla shall not any longer form part of the territory of that State." In other words, Bradshaw could retain even nominal control over Anguilla only if he made no waves.

Most Caribbean governments were very upset about all this. Not only was fragmentation occurring before their very eyes, but the pleasant fiction of associated statehood was being trampled in the mud. The final test of any independent government is its ability to enforce its decisions, and the children were being reminded that, however much they might play at independence, Mother was still in charge.

The least happy of the children was St. Kitts. On July 12, the St. Kitts Legislature passed a motion condemning the British action as "outrageous and illegal," which was perfectly accurate, and calling on other Caribbean Governments for support. Moral support was offered by Jamaica and Trinidad and the rest, and was as effective as it usually is.

Toward the end of July, heads and representatives of seven Caribbean Governments—Dominica, Grenada, Guyana, St. Kitts, St. Lucia, Trinidad and St. Vincent—met in Grenada, primarily to worry the bone of federation yet again, but also to consider the British action on Anguilla. Their statement, called "The Declaration of Grenada," plumped for federation on the one side and deplored the Anguilla Act 1971 on the other. Nobody paid much attention.

In London, the Act moved gracefully through the legal quadrille required for it to become law. The Anguilla Act 1971 was the enabling legislation that would permit an Order in Council, which in turn would do the actual colonizing of Anguilla. The Act became law with no trouble, the Order in Council was published on August 3, and Anguilla's two-year-old victory over the British was finally acknowledged on August 6.

The *Beacon* reported the famous victory under the headline "THOUSANDS OF ANGUILLANS ATTEND SWEARING-IN CEREMONY":

> Thousands of Anguillans, dressed in gay holiday attire, turned out on Friday morning to celebrate the first "Anguilla Day" which was marked by special ceremonies at the Court House for the swearing in of twelve members of the Council and the election of a Leader of the Anguilla Council.
>
> ... The other elected member of the Council, Mr. Wallace Rey, did not take the oath, but was seen among the crowd as the ceremony took place.
>
> Following the impressive ceremony, Anguillans in their thousands formed a procession and, headed by Council members and a steel band, marched to Ronald Webster Park. There an "Anguilla Day" service of praise and thanksgiving was held with Mr. Campbell Fleming as chairman. Mr. Ronald Webster spoke briefly to thank all concerned for their help over the past fifty months in bringing about the achievement of direct relationship with Great Britain; especially H. M. Government and succeeding Commissioners Mr. Cumber, Mr. Thompson and Mr. Watson.
>
> ... Friday was a public holiday and Anguillans were in a mood to celebrate a new era. Scores of private parties and public dances were being held, and on Sunday the Churches of Anguilla will hold special thanksgiving services.
>
> A special address by H. M. Commissioner and Mr. Ronald Webster, followed by a recording of the proceedings at the swearing-in ceremony and the Thanksgiving service in the park, will be broadcast by Radio Anguilla at 4 o'clock on Sunday afternoon.

Even in victory, of course, the Anguillans can't show a united front; there's Wallace Rey lurking around in the crowd instead of being up on stage getting sworn in as a Council member. But two weeks later the *Beacon* could report another happy ending:

MR. WALLACE REY TAKES OATHS

The thirteenth member of the Anguilla Council, Mr. Wallace Rey, who refused to be sworn in at the special meeting of the Council on 6th August, was sworn in on Tuesday August 17th. Mr. Wallace Rey took and subscribed the oaths of allegiance and office before H. M. Commissioner as prescribed by the Anguilla Order in Council. Mr. Rey did not take the oaths on August 6th when all the other members were ceremoniously sworn in, his reason being that he did not know what "law" he was swearing to.

And so the last piece clicked into place, and the Anguillan rebellion ended as it had begun—in confusion. The legal status of the island remained as baffling as ever, but all parties had agreed to ignore the legalities and simply get the job done. Anguilla remains technically one-third of the nation of St. Christopher-Nevis-Anguilla, but does not vote in that nation's elections, is not represented in that nation's Legislature, does not pay taxes to or receive funding from that nation, does not fly that nation's flag, does not feel itself bound by that nation's laws, and is not connected to that nation's Civil Service, Police Department or judiciary. Anguilla is definitely not a colony of Great Britain, but is governed by a British Commissioner appointed by the Queen.

In the two and a half years following the British invasion of Anguilla, the Royal Engineers worked like soldier ants across the island, building schools, paving roads, starting an electrification program, studying the water table, and generally tidying up the effects of the previous three hundred years of neglect. When they left, on September 14, 1971, they were technically the same invading army that had swept ashore on March 19, 1969, but never has an invading army been given a farewell to equal that written by Atlin Harrigan in the *Beacon:*

FAREWELL ROYAL ENGINEERS

Anguillans have learned with real regret of plans for the departure from our island of Royal Engineers. Their work is done and they are required elsewhere.

Since March 19, 1969, when the British Forces landed on the island, the presence of these friendly visitors has been increasingly welcomed. They came to prevent trouble and as a protection from our sister island of St. Kitts. Not only are they soldiers of the Queen, but they are experienced and capable engineers, electricians, mechanics, builders and development planners. They have put their time to good use, and the numerous additions, (in every development area) to the Anguilla scene are evidence of their ability along peaceful lines and their wish to serve another Commonwealth island.

The various buildings and other facilities built by the Royal Engineers during the last 30 months have been mentioned before, but their greatest contribution to Anguilla and the people of the island has been, perhaps, their friendly and cooperative attitude to the people, who will miss them and their ever-ready help.

Many Anguillans have made lasting friends of Royal Engineers' personnel.

The Beacon would like to pay tribute on behalf of all Anguillans, to the capable commanders of the British Forces on the island over the past two and a half years: Col. Norrie Giles, Col. John Waymark, Col. Robin Jukes-Hughes, Col. Bruce Brown, M.B.E. and last but certainly not least the present commander, Major Leslie J. Kennedy, R.E., and all their men.

The Royal Engineers came in peace and they go in peace. We thank them for their help and their friendships and we wish every member of the British Forces who has been on the island Godspeed and good fortune as the last contingent departs.

Bibliography

NEWSPAPERS:

Times (London), 1967–1971
Financial Times (London), 1967–1971
Daily Telegraph (London), 1967–1971
Daily Express (London), 1967–1969
Daily Mail (London), 1967–1969
The Guardian (London), 1968–1970
Sunday Telegraph (London), 1968–1969
Sun (London), 1969
Evening Standard (London), 1969
Sunday Times (London), 1969–1971
Evening News (London), 1969
Daily Sketch (London), 1969
The Observer (London), 1969
Daily Mirror (London), 1969
The People (London), 1969
Caribbean Business News (Toronto), 1971
Antigua Star, 1967
Guyana Graphic, 1968, 1969
Trinidad Guardian, 1968
Advocate-News (Barbados), 1968, 1969
Daily Gleaner (Jamaica), 1968, 1969
The New York Times, 1967–1971
Chronicle (San Francisco), March 1969
Sunday News (New York), 1970
Post (Washington, D.C.), 1971
Beacon (Anguilla), 1967–1971
Labour Spokesman (St. Kitts), 1967–1969
Democrat (St. Kitts), 1967–1969
The Conch Shell #1-7, and Research Papers #1-4, and Special Papers #1-2 (London, Toronto), 1968–1970

ARTICLES:

Anonymous, "Last Year's Bradshaw." *Private Eye,* London, March 28, 1969.
"Crabro," "Mr. Bradshaw's Chestnuts." *Spectator,* London, March 14, 1970.
Feigen, Gerald, Gossage, Howard, Newhall, Scott, Wade, Larry, and Gold, Herbert, "The

Log of the Anguilla Free Trade & Charter Company." *Scanlan's Monthly*, New York, April, 1970.

Harris, David, "Anguilla's Tradition of Independence." *Geographical Magazine*, London, June, 1969.

Hatch, John, "Who Wants Anguilla?" *New Statesman*, London, April 18, 1969.

Kohr, Leopold, "The Truth About Anguilla." *Spectator*, London, May 30, 1969.

Naipaul, V. S., "St. Kitts: Papa and the Power Set." *New York Review of Books*, New York, May 8, 1969.

Prior-Palmer, Diana, "The Prisoners of St. Kitts." *Spectator*, London, October 20, 1967.

Smithers, David, "Anguilla's UDI." *Venture*, London, October, 1967.

Updike, John, "Letter from Anguilla." *The New Yorker*, New York, June 22, 1968.

Watkins, Alan, "Mr. Stewart's Caribbean Jaunt." *New Statesman*, London, March 28, 1969.

Waugh, Auberon, "War of Whitlock's Ear." *Spectator*, London, March 28, 1969.

MAGAZINES:

Spectator (London), 1967, 1969, 1970
Private Eye (London), 1969
New Statesman (London), 1969
The Listener (London), 1969
West Indies Chronicle (London), 1969
Newsweek (New York), 1967, 1969
Time (New York), 1967, 1969
Life (New York), 1969
U.S. News & World Report (New York), 1969
Senior Scholastic (New York), 1969
Commonwealth European and Overseas Review (London), July, 1967

BOOKS:

Alexander, Andrew, and Watkins, Alan, *The Making of the Prime Minister 1970*. Macdonald Unit 75, London, 1970.

Bradshaw, Robert L., *The Present Crisis in the State of St. Christopher-Nevis-Anguilla*. Government Printery, St. Kitts, 1967.

Brisk, William J., *The Dilemma of a Ministate: Anguilla*. University of South Carolina, Columbia, South Carolina, 1969.

Marten, Neil, *Their's Not to Reason Why*. Conservative Political Centre, London, 1969.

Rickards, Colin, *Anguilla: Island in Revolt*. (In manuscript.)

PUBLIC DOCUMENTS:

Hansard. Lords and Commons, June 1967–June 1969.

Report of the Commission of Inquiry to Examine the Anguilla Problem. Her Majesty's Stationery Office, London, 1970.

Report of the St. Kitts-Nevis-Anguilla Constitutional Conference 1966. Her Majesty's Stationery Office, London, 1966.

Poetry:

Hollis, Christopher, "Battle of Anguilla." *Spectator,* London, April 4, 1969.
Updike, John, "Anguilla 1960." *New Republic,* New York, October, 1967.

Index

Also by Donald E. Westlake

Lightning Source UK Ltd.
Milton Keynes UK
UKHW010752050123
414875UK00004B/249